Social Security
for Decision Makers

DARSHAN,

DREAM

BELIEVE

ACT

ENJOY!

Social Security for Decision Makers

Charting Your Course to Retirement

By Peter D. Murphy

Published by
RockStar Publishing House
32129 Lindero Canyon Road, Suite 205
Westlake Village, CA 91361
www.rockstarpublishinghouse.com

Manufactured in the United States of America

Murphy, Peter
    Social Security for Decision Makers
    ISBN:
    Paperback: 9781937506766
    eBook: 9781937506773

Cover design by: Michael Short
Interior design: Scribe Inc.

Disclaimer: Securities and Advisory Services through United Planners
Financial Services, A Limited Partnership. Member: FINRA, SIPC.
OSJ Office: 901 Route 23 South, Pompton Plains, NJ 07444 (973) 831-
4424. APG and United Planners are not affiliated. This APG office is
independently owned and operated.

Author's URL: www.PeterMurphy1APG.com

Thank You!

To my wonderful wife, Lisa,
for inspiring (nagging) me to write this book

To Peter and Kathleen Murphy for
my education, work ethic, and empathy

To Mark Charnet, CEO/president of American Prosperity Group
(http://www.1APG.com)

To Patrick Carlson, illustrator (http://www.bbqlogos.com)

To Kelly Koepke, editor (http://www.kellykoepke.com)

To Karen Strauss, publisher at RockStar Publishing House
(http://www.rockstarpublishinghouse.com)

Contents

CHAPTER 1

Bottom Line Up Front (BLUF)

Isn't it better to know the ending at the beginning? This book is about concepts and decisions; it is not a numbers game for bean counters. We'll start with the forest and show you several paths to explore. It will help you make better retirement decisions, so the first order of business is determining your goals. Define your goals before reading this book, really!

I can't completely eliminate numbers, but I promise to minimize their use. The journey will be fun. Social Security and fun in the same sentence—stranger things have happened.

WHY YOU SHOULD READ THIS BOOK!

Social Security is the biggest piece of the retirement puzzle. Approximately 40% of the average retiree's income is her Social

Security benefit check. Because it's the largest piece, your decision on when to start collecting is important. You don't want to screw this decision up, so you should read the book.

This is a government-run program. In other words, it's more complicated than it needs to be and harder to understand than it should be. Don't believe me? Just log into the official Social Security Administration website (http://www.ssa.gov) and start reading. When you are done and understand it all, please give me a call and I'll send you the 10th edition of this book free, or maybe you can just help me write the 11th edition.

Uninformed decisions on your Social Security benefit and the lack of coordination of a spousal (or ex-spousal) benefit could cost you more than a hundred thousand dollars over your lifetime.

If you collect a Social Security benefit before full retirement age and continue to work, you may lose some of that Social Security income. Enough said for now. I'll write more on this later.

Are you married, divorced, or a survivor (a widow or widower)? If so, you have more options than your single counterparts and need to understand how these decisions will affect your retirement and legacy planning.

THE 90% SOLUTION

Have you ever run into people who can't make a darn decision? We all know them; some just plain won't make decisions and their circuitry will never change. Then there are the ones who always need more information, and just when you think they are completely overloaded with material, answers, and suggestions, they ask for more stuff. If you are one of those types, you won't get 100% of the information you want from this book. This book was created to inform those who want enough information to make a well-educated decision and move on. I'm not going to discuss Social Security brick by brick nor get into the bend points used to determine payment expectations. Offering more information will induce coma-like symptoms and confuse minds. Although I generally like to confuse people from time to time, this simple book will focus on the beef with no bun or condiments. After all, most of us don't want to understand every aspect of Social Security; we just want to make a good decision about claiming our earned benefits.

This book will answer common questions and provide scenarios to help you understand available options. It will open your eyes to the complexity of Social Security while simplifying your choices and suggesting appropriate solutions. This book will keep you safe—I promise!

MUST STAY!

If you were born in 1960 or earlier, this book is probably for you. As one of today's 78 million baby boomers, this book will inform you on Social Security essentials and help you make educated decisions about when to collect your benefit. There is a right solution for you; it's just not the right decision for everyone, so keep that in mind.

For single people, deciding when to begin social security benefits might take less effort, but everyone has options to consider. If you are divorced, the key question is, were you married to someone for at least 10 years? It must be one person, one time, for at least 10 years, or there will be no ex-spousal and no survivor benefit. It's a harsh rule, but if you are considering leaving your spouse, is it worth sucking it up for 10 years before divorce? I doubt it, but the choice is yours.

Survivors have too many options to consider. Yes, I did say "too many." Just the same, you need to understand your choices and know that you can undo, redo, and upgrade later in life. I know, it sounds confusing, but I'll turn the Social Security window less opaque in this short book. The key is that you will learn the available choices, understand how to evaluate them, and choose the right answer for *you*.

Married couples have many options also. This book will help you make excellent decisions to reach your goals. Understanding concepts such as the strategic use of a spousal benefit, why maximizing one of your two earned benefits is advantageous, and what happens when the first spouse passes away are paramount and could be worth tens of thousands of dollars or more.

If you are single or divorced and contemplating marriage, you should read this book. Getting married could increase your benefit or decrease it. Yes, that last sentence is correct. You could decrease your Social Security benefit if you remarry. I talk about love versus money in Chapter 9. There is no need to take a pay cut for love when shacking up is an option.

I love proactive planners. If that describes you, read this book and congratulations on getting an early start. The sooner you educate yourself, understand the concepts, and seek council, the more likely it is that you will reach your goal. Any plan is better than no plan, and frankly, most of us have no plan.

SHOULD GO!

Those born after 1960 should pass on this book. I appreciate you being superproactive, but the likelihood of Social Security benefits changing for you is high. Come back in a few years and try a more recent edition after Congress makes its adjustments. Additionally, cost-of-living adjustments and Medicare Part B premiums change annually. OK, the Medicare Part B stuff is more than I should have mentioned, as my purpose is to keep this book simple.

If you are seeking information on Social Security Disability Insurance (earned disability benefits) or Supplemental Security Income (welfare), this book will not meet your needs. Both of these benefit programs are important aspects of Social Security, but my purpose for this book is to keep it short, simple, and straightforward. If I included disability, family benefits (children benefits), and other miscellaneous aspects of Social Security, the book would be twice the size, too complicated, and not the one-day read I want it to be.

If you worked for an organization that did not participate in our Social Security system and you will receive a pension or lump sum payment from that organization, don't buy this book. I will not describe the "Windfall Elimination Provision" or "Government Pension Offset" for the same reasons I did not include disability benefits. The bottom line is this: even if you toiled in other jobs and contributed to Social Security, you will probably earn fewer benefits than others who paid the same amount into the Social Security system. If you aren't sure you fit into this category, check your annual Social Security statement (hard copy or online) to see if you have any "zero" paid amounts toward Social Security in years you worked. Generally, workers for some government, state, municipal, or education organizations fit this category.

If you will not pay 40 quarters in Social Security taxes, then do not read this book unless your spouse or ex-spouse (if married for at least 10 years) paid 40 quarters into Social Security. How many people do you know who paid fewer than 10 years of Social Security taxes, are not married, or weren't married for at least 10 years? I thought so!

THE MAJOR SOURCE OF
INCOME FOR MOST RETIREES

Yes, it is true. Social Security is about 40% of the average retiree's income. Any guesses on what comes in second place at approximately 25%? No, sorry, it is not pensions. No, wrong again, it is not savings. Yep, you guessed it: work. Yikes, it's kind of scary when you think about it—all the more reason to ensure you understand your Social Security benefit options now and create a plan for retirement.

Unlike fixed income retirement payments, Social Security is tied to an inflation index, meaning that payments received will increase over time. This annual cost-of-living adjustment (COLA) was added in 1975 and has kept Social Security's purchasing power from receding over time. I suggest you consider the value of your Social Security benefit in terms of today's dollar and expect it to somewhat keep pace with inflation during your lifetime.

Your decisions will dramatically affect the value of your Social Security income. We'll address various options in the chapters to come, but by delaying your benefit from age 62 to 70, your check may grow by 76%. You can also grow your benefit after you start collecting Social Security through continued work, remarriage, and survivor benefits. Planning is an integral part of Social Security and a necessary tool to maximize your goal for this earned benefit.

THERE IS NO RIGHT ANSWER

With all the options available, there is no right answer for everyone. There is just a correct answer for you, and this book will help you determine it. Remember, this is about retirement goals and not bean counting. Financially, it may make sense to wait until 70 to begin benefits, especially if you are healthy and have longevity in your family. But consider what you can do with the money at 65 compared with what you can do with the money at 85 (if you get there). Just food for thought. It's not all about the dollar; it's about your goals.

If you are married, you should consider what your spouse will be left with when you die. The higher of your two Social Security retirement benefits will last two lifetimes. Consider this with other income sources and assets in your planning.

CHAPTER 2

Will It Be There?

I didn't mean to scare you with the picture—OK, I did. But I apologize. I can't help but poke fun at the doomsday scenario and those who believe Social Security is bankrupt. It's certainly possible that we could lose our Social Security benefits, but it was also possible that we could have checked out at the end of the Mayan calendar. Fortunately (or unfortunately), we are still here. Social Security should be there for you also.

$2,732,334,000

It's a big number, and it's the Old-Age, Survivors, and Disability Insurance (OASDI) Trust balance at the end of 2012. For the purpose of our discussion, OASDI is the Social Security trust fund. It grew by $54.4 billion during 2012, and it is predicted to continue growing until 2021, until our sustained retiree growth rate begins draining our trust fund assets. Without congressional action, the trust fund could reach zero around 2033.

WHERE'S THE BEEF?

I loved that 1980s vintage Wendy's commercial (http://www .youtube.com/watch?v=R6_eWWfNB54), didn't you? Today's Social Security doomsters apply a variation of that same commercial slogan: "Where's the money?" So where *is* the money? Our Social Security trust funds are invested in special-issue short-term certificates of indebtedness and long-term bonds. According to the Social Security Trust Fund Data website (http://www.ssa .gov/cgi-bin/investheld.cgi), the average rate of return on this investment as of December 31, 2013, was 3.602%. I wish I could get that guaranteed rate of return from an AA+ rated company.

Our Social Security trust fund assets are not placed in a vault. They are invested as our government sees fit with a guarantee of return with interest. Companies you invest with do the same thing. The real question is, will the United States of America default on this debt? It's highly unlikely, and if it does, we'll have much larger problems to deal with than our Social Security checks.

If you worry about whether Social Security will be there when you retire, please don't. It will be there, and if you are more than 60 years old, the only change from today's program you will probably experience is a reduction in the cost-of-living adjustment. This is not a trivial matter, as cost-of-living adjustments help retain purchasing power in retirement. Congress is considering "tweaking" Social Security COLA, in addition to other options, to solidify our Social Security system. Changes are necessary and will take place. Let's not blow them out of proportion. You've paid into this program, are entitled to the benefit, and will receive it. Don't let the alarmists scare you.

10,000 A DAY

Any guesses? It's the number of US citizens reaching age 65 every day. Yes, there are approximately 78 million baby boomers, and all of us want to collect our Social Security someday. We also vote, so don't be shy in letting your congressional representatives know which solutions you like. They like their jobs and will thus like your suggestions. I'll discuss options later in this book.

You've probably heard that there will soon be just over two Social Security–paying workers supporting each retiree. With approximately 25% of our US population being baby boomers, it's not like we haven't seen this one coming for decades. That is why the trust fund is worth almost $2.8 trillion in 2014 and continues to grow. There is more good news for our Social Security program. Almost half our eligible beneficiaries begin collecting Social Security at age 62, which minimizes trust fund outlays over time. If I put on my green eyeshades and do a bit of break-even analysis comparing paychecks and life expectancy for 62-year-olds, the house (trust fund) wins against early collectors.

Another wild card is immigration reform. As it's a hot topic, we should see reform soon. Whatever Congress does, it should increase Social Security trust resources, improving program solvency.

Lastly, we like to live large—literally. Our overweight and obesity problems reduce life expectancy and will decrease Social Security outlays. Ouch, that may have hurt, but facts are facts. Obesity shortens life expectancy: I didn't make it up.

ZERO DOESN'T MEAN ZERO

What do you think would happen if the average American retiree lost 40% of her income? With 78 million baby boomers and approximately 10,000 each day turning 65 for the next 20 years, all of whom have the power to vote, do you think Congress may scrap this program or water it down much? Me neither. I didn't say it would be pain-free, but it's about time Congress felt some pain along with the rest of us.

Just because the trust fund could reach zero doesn't mean Social Security paychecks stop. Remember, people are still working. Workers and their companies will continue paying into our Social Security system. This worst-case scenario has Social Security benefits cut to about 75 cents on the dollar. That means if congressional gridlock remains, we'll lose 25% of our Social Security benefit starting around 2033. What is the likelihood of Congress taking no action? Pretty much zero. This isn't the first Social Security crisis we've experienced. Congress "fixed" Social Security in 1984 and again in 1993. It will do so again. The sooner the better, as small changes now are preferable to large adjustments later. The 1993 Social Security fix lasted 20 years, so hopefully the next adjustment will also. Congress will put in a fix and kick this can farther down the road. As for the next Social Security crisis, it won't matter for most of us baby boomers.

The actuarial deficit is 2.3%. What that means in English is that we must increase Social Security trust income (taxes/ earnings) and/or decrease expenditures by 2.3% annually to bring this program into balance. Is 2.3% really that big of a deal? The answer is no.

There are several credible proposals floating around Congress to adjust our Social Security program, and in the end, it will most likely be a combination of these "proposals" that gets approved:

- Increase the age required to receive "full retirement age benefits," which is currently 66 and grows to 67 for people born 1960 and later.
- Increase the amount of earned income subject to Social Security taxation. As of 2014, that ceiling was $117,000, and it increases annually based on wage growth.
- Increase the Social Security tax rate, which is currently 12.4% (6.2% by you and 6.2% by the company you work for). If you are self-employed, congratulations: you get to pay the full 12.4%.
- Use means testing. Social Security is already a wealth distribution tool. Those who contribute more receive a smaller percentage of their contributions back in benefits. Means testing is another way to distribute wealth.
- Tie the cost-of-living adjustment to an alternative (less beneficial) index than the one used today.

The last bullet is the one I'd whine to my congressperson about, as it has the largest negative effect on *you*. I don't like the second-to-last bullet, either. Why punish people who actually had a plan, saved money for retirement, and contributed to "their" Social Security retirement accounts?

Making Social Security more solvent for decades to come isn't that difficult. Go to the website of the American Academy of Actuaries (http://www.actuary.org) and select "the Social Security game." This is a great site where you can actually "test" your proposed solution. I combined three of the bullets listed and fixed our Social Security for the foreseeable future. I loved my solution, but maybe you won't. No worries, I don't plan to run for Congress. Visit the website and make your own adjustments and you'll find that small changes now will prevent problems down the road.

THE MORE COLA THE BETTER

Too many of us don't plan for retirement, and even fewer give inflation its due. At 3% inflation growth over a 20-year retirement, you'll need $1.82 to purchase $1.00 worth of goods in year 20, and inflation could be higher than 3% per year over the next 20 years. Please, please, please, consider inflation in your retirement planning. You will need to either spend more in retirement to offset the effects of inflation or reduce your lifestyle. Which do you prefer?

Adding a cost-of-living adjustment to our Social Security benefits in 1975 was the right thing to do. Thank you, Gerald Ford! The cost-of-living adjustment for Social Security should not go away, but Congress is considering changing the index it is tied to—that is, lowering your future benefit. Modifying COLA is the least favorite solution for *you* and also punishes current retirees who planned on the annual increases to keep up with inflation. OK, maybe some retirees didn't plan on it, but they certainly count on it now and have few options to make up the difference in retirement.

Squeaky wheels generally get greased. Most of us hate whiners, but in this case, make an exception. It's your money, and if you whine to get what's yours, that sounds fair, doesn't it? Our congressional representatives love to hear from us. At least that's what they say, so pick up the phone, write an e-mail, or send some snail mail voicing your displeasure with COLA adjustment for your friends, the 78 million baby boomers who all vote.

WE'RE ALL DOOMED

Damn the facts; USS *Doomsday* is full speed ahead. Social Security is a pay-as-you-go system, with $2.7+ trillion of assets averaging a guaranteed rate of return around 3.6% in 2014. The actuarial shortfall is 2.3%, and there are many proposals out there with myriad combinations to solve this problem.

Don't believe the scare tactics.

Include Social Security in your retirement planning. If you don't believe me, then go ahead and plan on its collapse, and take our government with it: military pensions, civil service pensions, Medicare, Medicaid, and the gamut of government-funded programs we rely on. Are you happy now? I think I saw a doomsayer smile!

OK, if it really happens and you want the satisfaction of giving me a piece of your mind, I'll be on the back of the ship featured at the start of this chapter. I recommend you bring a life preserver.

CHAPTER 3

Keep It Simple

My intent is to simplify a complicated issue enough to help you select the best Social Security benefit options and improve your retirement situation. I choose to do this by covering relevant Social Security features and using scenarios to describe various options through examples. You should also visit http://www.retirereadyseries.com and view the Social Security video presentation and/or attend a monthly Social Security webinar.

LET'S MAKE IT COMPLICATED

It amazes me how complicated we make things. Whether it's reading a phone bill, deciphering a financial statement, or understanding an insurance policy, things are more complicated than they used to be and more difficult to understand than they should be. Social Security is extremely complicated, yet many people sign up without seeking advice or knowing how to choose the best alternative to support their retirement goals. The Social Security representatives you deal with on the phone or in person are quite helpful. But they don't know you, your goals, or what you don't know. They are also overwhelmed with calls and forbidden to give financial advice. You may also sign up online but likewise need to understand your options before making such an important decision.

This book will help you make better decisions. However, I recommend you contact your financial advisor (or seek one if you don't have one) and verify that you have selected the best option to meet your retirement and legacy goals. Remember, you don't know what you don't know. Your financial advisor should know, and if he or she doesn't, look for a new one.

Almost 40 million retirees were collecting Social Security retirement benefits at the beginning of 2014, and the majority started early (before full retirement age). Only 4% of all recipients wait until 70 to maximize their Social Security benefits. I won't suggest that everyone wait until 70, but if more people understood the advantages of waiting, many would consider delaying benefits until full retirement age or later.

Single and divorced people who were married for fewer than 10 years should consider retirement goals, work status, health status, income needs, legacy desires, expected longevity, and children's ages in making Social Security income decisions. Divorced individuals who were married at least 10 years should also consider their ex-spousal benefits and potential survivor benefits. Married couples have even more to consider in coordinating benefits between themselves and planning for a survivor benefit. I could go on and on, but I'm already starting to lose you. The bottom line is that this book and its scenarios will describe options you should consider.

Medicare is available to most of us at age 65. If you are already collecting Social Security, you will be automatically enrolled for Medicare Part A and Part B. Part B requires a monthly premium deducted from your Social Security monthly payment. For most people, that amount was $104.90 per month in 2014. It varies annual and generally goes up from year to year. There are also income-related adjustments if your income reaches certain thresholds. Plan ahead and talk with your tax advisor about this issue. You may decline Part B coverage, but that is generally a very bad idea unless you are covered by another health plan. Medicare Part B is heavily subsided by general tax revenue, so please do not decline this coverage before talking to a heath care professional and your financial advisor.

Social Security is a wealth distribution tool as well as a retirement plan. These annuity benefit payments are based on individual contributions. Determining your earned benefit is fairly complicated and depends on bend points that dilute benefits for higher contributors. I point this out so you will understand that the benefits earned by high and moderate contributors isn't much different and that low-wage earners receive a higher percentage of their contributions in monthly benefits. This compromise between a retirement plan for individual contributors and a wealth distribution tool to help the less fortunate was the foundation for Social Security's creation in the 1930s.

ACRONYM SOUP

Our government loves acronyms, and Social Security has plenty of them: PIA, FRA, WEP, GPO, COLA, and so on. We won't discuss many of these throughout the book, with the exception of cost-of-living adjustment (COLA) and full retirement age (FRA). I refer to COLA to let you know that your benefit will, for the most part, keep up with inflation. This growth is essential to maintain purchasing power as we age. When I discuss particular scenarios starting with the next chapter, I disregard this growth to keep it simple. Just remember that your benefit will increase to help maintain your Social Security income purchasing power.

Full retirement age (FRA) is based on your birth year. If you were born in or between 1943 and 1954, your FRA is 66. If you were born before 1943, your FRA is less than 66 (65 for people born in 1937 or earlier), and if you were born more recently than 1954, then your FRA is beyond age 66, gradually stepping up two months per year until reaching a maximum of 67 for those born in year 1960 or later. If your FRA is 66, you will receive 100% of your earned benefit at age 66, and if your FRA is 67, you have to wait an additional year to receive 100% of your Social Security benefit. You may think this is unfair, but at least you are younger and should have more life ahead of you. Want to trade places? Thought not.

I use 66 as the full retirement age for all scenarios. It keeps the math simple and will help you concentrate on the concept. The key point here is that full retirement age equals 100% of earned benefit. If you start sooner, you get less, and if you wait longer, you get more. For earned benefits, you may start as early as age 62 or wait until age 70 to maximize your benefit.

My favorite part of Social Security is the cost-of-living adjustment! Inflation can devastate a retirement plan. At 3% inflation, you will need to double your income to buy the same stuff 24 years from now, and many of you will be alive 24 years from now. COLA will protect your Social Security purchasing power, and because you cannot outlive your benefit, your longevity is protected also.

We could dig down much deeper, but adding more ingredients would spoil this simple dish and defeat the purpose of my book. A confused mind will not make a decision, and you must make a decision. My job is to get you there by simplifying the complicated.

WHAT YOU NEED TO KNOW

Almost every decision on when and which Social Security benefits to take will be compared to waiting until full retirement age. This is a benchmark we deviate from in upcoming scenarios to explain why. Options increase dramatically if we wait until full retirement age, as you will soon learn.

Most of us want things right now! As a group, we don't like to wait, thus many people sign up for Social Security as soon as they are eligible for benefits. There are many detriments to this strategy. If you start benefits before full retirement age, you won't have the option of collecting a spousal benefit while delaying earned benefits. If you work, you could lose a portion of your Social Security income until you reach full retirement age, although your benefit will be recalculated at full retirement age, adding lost benefits back into future benefit payments. If you are married and the higher of the two wage earners, collecting early benefits will diminish the survivor benefit, possibly leaving you or your spouse short of income after one of you passes. The highest Social Security benefit for a couple performs like a joint annuity and will last two lifetimes, while the smaller benefit will be lost upon the death of the first spouse.

By delaying benefits, you will receive a bigger check for the rest of your life, and if you delay until full retirement age or longer, you are better able to coordinate spousal benefits to realize your family goals. If you are divorced and eligible for an ex-spousal benefit, you can coordinate ex-spousal benefits at full retirement age, similar to a married couple.

Survivors are treated differently, and the rules allow more flexibility to help offset the loss of your loved one. A survivor may start benefits at age 60 and will maximize her survivor benefit by waiting until full retirement age. A survivor is also able to start her earned benefit or survivor benefit before full retirement age and switch benefits later in life; the same holds true for a divorcee eligible for a survivor benefit.

DON'T MEMORIZE THE NUMBERS

If you focus on the numbers, you will miss the big picture. Understand the concepts and options first and then choose a couple of solutions that meet your needs. Plugging in numbers is the last step, not the first. I will use a $1,000 benefit as the full retirement age benefit for all single and divorced individuals. It makes the math and comparisons easier to comprehend. Because most of you will have a full retirement age benefit greater than $1,000, it should make you feel pretty good. If you have less, sorry.

This book is about forest to trees to leaves. Take off the green eyeshades for now and read through the scenarios first. Concentrate on the options and move from chapter to chapter as they build on themselves. When you finish, you will be at the point where you can select the best choices to meet the goals you determined before reading this book. You did that, didn't you? If not, stop reading the book and do it now.

FOCUS ON CONCEPTS

As mentioned a few times, begin with the end in mind: your retirement goals! Because Social Security is the largest income source for most retirees, consider it within the context of your overall retirement plan. Remember that you can't outlive it, that you can't pass it on to anyone other than your spouse (or maybe an ex-spouse), and that it will retain most of its purchasing power as you age. The decision to start early or wait should be considered in the context of your overall retirement plan.

You do have a plan, don't you? Good. Because most budding retirees don't, that puts you a step above the rest. After all, it's hard to make good retirement income decisions if you don't have a path to success. Good decisions are hard to make if you don't know how much money you need and when you need it in retirement. Please, please, please create a plan before making a decision on this significant portion of your retirement income.

Know your goals and prioritize them for retirement. It is foolhardy to expect plans to execute perfectly. Hopefully your plan is conservative and you'll get to add instead of subtract retirement desires.

The following is Retirement Planning 101:

- Determine your goals.
- Create a plan.
- Execute the plan.
- Review the plan.
- Revise the plan.

Now, that doesn't seem difficult or complicated. You can do it!

CHAPTER 4

Start Early or Wait

FOR INDIVIDUALS AND DIVORCEES WITH FEWER THAN 10 YEARS OF MARRIAGE

All right, we are finally here. We begin to compare scenarios! We start with individual cases, and there is no right answer for everyone, only a right answer for you. Let's get started with what most people have done, cover the plusses and minuses, and help you make a decision.

73%

This is the percentage of people who begin their Social Security benefit before full retirement age (FRA). The most common age to begin benefits is 62, and it guarantees the lowest monthly lifetime payment. If starting benefits early coincides with a well-thought-out retirement plan, great. If not, it probably isn't the right choice, because it may not provide adequate resources to protect your longevity.

If your FRA benefit is $1,000 per month and you begin at age 62, your monthly check will be $750. Payments start four years early, but the 25% haircut costs you in the long run. Without considering cost-of-living adjustments (COLA) and assuming you spend the Social Security check (rather than invest the money), the "break-even" age is 78, which means that if you live beyond age 77, you'd earn more money from Social Security by waiting until full retirement age (66) to begin collecting benefits. Adding expected COLA reduces the break-even age.

OK, now you know the break-even age and can plan accordingly.

STARTING EARLY: THE GOOD

If Social Security isn't a big portion of your retirement plan and you want to see the glaciers before they melt away, then starting early might be your plan of choice. Additionally, most of us will be able to do more in our 60s than in our 80s and, as my sister always reminds me, "If you don't have your health, the rest doesn't matter." Having the money to enjoy retirement while you can enjoy retirement is important, and if starting Social Security before full retirement age allows you to enjoy your retired years, wonderful.

STARTING EARLY: THE BAD

If Social Security is a significant portion of your retirement and you do not have a pension, another annuity, or significant retirement assets to accommodate your desired lifestyle, then beginning Social Security benefits early could be a very bad idea! If you plan to continue working and decide to collect Social Security benefits before full retirement age, you will be subject to the "earnings test." This could reduce or eliminate your monthly Social Security paycheck until you reach full retirement age. Delaying your Social Security from 62 to 66 is like receiving a 7.2% compound return on your paycheck. That is pretty good, and I don't know anywhere else that you can get that type of guarantee; spending down other assets while delaying Social Security benefits is less risky and may be a better long-term solution.

STARTING EARLY: THE UGLY

Yes, it could be worse. If you live longer than expected, don't have a pension or another annuity, and run out of other financial assets before you run out of life, options are limited. Social Security may become your only source of revenue. Thus starting this benefit early could be devastating. The difference between beginning at 62 and waiting until 70 is a 76% increased monthly payment.

STARTING EARLY: THE UNEXPECTED

If you begin Social Security benefits before full retirement age and earn income above a certain amount, you will lose a portion of your Social Security payment until you reach full retirement age. Your benefit will be recalculated at full retirement age and adjusted for withheld payments. However, it might be smarter to wait based on your earnings expectations.

27%

If 73% of Social Security retirees begin collecting benefits early, then 27% wait to collect their Social Security benefit checks until full retirement age or later. There are advantages for those who wait!

FULL RETIREMENT AGE: THE GOOD

The good news is that you will now receive 100% of your full retirement age benefit, not a lesser amount based on an early start. If you worked between the ages of 62 and 66, you weren't penalized by having Social Security benefits withheld based on income. You might have actually increased your full retirement age benefit by working longer (assuming you broke into your 35 highest years of earnings). You have undoubtedly increased your retirement income and should be able to take advantage of these additional resources in reaching your retirement goals.

FULL RETIREMENT AGE: THE BAD

You've probably worked an additional four years or used up savings to support yourself in retirement between 62 and 66. If your goals included a family legacy and you pass before your mid- to late 70s, then your beneficiaries might be left with less money. If your health decreased significantly between 62 and 66 and you can no longer enjoy some of those items on your bucket list, then perhaps starting earlier would have been a better idea. Getting a physical or wellness checkup each year should assist with making the best decision.

FULL RETIREMENT AGE: THE UGLY

You die at 65 and 364 days. This is as ugly as it gets, because you will not collect any Social Security benefits. At least you won't know you made a bad decision—but all your friends will!

4%

A small percentage of individuals wait until 70. Doing so maximizes your monthly Social Security check. I generally recommend this strategy for the highest-earning partner in a marriage, but it's a toss-up for recipients who are single or divorced (with fewer than 10 years of marriage).

WAITING UNTIL 70: THE GOOD

Congratulations, your paycheck is 32% larger than what you would have received at full retirement age and 76% higher than if you began Social Security at age 62. By waiting, you have maximized your Social Security income checks for life! If you have a pension or additional annuity, you should be in pretty darn good shape. If you don't, at least you have maximized your Social Security and there is less of a burden on your remaining investments.

WAITING UNTIL 70: THE BAD

Money doesn't matter much if you don't have your health. Creating a plan to begin Social Security at 70 is just a plan. Monitoring your heath is essential. Declining health might suggest you should initiate Social Security payments before age 70. Your health and retirement goals are more important than maximizing your Social Security paycheck. Keep things in perspective.

WAITING UNTIL 70: THE UGLY

You die between full retirement age and 70.

One note: You can file for and suspend your Social Security benefit at full retirement age. It will allow you an option to backdate your payments to full retirement age. If you are terminally ill at 69, you can file for and collect all the missed Social Security payments from when you suspended benefits to your current age. It'll be one big check and you can have a huge party. You are terminally ill, though, and that's not much of a trade-off.

SCENARIO 1: KEVIN

Kevin makes plenty of money and saves a good percentage of his income for retirement. His health is average, his eating habits are inconsistent, he doesn't exercise much, and he works a lot of hours in a very demanding environment. Kevin plans to retire at 62. His retirement goals include travel, and he owns a primary and a vacation home. He is unmarried and has no long-term relationships.

Kevin plans to begin his earned Social Security benefit at 62. He is motivated to retire early to reduce stress and focus on his health. He will be debt-free at retirement and have enough assets to enjoy the type of retirement he desires. Although Kevin isn't primarily concerned with leaving a legacy, he plans to start his Social Security benefit at 62 and delay using other retirement assets, which will maximize a death benefit for his niece and nephew should Kevin die prematurely.

SCENARIO 2: ELIZABETH

Elizabeth is in her second career. As a retired Massachusetts state trooper, she has a pension, although it does not provide a cost-of-living adjustment to protect the pension's purchasing power. She is self-employed and likes her job. She eats well and exercises when she has time. She is unmarried and has no children.

Elizabeth likes to travel and spend time with her many friends. She is an avid New England Patriots fan and enjoys her "toys." Saving isn't her strong suit, but she owns some rental property and has significant cash value in a life insurance policy she plans to use in retirement. Like many of us, she wants to maintain her current lifestyle in retirement.

Because she enjoys working and is in good health, she plans to wait until 66 to retire. Waiting until 66 to start Social Security will provide her with 100% of her full retirement age benefit and keep her from being susceptible to the Social Security earnings test. She will not be debt-free at retirement, increasing her monthly cash flow needs.

Elizabeth enjoys life and will not sacrifice her lifestyle between 66 and 70 for a more generous Social Security payment. She has a good plan and believes starting Social Security at full retirement age is an excellent compromise.

SCENARIO 3: SEAN

Sean is a retired schoolteacher and in a second career. He is single with no children and didn't save much during his teaching career. He is seven years into a second career and was recently selected as a clerk magistrate for a municipality. It pays well and will produce a nice pension when Sean retires. Sean is a bit of a spendthrift, and he has struggled to save money throughout his life. He is afraid of running out of money in retirement and plans to work until 70 to maximize his municipal pension. He likes his free time, enjoys travel, and spends most of his time with friends. He likes to eat out and tends to overeat from time to time. He is in good health and exercises regularly. Longevity runs in his family.

Because Sean enjoys his job and fears running out of money before running out of life, he wants to work until 70 and delay receiving Social Security benefits until then. Sean met with a financial retirement planner who indicated Sean could retire from his municipal job at 66 and easily meet all his retirement goals. Sean may reevaluate at 66 but currently plans to remain at work until 70. He will be debt-free at retirement and will maximize his Social Security income at 132% of the full retirement age benefit.

Sean has many options based on his retirement analysis. He will monitor his health situation and use the generous vacation time provided by his current employer until calling it quits at 70. He can always accelerate his retirement by four years without compromising his retirement plans.

CHAPTER 5

Tapping into Someone Else's Benefit

FOR MARRIED COUPLES, DIVORCED INDIVIDUALS WITH AT LEAST 10 YEARS OF MARRIAGE, AND SURVIVORS

Options multiply for married couples, divorced individuals with at least 10 years of marriage, and survivors. The next three chapters will discuss your alternatives and provide many scenarios to help solidify the material. The key point at this stage is to understand that some people have the option to tap into someone else's earned benefit regardless of their own earned benefit size. Thus a higher-earning woman may take a spousal benefit on her lower-earning husband's Social Security benefit, and there are some good reasons to do so. Really.

MARRIED

You are probably aware that Social Security provides a spousal benefit, although too many married couples who attend my seminars are not. Based on recent law changes, marriage between same-sex partners is now recognized by our federal government, meaning that Social Security benefits apply to married same-sex partners just as they apply to married opposite-sex partners. For the point of discussion, you can replace "Lisa" in the following examples with "Fred" and the situations will be identical. Just don't call my wife Fred; she prefers Lisa.

My wife, Lisa, never worked a day in her life. All she did was raise our 12 kids (slacker). Even though she didn't earn one darn penny, she is entitled to a spousal benefit because we are married. If my full retirement age benefit is $1,000 per month and Lisa begins Social Security at age 62, she will receive 35% of my full retirement age benefit ($350 per month). If she waits until her full retirement age, the benefit will increase to 50%, or $500 per month. I must have filed for (or filed and suspended) my Social Security payments for Lisa to be eligible for this spousal benefit.

Lisa's spousal benefit is based on when she applies and not when I apply, so whether I start early, collect at full retirement age, or delay benefits until 70, it will have no effect on Lisa's spousal benefit. Lisa's spousal benefit is maximized at her full retirement age! This is a key point to remember, so I'll state it again. Spousal benefits are maximized at full retirement age.

DIVORCED

Divorced individuals who were married for a minimum of 10 years (to one person) and remain unmarried are eligible for an ex-spousal benefit. This is a significant benefit and one that many people aren't aware exists. Remember, you must have been married to a person for a minimum of 10 years: 9 years and 364 days gets you zilch. It begs the question whether you should suck it up for 10 years before calling it quits—seriously. Marrying the same person twice for a total of 10 years won't work either, unless the second marriage takes place before the end of the calendar year following your divorce. To collect an ex-spousal benefit, your ex-spouse must be at least 62 but isn't required to file for benefits (as long as you've been divorced for two years). Your ex won't know you are filing, as it's none of his business, so there's no need to worry about receiving hate mail or unwanted phone calls. Ex-spousal benefits aren't split, so if your ex was married at least 10 years multiple times, both you and the other ex-spouse(s) are entitled to full ex-spousal benefits. Any current spouse is also eligible for a spousal benefit. No wonder Social Security rules need some updating.

Spousal and ex-spousal benefit payments can be coordinated with your earned benefit. We'll cover those details in Chapter 7.

If you remarry, the ex-spousal benefits will stop. You may want to ask your significant other (preferably before proposal time) what his Social Security full retirement age benefit is before tying the knot. It may make the difference between hitching up and shacking up. My advice is to upgrade your benefit or shack up. The money will retain its value, whereas your love might not!

SURVIVOR

We all pass, and it generally doesn't happen at the same time for a married couple. There will be a survivor, and the planning decisions you make about beginning Social Security benefits have a dramatic impact on the survivor. When the first spouse passes, the smaller Social Security monthly payment will stop and the larger benefit will remain. I suggest you strongly consider maximizing this payment, as it performs like a joint annuity and will last two lifetimes.

Survivorship doesn't follow the same rules as spousal and ex-spousal benefits, making it more complicated to explain. Survivors may begin receiving survivor Social Security benefits as early as age 60 and simultaneously delay their own earned benefits until 70. Alternatively, a survivor may begin her earned benefit at 62 and delay the survivor benefit until it is maximized at full retirement age. The "earnings test" is still applicable to receipt of Social Security benefits prior to full retirement age. Lastly, the survivor benefit is dependent on when both spouses begin Social Security income, unlike the spousal and ex-spousal benefits.

Ex-spouses are also entitled to survivorship income. The marriage must have lasted at least 10 years, and the survivor must remain unmarried until age 60 to become survivor-benefit eligible. Survivorship is complicated enough to dedicate an entire chapter to how it works. Chapter 6 will tackle these benefits in detail.

SCENARIO 4: BILL AND TINA

Bill and Tina are happily married and the same age. Both lead sedentary lifestyles and are overweight. Bill works for the government, has a well-paying job, and will receive a small pension. He is a conservative investor but has consistently contributed to his thrift savings retirement account, creating a nice nest egg for retirement. He's also been paying into Social Security his entire career. Tina works part time, which provides extra money to fund the couple's discretionary spending habits while earning a small Social Security benefit. Bill and Tina have two grown children who have left home and are employed (if we could all be so lucky).

Let's compare three retirement situations, assuming Bill's full retirement age Social Security benefit is $1,000 per month and Tina's is $200 per month.

Plan A: Bill and Tina retire at 62 and begin Social Security benefits immediately. In Plan A, Bill will receive a $750 monthly Social Security payment (75% of full retirement age benefit), and Tina will receive a $360 monthly check (combination of earned and spousal benefit).

Plan B: Bill and Tina retire at 66 and begin Social Security benefits immediately. In Plan B, Bill will receive a $1,000 monthly Social Security payment (full retirement age benefit), and Tina will receive a $500 monthly check (50% of Bill's full retirement age benefit).

Plan C: Bill and Tina retire at 66. Bill files and suspends his benefit until age 70. Tina begins her Social Security income immediately. In Plan C, Bill will receive a $1,320 monthly Social Security payment starting at age 70 (maximizing his Social Security income), and Tina will receive a $500 monthly spousal benefit at retirement.

Comparing spousal benefits indicates the smallest amount Tina will receive is $360 per month at age 62. The spousal benefit is maximized at age 66 and equals $500 per month.

SCENARIO 5: TINA THE SURVIVOR

Bill maintained his sedentary lifestyle in retirement, which led to heart disease and an early demise at age 75 (sorry Bill, but none of us are getting out of here alive). Let's compare the same three plans after Bill passes.

Plan A: Bill and Tina retire at 62 and begin Social Security benefits immediately. When Bill passes at age 75, Tina will lose her $360 Social Security benefit and start collecting a survivor benefit. Here is where the survivor benefit is a bit tricky. Even though Bill started his benefit at age 62, the minimum survivor benefit is 82.5% of Bill's full retirement age benefit. So Tina's monthly survivor check will be $825, not $750. This begs the question why, but we won't go down that road, or you'll want to jump out of the car.

Plan B: Bill and Tina retire at 66 and begin Social Security benefits immediately. In this scenario, Tina will lose her $500 per month spousal benefit and receive a monthly $1,000 survivor benefit.

Plan C: Bill and Tina retire at 66. Bill files and suspends his benefit until age 70. Tina begins her Social Security income immediately. In Plan C, Tina will lose her $500 payment and collect a monthly survivor benefit check of $1,320.

Comparing survivor benefits shows the lowest monthly payment is $825 while the maximum available is $1,320. The latter amount is 60% higher than $825. Which check would you want?

SCENARIO 6: TINA THE EX-WIFE AND SURVIVOR

I guess Bill and Tina weren't happily married after all, and the relationship ended in divorce. The marriage was so bad toward the end that Tina vowed to remain divorced for the rest of her life. Because Tina was married to Bill for well over 10 years, she will receive an ex-spousal benefit and upgrade to a survivor benefit if she outlives Bill. In comparing Tina the ex-wife and survivor with plans A through C, Tina's incomes would be identical to those of Tina the spouse and Tina the survivor. Because Tina was collecting an ex-spousal benefit when Bill died at age 75, Social Security was aware of the marriage and upgraded Tina to a survivor benefit. Sending holiday cards to your ex-spouse and awaiting a nondeliverable mail return is a great back up plan—just in case.

CHAPTER 6

Making Your Benefit Last Two Lifetimes

I love joint annuities because they last both spouses' lifetimes. This chapter is about survivors and helping you make the best benefit decision for your family.

BIGGER IS BETTER

Perhaps bigger isn't always better, but I'll take a bigger paycheck any day of the week. When it comes to Social Security benefits,

I often recommend that the highest-earning spouse wait to start her earned benefit at age 70. Simple math suggests this is a great decision for married couples, as this payment will last two lifetimes and most likely exceed the break-even age of waiting to maximize this benefit. Considering that the highest-earning spouse might collect a spousal benefit from 66 to 70 is frosting on the cake. Maximizing this benefit isn't always the right answer, but it's a great place to start the analysis.

When making decisions on starting the highest earner's benefit, it's best to remember that it affects both spouses. It's critical to make this decision with survivor cash-flow needs in mind, too. I always run an analysis with the primary wage earner dying at a relatively young age to view a bad (if not worst) case scenario. It's better to plan for the worst and happily enjoy the expected than to plan for the best-case situation and leave your survivor destitute. Don't leave your survivor's outcome to chance. Have a plan. It's often better to start the lowest wage earner's benefit early if needed to enjoy retirement and allow the larger benefit to grow and protect your longevity.

LIFE EXPECTANCY

How long can you expect to live once you reach 65? Well, if you are a man in average health, that age is 82. If you are a woman, you can expect to live until 85. Couples tend to outlive their single counterparts. For a 65-year-old couple, there is a 50% chance that the survivor will reach age 92.

As we previously discussed, most of us would rather have the money early in retirement when we can enjoy it rather than delay benefits to protect our mid-80s and beyond (if we get there). Just the same, I have yet to meet anyone who prefers to run out of money before running out of life, so protecting longevity is an important consideration. I suggest that maximizing the highest wage earner's benefit is a relatively easy solution if other assets are available in early retirement. The risk to Social Security is miniscule (doomsday scenario), delayed benefits grow regardless of stock and bond market performance, and these guaranteed lifetime payments receive cost-of-living adjustments. Thus maximizing the highest wage earner's Social Security payment is an ideal strategy to protect survivors.

NO ONE IS GETTING OUT OF HERE ALIVE

OK, since none of us will live indefinitely, let's do a little number crunching to find break-even points. We'll disregard the cost-of-living adjustment (COLA) and focus on the survivor benefit. Just remember that any COLA will add more income to a bigger benefit and reduce the break-even age. The break-even analysis also assumes you are spending Social Security payments and not investing the money.

Let's pick on Bill and Tina again (from Chapter 5). Forget about the divorce; we'll leave them happily married and enjoying a carefree retirement. Recall that Bill's full retirement age benefit was $1,000 per month. In Plan A, Bill started his Social Security at age 62. In Plan B, he began the benefit at full retirement age (66). In Plan C, Bill waited and maximized his benefit at age 70. His age 62 benefit would be $750 per month; age 66 benefit would be $1,000 per month; and at 70, the monthly check would be $1,320.

Ready, set, go. Plan A (62) is in the lead, collecting $750 per month, and it remains there until Plan B (66), collecting $1,000 per month, passes Plan A when Bill turns 78. Plan B then takes the lead until Plan C (70), collecting $1,320 per month, passes Plan B when Bill reaches 82.5 years. If either Bill or Tina lives past 82.5, then delaying Bill's benefit to age 70 will earn them more in Social Security benefits.

Rarely are both spouses the same age. If the higher-earning spouse is also the older spouse, the analysis looks even better. Let's shave three years off Tina's age and have another look. When Bill turns 82.5 (break-even age for maximum delayed benefit), Tina would be 79.5 and may have plenty of tread left on her tires. That big Social Security check could go a very long way toward protecting her lifestyle if Bill, as expected, predeceases her.

WHAT'S IN IT FOR YOU?

Protecting the survivor's longevity provides a host of benefits. Primarily, it maximizes the survivor's Social Security benefit for life, reducing the likelihood of her becoming destitute and needing government support to survive. It should assist your spouse in maintaining financial independence after you are gone. It allows your children to focus on their children and not their parent. Lastly, it is a great example to set for your children. You may even seem wiser than deserved.

CHAPTER 7

Coordinating Benefits

Most people only consider Social Security benefits as individual benefits and leave money on the table. But it is your money, earned by paying into the Social Security system for your entire working career, and you are entitled to it. In this chapter, we'll discuss your benefit coordination options and run through several scenarios.

PUTTING THE PIECES TOGETHER

Now that we have covered individual, spousal, ex-spousal, and survivor benefits, it's time to put it all together to ensure that you optimize them in supporting your retirement plan. Each person is unique and will have different retirement goals. As such, we will cover benefit coordination alternatives for early, mid, and late benefit selection periods. At this stage, it is assumed that

you have a plan and know what you want in your life once retired. You should realize where the income challenges exist, and
this chapter will help you make smart decisions about Social
Security. The problem is that you don't know what you don't
know. This chapter will demystify your coordination options
and help you choose the best strategy to realize your personal
retirement goals.

MARRIED, DIVORCED, OR WIDOWED

Whether you are married, were married for at least 10 years to
the same person, or are a survivor, you are eligible to tap into
someone else's benefit. For married and divorced individuals,
these options are very similar. Survivors have more alternatives.
Please refer to Table 1.

If you are married or were married at least 10 years, the key
decision point is at full retirement age (66). If you begin benefits before full retirement age, you will receive a combination
of your earned and spousal (or ex-spousal) benefits. You have
no options. However, if you wait until 66, you are able to begin
a spousal (or ex-spousal) benefit and allow your earned benefit
to grow.

Table 1. Social Security benefit age decision points

Age 60	Age 62	Age 66	Age 70
Earliest survivor benefit age	Earliest earned, spousal and ex-spousal benefit age	Full retirement age / maximum spousal, ex-spousal, and survivor benefit age	Maximum earned benefit age

This is a key point to maximizing a working couple's Social Security benefits. At full retirement age, one spouse may have the option of collecting a spousal benefit while postponing and maximizing her own earned benefit. The caveats are that both of you must be at least 62 years old and have filed for Social Security benefits. Additionally, couples cannot collect spousal benefits simultaneously, so only one spouse may collect at a time. Remember, at full retirement age, you can file for and suspend your benefit, making your spouse eligible for a spousal benefit.

If you are divorced and were married for a minimum of 10 years, you have similar options at age 66. You can begin your ex-spousal benefit and allow your earned benefit to grow. Unlike a married couple, your ex only needs to be 62 or older. His filing isn't necessary for you to receive an ex-spousal benefit unless your divorce took place within the last 2 years. Coordinating benefits is just as important for you as it is for married couples.

If you are collecting an ex-spousal benefit and remarry, you will lose your ex-spousal benefit and become immediately eligible for a new spousal benefit. The key word to remember here is *upgrade*. If your second marriage doesn't work out and you divorce, you can return to collecting your previous ex-spousal benefit. If the second marriage lasted 10 years or longer, you can choose between the ex-spousal benefits and select the higher of the two payments. Sorry, you are not eligible to collect both!

For survivors, the rules are quite different. A widow (or widower) may begin a survivor benefit as early as age 60 and may postpone her own earned benefit to as late as 70 (maximizing her earned benefit). Alternatively, a survivor may file for her earned benefit as early as age 62 and postpone her survivor benefit until age 66 (maximizing the survivor benefit). The key point to remember here is that survivors do not have to wait until full retirement age to coordinate their earned and survivor benefits. Don't forget that Social Security benefits collected before full retirement age are subject to the Social Security earnings test.

FULL RETIREMENT AGE OPTIONS

Full retirement age is the most critical time in Social Security benefit options for married couples and divorced individuals who were married for a minimum of 10 years. As previously mentioned, there are no coordination options before full retirement age for these two categories of individuals. At full retirement age, the spousal benefit is maximized and you are now eligible to choose between your spousal (or ex-spousal) and your own earned benefits. This is a wonderful opportunity to delay your earned benefit, allowing it to grow at 8% simple interest per year to age 70 while collecting a spousal benefit at the same time. It's almost like having the best of both worlds: collecting benefits and growing benefits. Single counterparts must choose between collecting or growing benefits. If you are the higher wage earner, using this strategy also maximizes your survivor benefit, making you a trifecta winner!

Survivors have the advantage of coordinating benefits as early as age 60. The earnings test influences decisions before full retirement age, though. As a reminder, earning more than $15,480 per year in 2014 (tied to wage growth in future years) will reduce your Social Security benefit check. At 60, a survivor is entitled to 71.5% of either the deceased's full retirement age benefit, early benefit, or delayed benefit, depending on the age at death and whether the deceased was already collecting earned benefits. Yes, it's bit confusing.

If the survivor is still working and has an earned benefit similar to the survivor benefit, a great option is to begin the survivor benefit at 66, when the benefit is maximized and the earnings test no longer applies. This allows the survivor to delay receipt of her own earned benefit until age 70, maximizing her lifetime Social Security benefit.

If the survivor is unemployed or working but with a much smaller earned benefit, then it might make more sense to start the earned benefit at age 62 and allow the survivor benefit to maximize at full retirement age before beginning this lifetime income stream.

If the survivor is at or over full retirement age, it simplifies the decision-making process, as we can disregard the earnings test considerations.

The last point before we tackle scenarios is age. Significant age differences between spouses (and ex-spouses) eliminate coordination of benefit opportunities for the older applicant. The younger applicant must be at least 62 in order for the older applicant to consider a spousal (or ex-spousal) benefit. A survivor, on the other hand, may coordinate earned and survivor benefits based solely on her age.

SCENARIO 7: LEE AND BROOKE

Lee and Brooke are happily married. Both are employed in similar professions with comparable salaries and Social Security earned benefits. This couple's dilemma is age. Lee is 13 years older than Brooke. Lee is in great physical shape and has longevity on his side. In planning for the future and retirement, Lee plans to work until 66, and Brooke will retire on Lee's 70th birthday. She will be 57 years old. This is a compromise based on their age differences and should afford the couple quality time together in retirement. Lee will earn a small pension during his career; however, Brooke will not. Lee plans to take his pension as a joint lifetime annuity, accepting a reduced benefit but protecting the income stream for Brooke's lifetime. This couple hasn't done a good job of saving, but they are willing to change to meet their retirement goals. They plan to be debt-free at Brooke's retirement.

What are the best Social Security options for this couple? Should Lee start his Social Security at 66 or 70? And what about Brooke?

Because Lee will start his pension at 66 while Brooke continues to work, it makes sense for him to delay his Social Security benefit until 70. This will maximize his earned benefit and the couple's survivor benefit. Because Brooke will not have reached the age of 62 when Lee reaches full retirement age, there is no option for him to collect a spousal benefit.

Brooke will reach 62 when Lee is 75 years old. This will be her first opportunity to collect Social Security benefits. Although she is retiring early and will stop contributing to Social Security at age 57, her own earned benefit will remain bigger than her spousal benefit. If she starts her earned benefit at 62, she'll receive 75% of her earned benefit. If Brooke waits until full retirement age, she'll get 100% of her earned benefit, but Lee will then be 79 years old.

Thinking about just Brooke for a minute, the break-even age (without considering cost-of-living adjustments) between Brooke starting benefits at 62 and 66 is age 78. When Brooke is age 78, Lee will be 91. OK, Lee is in great shape today, but the likelihood of him reaching 91 is less than 50% (sorry Lee—facts are facts).

When Lee passes, Brooke will lose her earned benefit and begin collecting her survivor benefit. In this situation, a prudent choice would be for Brooke to start collecting her earned benefit on the day she turns 62.

Lee starting his earned benefit at 70 and Brooke beginning her earned benefit at 62 is a great plan for this couple.

SCENARIO 8: TYLER AND AUBREY

Tyler and Aubrey were college sweethearts. They are happily married and the same age. Tyler is self-employed and Aubrey assists Tyler but doesn't earn a salary. They make good money and are saving for retirement; Tyler is paying into the Social Security system, whereas Aubrey is not (because she isn't receiving a salary). They plan to retire at 66, travel, and spend time with their son, daughter, and grandchildren. They will be debt-free at retirement or work longer to obtain this retirement goal. Tyler's heath and family longevity are average; Aubrey stays fit and has family longevity on her side. This couple will not have a pension and will depend on their individual retirement accounts (IRAs) and Social Security to fund retirement.

What are some credible Social Security options for this couple?

Let's start with the easy one. Aubrey should begin her Social Security upon Tyler's retirement. She will be at full retirement age, and the spousal benefit will be maximized. As for Tyler, he has the option of beginning his Social Security benefit at retirement, or he can delay his benefit. It would reach a maximum amount at age 70.

If Tyler decides to begin his benefit at 66, it would initially reduce the amount needed from his and Aubrey's IRAs to fund the couple's desired lifestyle. Delaying the benefit would ensure an 8% simple income growth, increasing his future Social Security income. The break-even age between Tyler starting his benefit at 66 and waiting until 70, without considering cost-of-living adjustments, is 82.5. Adding cost-of-living adjustments will lower this break-even age. Tyler doesn't think he'll be around at 82.5 but knows his benefit will turn into a survivor's benefit upon his death and last two lifetimes. As there are no guarantees that his and Aubrey's IRA investments will grow, Tyler plans to eat into his IRA and turn on his Social Security benefit at 70.

Aubrey starting her spousal benefit at 66 and Tyler waiting until 70 for his earned benefit is a great selection for this couple.

SCENARIO 9: TIM AND LAUREN

Tim and Lauren are unmarried partners. They maintain active lifestyles and have good jobs. Tim works for a company that offers a 401(k) plan with matching contributions but no pension. Lauren is self-employed and a good saver. They have a dog but no children. Lauren is one year older than Tim. Both have good Social Security benefits, but Tim's benefit is slightly larger than Lauren's. Both plan to retire when Lauren turns 66 (full retirement age).

They love to travel and recently returned from a trip to Kauai, where they kayaked the Nā Pali coastline and went skydiving. These adventurers plan to increase their traveling and have a very active retirement. As there are no children, their legacy isn't very important to them.

What are some options for this couple?

As single people, there are no spousal benefits. This couple would rather spend more money up front enjoying travel and adventure at the cost of a less comfortable late-term retirement. To supplement cash-flow needs in early retirement, it makes sense for at least one of them to begin Social Security benefits at retirement. If we knew who was going to die first, the decision would be an easy one: we'd start that person's benefit first. Lauren is likely to outlive Tim, but this is a difficult decision. The best answer? Get married!

OK, they get married before retirement. What are the options now?

There are several credible choices.

Tim and Lauren: Option 1

Let's start with maximizing the biggest benefit: Tim's. To maximize it, Tim would have to wait until 70 to start his earned benefit. With this premise, Lauren should start her benefit immediately to reduce other retirement cash-flow requirements. Tim isn't at full retirement age, so he needs to wait until his 66th birthday before filing for his spousal benefit. This will net him 50% of Lauren's full retirement age benefit from age 66 to 70 while allowing Tim's earned benefit to grow. At 70, Tim would switch to his own earned benefit.

Option 1 provides a good early retirement Social Security income and maximizes the survivor benefit.

Tim and Lauren: Option 2

Tim and Lauren both decide to maximize both Social Security benefits. In this case, all spending during the first year of retirement will come out of this couple's retirement savings. When Tim turns 66, Lauren would file and suspend her earned Social Security benefit. Immediately afterward, Tim would file for his spousal benefit. Both spouses cannot simultaneously collect a spousal benefit. Although Tim's earned benefit is slightly larger than Lauren's earned benefit, Tim would collect four years of spousal benefit, whereas Lauren would only collect three years of spousal benefit before reaching age 70. In this situation, having Tim collect the spousal benefit would create more income. When Lauren turns 70, she would start her earned (and maximized) benefit. When Tim reaches 70, he would file for his own earned benefit.

Option 2 maximizes the couple's Social Security monthly income when Tim turns 70. The drawback is a much-reduced Social Security benefit for the first five years of retirement. If this couple saves enough and isn't concerned about drawing on their other retirement assets, Option 2 best protects their longevity.

Tim and Lauren: Option 3

Tim and Lauren decide to maximize Lauren's Social Security benefit and increase their early retirement income. In this situation, Tim would start his Social Security benefit immediately at age 65 and Lauren would file for her spousal benefit. At 70, Lauren would file for her own earned (and maximized) Social Security benefit.

Tim would continue receiving his current benefit. He is not allowed to suspend his earned benefit and collect a spousal benefit because he initiated Social Security benefits before full retirement age. Yes, it's a bit complicated.

Compared to the other options discussed, Option 3 provides more near-term retirement income for this couple and maximizes Lauren's Social Security benefit. Because Lauren's benefit isn't as high as Tim's, this option doesn't protect longevity as well as Options 1 or 2.

Tim and Lauren: Option 4

This is the last one for Tim and Lauren—promise! Tim and Lauren decide to just go for it and immediately maximize their near-term Social Security incomes. Lauren starts at 66 and Tim begins at 65. This will create the highest Social Security benefit in early retirement. It does eliminate any spousal benefit collections and minimizes the survivor benefit and longevity protection.

Option 4 is my least favorite, but it is one all too often chosen under these circumstances. Personally, I'd go with Option 1, as I believe it's the best value selection.

SCENARIO 10: LOIS LANE

Lois is divorced, works for a large newspaper company, and earns an average salary. She was married to Clark, who was her superman, but he left her for a younger woman after 15 years of marriage. Lois was heartbroken. Clark was in the movie business and made a lot of coin. He will receive an outstanding Social Security benefit. If Lois outlives Clark, she will receive a great survivor benefit. Clark keeps himself pretty fit and has longevity on his side, but he has a dangerous job and isn't getting any younger. He's also severely allergic to kryptonite, and too much of it could kill him. P.S. Lois doesn't own any kryptonite.

Lois is a good saver but is addicted to purchasing clothes and getting manicures, pedicures, and eyelash extensions. She rents an apartment and is debt-free. She will not have a great deal of savings in retirement, so maximizing her Social Security income is important. As such, she is planning her retirement around her Social Security benefit. With this in mind, her best option is to work until 66, begin her ex-spousal benefit, and then switch to her own earned benefit at age 70, when it is maximized and slightly larger than her ex-spousal benefit.

Recently, a fellow newspaper colleague, Jimmy Olsen, asked Lois to marry him. She was obviously flattered and likes Jimmy. Unfortunately, Jimmy's Social Security benefit is much lower than her ex-husband Clark's benefit. Marrying Jimmy would reduce her expected Social Security income between the ages of 66 and 70. Lois thanked Jimmy for the proposal but turned him down. She suggested they shack up instead and marry when Lois turns 70. They do marry when Lois turns 70.

If Clark predeceases Lois after she marries Jimmy, Lois is still eligible to upgrade to Clark's survivor benefit, because she married Jimmy after she turned 60.

SCENARIO 11: DOROTHY

Dorothy is a widow. She was married to Frank, who passed on at a relatively early age. Although Dorothy worked prior to meeting Frank, she left the workforce to help Frank with his law practice. She wasn't paid during this time and earned a very small Social Security benefit. Frank passed when Dorothy was 61 years old. Dorothy immediately started her (reduced) survivor benefit to supplement the retirement savings she and Frank created. At 61, Dorothy didn't have an option to start her own earned benefit, and because it was such a small amount, it wasn't worth waiting until age 62 and delaying her survivor benefit to age 66 (and maximizing it).

When Dorothy was 66, she remarried. Her second husband, Peter, was retired and had a pension and a Social Security benefit. As a survivor, Dorothy had options: she could keep her survivor benefit or take a spousal benefit based on Peter's Social Security earnings. Because Frank's survivor benefit was larger than the expected spousal benefit, she kept the survivor benefit.

Dorothy outlived her second husband. He died when Dorothy was 76 years old. She was then entitled to a survivor benefit based on Peter's Social Security income. Comparing benefits, Peter's survivor benefit was slightly larger than Frank's, so Dorothy switched to the highest survivor benefit.

CHAPTER 8

Taxes, Taxes, Taxes

Two of the largest concerns you should prepare for in retirement are inflation and taxation. We've discussed the importance of retaining Social Security cost-of-living adjustments, and now we'll talk about Social Security taxation.

Many people believe taxation of Social Security benefits is a double tax. I don't. I look at Social Security as a tax-deferred savings plan similar to a 401(k). My contributions (and matching company contributions) aren't much different from a 401(k), with the exception that they are forced on us. Unlike the 401(k), Social Security will provide me (and my spouse) a lifetime joint annuity payment with cost-of-living adjustments. It is a wealth distribution tool as well as a "retirement plan," so people who earn a lot will get a smaller monthly percentage of contributions back compared to lower-earning (and contributing) members. Sorry for the diatribe. Back to business.

DON'T SHOOT THE MESSENGER!

I didn't make the rules; I'm just informing you that your Social Security payments will most likely be taxed. The maximum amount of Social Security income that can be taxed is 85%, and it is taxed at your marginal tax rate. If you are in this category, where 85% of your Social Security benefit is taxed, congratulations! You should have enough money to enjoy your retirement.

IN THE BEGINNING

In 1935, the Social Security Act was signed into law. It was set up as a self-funding program with the expectation that it would never need general tax revenue to survive. Benefits were tax exempt, and it worked as advertised for decades.

Demographic changes, particularly reduced worker-to-Social Security beneficiary ratios and extended life expectancies, required adjustments to keep Social Security solvent. Taxation would be one of the many adjustments. The original act didn't provide for the automatic cost-of-living adjustments that we currently enjoy, either, so some of the changes were favorable.

TODAY

Up to 85% of your Social Security Benefits could be taxed. I could educate you on all the law changes and how we got here, but probably all you want to know is how much of your benefit will be taxed. Let's get going.

PROVISIONAL INCOME

Taxation of your Social Security is based on your *provisional income*. You've probably never heard this term. New names generally aren't a good thing, especially when they deal with taxes. This name is no exception to that rule.

> Provisional income = adjusted gross income (AGI) + 1/2 of your Social Security benefit + tax-exempt interest.

There are a few other items, but this definition covers it for most of us.

Tax-exempt interest includes municipal bond tax-fee interest payments. Although these bond interest payments aren't taxed (directly), they do contribute to the taxation of your Social Security benefit.

Thought you were being smart by purchasing muni bonds and accepting the lower, nontaxed interest payment? Whoops, maybe that wasn't such a smart idea. Remember, don't shoot the messenger. **Note:** Roth IRA earnings do *not* contribute to your provisional income.

FIXED THRESHOLDS

Fixed is the key word here. The thresholds we discuss are fixed, not tied to inflation or wage growth. So as your income needs grow to keep up with rising costs, the thresholds that determine how much of your Social Security benefit is taxed don't increase, meaning that more of your Social Security income will be taxed in the future, unless you are already paying taxes on 85% of your benefit.

SCENARIO 12: PETER AND LISA

Peter and Lisa are married. They are retired and currently living on Peter's pension and Lisa's Social Security benefit. Although they have savings, they aren't needed at this time. Their adjusted gross income is $75,000, and Lisa's Social Security benefit is $12,000. They did not earn any tax-exempt interest this year. How much of Lisa's Social Security benefit will be taxed?

Provisional income = $75,000 (AGI) + $6,000 (1/2 of Lisa's Social Security benefit) = $81,000.

Using Table 2, Peter and Lisa are $37,000 above the $44,000 threshold. They also have $12,000 between the $32,000 and

Table 2. Social Security taxation

Status	Provisional income	Taxable % of Social Security benefit
Single	< $25,000	0
	$25,000 to $34,000	50
	> $34,000	85
Married	< $32,000	0
	$32,000 to $44,000	50
	> $44,000	85
Married filing separately (living with spouse)	All	85

$44,000 thresholds. To figure out the taxation on Lisa's Social Security benefit, we multiply $37,000 by 0.85 (85%) and multiply $12,000 by 0.50 (50%). Then we add them together.

$37,000 × 0.85 =	12,000 × 0.5 =	$31,450 + $6,000 =
$31,450	$6,000	$37,450

We now compare the $37,500 to 85% of Lisa's Social Security benefit, which is $10,200 ($12,000 × 0.85). Social Security taxation is limited to 85% of the annual benefit received. Thus Peter and Lisa would add the lower amount ($10,200) to their adjusted gross income of $75,000. This additional $10,200 would be taxed at their marginal income tax rate.

The key takeaway is that Peter and Lisa have a moderate income, but they easily maximized taxation on their Social Security benefit.

SCENARIO 13: JIM AND DEB

Jim and Deb are married. They are in a phased retirement. Jim is collecting his Social Security benefit while Deb continues to work and pay the bills. Deb has a secure but low-paying job. Her work allows them to leave their other retirement assets intact for the time being. Their adjusted gross income is $40,000, and Jim's Social Security benefit is $12,000. They did not earn any tax-exempt interest this year. How much of Jim's Social Security benefit will be taxed?

Provisional income = $40,000 (AGI) + $6,000 (1/2 of Jim's Social Security benefit) = $46,000.

Using Table 2, Jim and Deb are $2,000 above the $44,000 threshold. They also have $12,000 between the $32,000 and

$44,000 thresholds. To figure out the taxation on Jim's Social Security benefit, we multiply $2,000 by 0.85 (85%) and multiply $12,000 by 0.50 (50%). Then we add them together.

$2,000 × 0.85 =   12,000 × 0.5 = $1,700 + $6,000 =
$1,700 $6,000 $7,700

We now compare the $7,700 to 85% of Jim's Social Security benefit, which is $10,200 ($12,000 × 0.85). Jim and Deb would add the lower amount ($7,700) to their adjusted gross income and pay taxes on $7,700 of their Social Security benefit at their marginal income tax rate.

SCENARIO 14: LUIS

Luis is divorced and was previously married for more than 10 years. He is 67 years old. He is frugal and saved a significant portion of his earnings during his working years. His frugality was the cause of his divorce (at least that's what Luis claims). His favorite investment vehicle during his working years was a Roth IRA, following the 1997 Taxpayer's Relief Act, which established Roth IRAs. He maximized his contribution every year. He currently has 60% of his retirement assets in a Roth account. This Roth IRA provides Luis tax-exempt income, which is treated very differently than municipal bond tax-exempt interest. The bottom line is that Roth IRA earnings do *not* contribute to your provisional income.

Luis's ex-wife is over the age of 62, and Luis is currently collecting his ex-spousal benefit, allowing his own earned benefit to grow. He hates paying taxes and adjusts his income to minimize taxation. His adjusted gross income is $21,000, and Luis's ex-spousal Social Security benefit is $6,000. He did not earn any municipal bond tax-exempt interest this year. How much of Luis's Social Security benefit will be taxed?

> Provisional income = $21,000 (AGI) + $3,000 (1/2 of Luis's Social Security benefit) = $24,000.

Using Table 2, Luis's provisional income is below the $25,000 threshold. As such, he will pay no taxes on his $6,000 Social Security benefit.

Although Luis's taxable income is low, he lives on much more. He supplements his taxable income with an additional $26,000 taken from his Roth account. Because Roth money isn't taxed and doesn't contribute to his provisional income, Luis eliminates taxation on his Social Security benefit without reducing his lifestyle.

SCENARIO 15: RICH AND LYDIA

Rich and Lydia are married. They took an early retirement at age 60. Rich had a well-paying job, and Lydia was a stay-at-home mother with no earned Social Security benefit. Both turned 66 this year and decided to begin Social Security benefits. Rich started his full retirement age benefit, and Lydia began her spousal benefit. As in previous years, Rich left his retirement accounts alone. He prefers to let them grow tax deferred for the time being while he creates income for a well-funded municipal bond investment portfolio. He enjoys the tax-exempt income it provides.

Rich and Lydia's adjusted gross income is $0, Rich's Social Security benefit is $24,000, and Lydia's spousal benefit is $12,000. They earned $40,000 in tax-exempt interest this year from their municipal bond portfolio.

How much of Rich and Lydia's Social Security benefits will be taxed?

Provisional income = $0 (AGI) + $18,000 (1/2 of Rich and Lydia's Social Security benefit) + $40,000 (tax-exempt interest) = $58,000.

Using Table 2, Rich and Lydia are $14,000 above the $44,000 threshold. They also have $12,000 between the $32,000 and $44,000 thresholds. To figure out the taxation on their Social Security benefit, we multiply $14,000 by 0.85 (85%) and multiply $12,000 by 0.50 (50%). Then we add them together.

$14,000 × 0. 85 = $11,900	12,000 × 0.5 = $6,000	$11,900 + $6,000 = $17,900

We now compare the $17,900 to 85% of their combined Social Security benefit, which is $30,600 ([$24,000 + $12,000] × 0.85). Rich and Lydia would add the lower amount ($17,900) to their adjusted gross income and pay taxes at their marginal income tax rate. This caught Rich by surprise, as he didn't expect to pay taxes on Social Security income at all.

MY HEAD HURTS

Did you enjoy the last section? Me neither. Too much math. But the scenarios should have made comprehension a bit easier. Just focus on the big picture. The fixed thresholds mean that more of your Social Security income will be taxed as inflation requires increased spending to maintain your lifestyle. If you want to reduce Social Security taxation, there are three basic options.

REDUCING SOCIAL SECURITY TAXATION

Eliminate/Reduce Debt

Eliminating debt decreases your required living expenses without reducing your lifestyle expectations. Reducing expenses helps also, but eliminating debt should be the goal!

Minimize Your Adjusted Gross Income

There are many ways to do this without negatively affecting your lifestyle. I'll cover a few favorites.

1. Eliminate debt, which reduces fixed income needs.
2. Consider Roth IRA investments. This money is collected by you tax-free in retirement and will not affect your provisional income.
3. Borrow against permanent life insurance policies. This offers another option for receiving tax-exempt money that will not impact your provisional income.
4. Consider moving to a location with a lower cost for the lifestyle you desire. As an example, the fixed cost of living in New York City is pretty darn high compared to the national average.

Delay Your Social Security Benefit

The maximum amount of Social Security income taxed is 85%. If you are in this category, congratulations! You won't go hungry, and you can still reduce taxation by delaying benefits. A full retirement age (FRA) benefit of $1,000 pays $1,320 if delayed to 70 years of age.

At FRA (66), 85% of $1,000 is $850, meaning that $150 of the $1,000 is *not* taxed.

At 70, 85% if $1,320 is $1,122, meaning that $198 of the $1,320 is *not* taxed.

You may not think the difference is all that important, but $48 per month is $576 per year. Throw in annual cost-of-living adjustments and multiply by the number of years you (and your spouse) expect to live. Now the number gets much bigger. If you don't like paying extra taxes, this strategy helps. Everything adds up!

KEEP IT SIMPLE, SHIPMATE (KISS)

I believe in the KISS principle. Planning to pay taxes on 85% of your expected Social Security income is a conservative approach to retirement planning. Could it get worse? Perhaps Congress will decide to tax an even higher percentage of our Social Security income, but I don't think so. As my hiking buddy says, "Pack for bear and hope for squirrel." You won't be disappointed if you plan to pay taxes on 85% of your Social Security benefit.

Chapter 9

Redos and Upgrades

Too many of us believe that beginning Social Security benefits is the last Social Security decision we have to make. This would be a mistake. Like the rest of your investments and income, Social Security planning should be considered periodically: in preparation for a life change or when your spouse or ex-spouse passes.

LIFE AFTER FULL RETIREMENT AGE

1. When you reach full retirement age, Social Security benefit options multiply. If you began benefits earlier

in life, you can suspend payments at full retirement age and let your future benefits grow by 8% per year until age 70.

2. You can file for and suspend benefits at full retirement age and then change your mind any time before age 70 and ask for a lump sum of the delayed benefits.

3. You can file for and suspend benefits at full retirement age to delay your Social Security income but allow your spouse to collect a spousal benefit.

4. You can "restrict" your Social Security income to your spousal benefit at full retirement age provided your spouse is at least 62 and has already filed. If you are filing for an ex-spouse's benefit, she must be at least 62, and her filing for Social Security benefits isn't a requirement.

5. You can shift from a spousal benefit to your own earned benefit anytime between 66 and 70. The longer you wait, the higher your earned benefit will grow (up to 32% at age 70).

SCENARIO 16: ROGER

In 2008, at age 63, Roger lost his job after the US housing market crashed. As a typical American, he hadn't saved much for retirement and decided to begin his Social Security benefits immediately. His persistent job searching paid off. At 65, he found a position that would cover his annual living expenses and actually allow him to somewhat rebuild his retirement savings. At 66 (full retirement age), he suspended his monthly payments. He allowed his benefit to grow by 8% per year and restarted his Social Security income at age 70, maximizing his future benefit.

SCENARIO 17: JILL

Jill filed for and suspended her $1,000-a-month full retirement age Social Security benefit at 66 and then at age 69 discovered she had terminal cancer. She decided to immediately begin her Social Security benefit and backdate the application to when she "suspended" payments at 66. She began collecting $1,000 per month at age 69 and also received a check for $36,000 ($1,000 per month × 12 months × 3 years). She was able to complete several of her bucket list items before becoming too ill to travel.

REMARRIAGE

If you remarry, your benefit could go up, stay the same, or be reduced. It depends on your earned benefit, your ex-spousal benefit, and your new spouse's benefit. Complicated, huh?

LOVE VERSUS MONEY

Call me heartless (you won't be the first—or the last). I'm just providing the facts, and you make the decision. It's always best to know what will happen when you say "I do." Remember that phrase "to have and to hold from this day forward, for better or for worse, for richer or for poorer"? Well, most of us don't plan on the "for poorer" part. Saying "I do" might be an instant downgrade if you are collecting an ex-spousal benefit that is higher than your future spousal benefit.

SCENARIO 18: LIVING THE LIFE OF RILEY

Riley was married for 15 years but, at age 60, left his wife, Kelly, for a younger woman. Kelly was 64 at the time, had a great-paying job, and maximized her Social Security contributions. Riley bounced around from job to job during his life and didn't work the 40 quarters necessary to earn a Social Security benefit. However, he was good looking. Riley immediately moved in with his girlfriend, Nancy. He worked part time as a handyman, getting paid mostly under the table, and survived off Nancy's income. Riley started his Social Security as soon as he turned 62, collecting his ex-spousal benefit. He is now 65, and Nancy is 62. They plan to retire, get married, and enjoy travel. Nancy is a high school teacher in Texas, and she never paid into the Social Security System.

The big day comes when Riley and Nancy are married. Riley immediately loses his ex-spousal Social Security benefit. He is not eligible for a spousal benefit because Nancy never paid into Social Security, and because Riley hadn't contributed 40 quarters, he will receive zilch in future Social Security benefits. Most of us don't care because we don't like Riley.

The key point is that a divorcee could lose Social Security income if she remarries because her ex-spousal benefit will be replaced with the "new" spousal benefit. Do the math before reciting the "for richer or poorer" section of your vows.

Riley 2: Shacking Up

We don't like Riley, but that doesn't mean he's an idiot. He and Nancy quickly divorced, making Riley immediately eligible for his previous ex-spousal benefit. Then they traveled the world and had a lot of fun together. When his ex-spouse Kelly predeceased him, Riley upgraded to his survivor benefit, which more than doubled his Social Security income. He also inherited Nancy's pension when she died shortly thereafter. He lived to 100 and enjoyed a worry-free life.

In all seriousness, know the Social Security facts before committing to remarriage. Your ex-spousal benefit will stop, and your spousal benefit begins upon remarriage. The same goes for your new spouse, so do a little planning beforehand.

SURVIVOR

The critical age to remember is 60. A survivor may start her benefit at age 60 (earlier if disabled or when young children are involved) and simultaneously delay her own earned benefit. On the other hand, she may collect her own earned benefit at 62 and delay the survivor benefit until age 66 (when it is maximized).

An ex-spouse (previously married for at least 10 years) receives the same survivor benefits and options at age 60.

SCENARIO 19: LUCY

Lucy was married to Ricky for 13 years before they divorced. At age 60, Lucy married Fred. Ricky died when Lucy turned 64 years old, making Lucy eligible for Ricky's survivor benefit even though she was married to Fred. It's a head scratcher, but it's really true!

Lucy 2

This is the same situation as the first, except Lucy and Fred married when Lucy was 59. Because she married Fred before the age of 60, she was not entitled to Ricky's survivor benefit when he died.

Lucy 3

This is the same situation as in Lucy 2. Fred's infatuation with redheads diminished. He divorced Lucy and returned to his previous wife, Ethel. Lucy immediately became eligible for Ricky's survivor benefit when her divorce with Fred was finalized.

WIDOWED TWICE OVER

The survivor has more options. She can collect Social Security income based on her own earned benefit, her first deceased husband's survivor benefit, or her second deceased husband's survivor benefit. If she remarries, then a spousal benefit based on her current husband is another option. Reread the section titled "Scenario 11: Dorothy" in Chapter 7.

SURVIVOR × 3

Never marry someone who has survived two spouses. It would be bad luck.

STILL WORKING IN RETIREMENT

Approximately 25% of the average US retiree's income is earned money (meaning that many retirees are still working). The critical age to remember is 66 if you plan to work and collect Social Security benefits at the same time. At 66 (full retirement age), you are not penalized for working and simultaneously collecting Social Security benefits. Before 66, your benefits are reduced if you earn more than a certain amount of income. It doesn't matter if you are collecting survivor, spousal, ex-spousal, or earned Social Security benefits; if you collect before full retirement age and you earn too much, your Social Security income is reduced.

P.S. Earnings = *work*. You are not penalized for pensions, investment income, royalties, inheritances, real estate income, gifts, and a host of other income sources.

I could make this section very complicated and explain all the rules, but you are near the end of this book, and I've confused you enough. Suffice it to say that if your Social Security benefits are reduced because you earn more money than the allowed threshold, you will get increased future monthly benefits based on these withholdings after you reach full retirement age. You can earn millions at full retirement age and beyond without a Social Security benefit reduction.

The bottom line is that if you plan to work in retirement and need Social Security before 66, then start it. If you can wait until full retirement age to begin your Social Security benefit, it's a better alternative.

SCENARIO 20: WARD AND JUNE

Ward and June are lifelong partners and just celebrated their 50th wedding anniversary. They are doing well and enjoying retirement. Their two boys are grown.

Several years ago, their youngest son, Theodore, lost his job in the movie industry and moved back home for a short stint. It was actually 2 years. It seems short compared to 50 years of marriage, but at the time, it seemed like a very long period. Theodore went back to school, got a psychology degree, and used his connections to get back into the movie industry, where he helps actors with their personal problems.

Due to Theodore's unexpected arrival and the additional family cost of supporting their son with living and tuition expenses, Ward and June decided to begin Social Security benefits earlier than planned. At the time, Ward was 64 years old, retired, and collecting a nice pension. June was 63 years old and a stay-at-home mom for most of her life. After the boys left home, she earned her nursing degree and worked at the local hospital for 12 years. When Theodore returned home, she was semiretired, working part time at the hospital, and earning approximately $25,000 per year.

Although Ward and June planned to maximize the family's survivor benefit (Ward's Social Security income at age 70), they decided the best option to increase current income and reduce Theodore's school debt was for Ward to begin his Social Security early.

Even though June was working at the time, her earned income didn't affect Ward's Social Security benefit. Ward had income from a pension, but not any earned income. He received a reduced Social Security benefit due to his age, but no additional money was withheld because he had zero earned income. His Social Security payments during the next two years paid for Theodore's tuition and kept Ward and June from touching their retirement nest egg.

Once Theodore earned his degree and left for California and his new job, Ward suspended his Social Security benefits (he was 66) and allowed his future Social Security benefits to grow at 8% per year. He recently restarted his benefits at 70. June started her spousal benefit at 66 (maximizing this benefit) and plans to switch to her own earned benefit next year when she turns 70.

This scenario discussed numerous Social Security decisions made by Ward and June. They were fortunate that their oldest son, Wally, worked for the Social Security Administration and knew the ropes. Social Security isn't as black and white as many of us believe.

INCREASING SOCIAL SECURITY IN RETIREMENT

Many of us will not increase our own earned Social Security benefits during retirement; however, it can be done! Our government is happy to collect Social Security contributions every time you earn a paycheck, so you'll continue to pay into the system for as long as you work, regardless of age. Ageism doesn't exist when it comes to paying taxes.

Some of us like our jobs; others aren't so fortunate. For those that get fed up with their employment and transition into something they love to do, there is usually a cost. It might just be the paycheck. Fun jobs and pay tend to be negatively correlated. Yes, there are exceptions to the rule.

THIRTY-FIVE IS THE MAGIC NUMBER

Social Security only looks at your highest 35 years of contributions (adjusted for wage growth). So if you pay into the Social Security system for 45 years, your earned benefit is based on the highest 35 years of contributions. But thank you for paying in those extra 10 years and helping out the slackers. Of course, if you haven't paid into Social Security for 35 years, every year you continue to contribute, you earn a bigger Social Security paycheck.

SCENARIO 21: CHUCK

Chuck is a workaholic. He began working on his family farm at age eight and started receiving earned income (paying into Social Security) at 16. A successful, college-educated agribusiness executive, Chuck earned millions during his 50-year working career and now teaches as an adjunct professor at a prestigious local university. He's paid very well for his part-time work. He continues to pay 6.2% of his earnings (along with a similar contribution from the university) into the Social Security system. Because Chuck will not break into his top 35 years of earnings, his continued contributions will not earn him an extra penny in Social Security income. He doesn't mind, as he enjoys sharing his corporate American life experiences with young men and women, helping ready them for the real world. His business experiences help balance other university academics who lack Chuck's corporate background.

SCENARIO 22: KATHLEEN

Kathleen is married to Peter, and they had six children. She began a teaching career after her youngest son entered elementary school. Peter worked for a state government agency and earned a good pension but never paid into our Social Security system. Kathleen worked 26 years as a schoolteacher and paid into the Social Security system before retiring at the age of 66 and beginning her Social Security benefits. After a year of retirement, she missed teaching children (actually, she found it hard to be around Peter all day long, but don't tell Peter). She obtained part-time employment with a private elementary school in her hometown and, through her new employment, began contributing to the Social Security system again. Because she had worked fewer than 35 years, she will experience increased Social Security benefits based on her new contributions.

On a side note, Peter is ineligible for a spousal benefit due to the size of his pension. The government pension offset comes into play here. I promised not to talk about it in this book, but I couldn't help myself in mentioning it once.

CHAPTER 10

Do It!

I'm done with the Social Security education, but the class isn't over. All the information in the world will make you wise but not make you move. You've probably heard the saying "knowledge is power," but it really isn't true if you don't use the knowledge. I mentioned early in this book that underestimating taxes and inflation can decimate your retirement. Well, there is an obstacle 100 times larger than those combined perils: procrastination. I witness it all the time, every day, where people like you and I can't decide. Instead of making the future happen, they just let it happen without planning, which usually isn't the best plan!

THIS ISN'T ROCKET SCIENCE

Retirement income planning isn't rocket science. If you follow just five basic steps, you'll be OK: act, determine goals, put together a plan, execute the plan, and revise the plan. You can count these steps on one hand—or one foot, if you prefer.

PIE

Most of us like pie, so let's pretend our retirement income is a pie; you pick the flavor. My favorite is blueberry, but it tends to be a bit runny. Approximately 40% of the average US retiree's pie consists of Social Security; it's a very big piece. Maybe too big. But it's not the whole pie. Don't forget the rest. If you add more ingredients, perhaps you can reduce the Social Security slice. We all like variety, don't we? The more flavors the better. Pensions, retirement savings, real estate, annuities, royalties, life insurance cash value, nonretirement investments, and even work add ingredients to our pie.

BIG PIE VERSUS SMALLER PIE

If we have a lot of debt, we need a big pie. Less debt means we can live on less pie, and no debt means we need a much smaller pie. A small pie without debt reduces risk and taxes and could increase quality of life. There is no penalty for having no debt and a big pie! As mentioned previously, becoming debt-free in retirement should be a goal.

EVERY YEAR WE NEED MORE PIE

Costs generally go up, not down. Over time, we'll need more pie to survive and enjoy life. Twenty years into retirement, we'll need approximately twice the income to enjoy the same retirement we began with, and the average retiree lives approximately 20 years after retirement! If we live on the same income each year, then halving our lifestyle is only the other choice. Which option do you prefer?

BAKE YOUR PIE EARLY

Too many of us don't start baking our pie until retirement is upon us. You may not have enough of the right ingredients if you wait too long—and you *will* need pie. If you haven't considered retirement yet, start now, and I mean right now. If you have a financial advisor, ask her to run a retirement analysis on you. If you don't have an advisor, get one or contact the company that invests your money. Remember, you don't know what you don't know. Retirement planning is too important to go it alone, so at least get a second opinion from a licensed professional if you tend to be stubborn and pig-headed like me. Take some financial and retirement classes, which most universities, colleges, and community colleges offer. It'll reiterate that you don't know what you don't know.

MAKE THE PIE LAST

The pie must last longer than you do. Plan on making a big enough pie to last your lifetime. This brings us back to the previous section: Bake your pie early.

FIVE BASIC STEPS TO RETIREMENT PLANNING

Step 1: Act

There are three types of people in the world: proactive, reactive, and inactive. Which one are you? The first two categories have a chance; the last one isn't reading this book. If all you do is read this book and nothing else, I haven't achieved my goal and neither have you. Do something, and do it today! I mean right now. Make a decision and don't second-guess yourself. Now don't you feel better?

Step 2: Determine Goals

You should have completed this task before reading the book. If you did, then you may want to tweak those goals based on the information you learned here. Your retirement is a living, breathing entity, and it needs care and feeding during your lifetime. If you have yet to complete your goals, do it now. Read Step 1 again if necessary! The following is a list of items to help you determine your goals:

1. What is your destination?
2. When are you going?
3. Who's coming along?
4. How much will it cost?
5. How long will it take?
6. What's your Plan B? (You need a backup plan.)
7. What's your Plan C? (Some of us need two backup plans.)

Step 3: Put Together a Plan

This is where most people come up short, because they decide to go it alone. It amazes me how many very successful and well-educated people plan their retirement by themselves when these very decisions have such a significant impact on the last 20%–25% of their lives. We go to doctors for annual physicals because these experts can better determine our health needs. Would you ever reset a broken bone by yourself? Of course not: it seems almost ludicrous to make such a suggestion. If we treated our financial health with the same regard as we treat our physical and mental health, many of us would better enjoy the latter years of our lives.

Once we take action, we should look ahead and be realistic. I believe in the adage "measure twice and cut once." Remember that you don't know what you don't know, so please seek counsel.

Step 4: Execute the Plan

We might as well execute the plan we created, or it wouldn't be of much use. For most of us, preparing for retirement will be a long journey covering decades; for others, retirement may only be a few years away. Don't get distracted and take a lot of side trips along the way. This doesn't mean you should only focus on retirement; it means you must remember your retirement priorities so you will actually realize them. Too many of us have a short-term focus. Don't fall into this trap. The sooner you begin implementing pieces of the plan, the earlier you will reach your goals. Persistence is the key to success once you execute the plan. It will be worth the effort!

Step 5: Revise the Plan

I love Bill Belichick. For those of you who don't know him, he is the head coach of the New England Patriots. Arguably, he will be remembered as the most successful National

Football League coach—ever! OK, I'm a New England Patriots fan, so perhaps I'm a bit biased, but he is a great coach nonetheless.

Do you think Bill Belichick and the Patriots have a winning plan before the game begins? Of course they do. They have already completed Steps 1–4, as have all the other National Football League teams and coaches in preparing for each game. Why are Belichick and the Patriots so darn successful? I'll argue that it's the way they handle Step 5. Just watch the team perform after half time and recognize the adjustments they have made.

Life evolves and retirement goals may change. Your retirement plan requires adjustments along the way. I encourage my clients to meet for a retirement analysis review annually. No one needs to obsess daily or monthly on "how goes it," but annual reviews on something so darn important are prudent. Modifications and course corrections are necessary to realizing success.

There will be times in our lives when we run into bad weather and restricted waterways. They can slow us down or perhaps force us to take an alternative retirement route, but keep your eye on the destination. Plan management is expected. Lean on your trusted advisors to help you navigate around or safely through existing hazards.

This trip should fun, and if you enjoy yourself along the way, you are more likely to stick with the plan. Celebrate each victory en route to retirement: ending credit card debt, paying off a car loan or home mortgage, reaching a financial objective in your retirement account, and getting your children off the dole come to mind.

This book contains the requisite information for most of us to make a darn good decision on when to begin our Social

Security benefit. If you need more specifics on a personal situation, I suggest you speak with your financial advisor or attend one of my monthly Social Security webinars. Your feedback on ways to improve this educational resource is encouraged. Please visit http://www.retirereadyseries.com for details.

CPSIA information can be obtained
at www.ICGtesting.com
Printed in the USA
FSOW02n1531261114
3582FS

ISBN 978-0-282-26950-0
PIBN 10845995

English
Français
Deutsche
Italiano
Español
Português

www.forgottenbooks.com

Mythology Photography **Fiction**
Fishing Christianity **Art** Cooking
Essays Buddhism Freemasonry
Medicine **Biology** Music **Ancient**
Egypt Evolution Carpentry Physics
Dance Geology **Mathematics** Fitness
Shakespeare **Folklore** Yoga Marketing
Confidence Immortality Biographies
Poetry **Psychology** Witchcraft
Electronics Chemistry History **Law**
Accounting **Philosophy** Anthropology
Alchemy Drama Quantum Mechanics
Atheism Sexual Health **Ancient History**
Entrepreneurship Languages Sport
Paleontology Needlework Islam
Metaphysics Investment Archaeology
Parenting Statistics Criminology
Motivational

ECLECTIC SCHOOL READINGS

THE STORY OF
THE GREAT REPUBLIC

BY

H. A. GUERBER

DEPARTMENT OF EDUCATION
LELAND STANFORD JUNIOR UNIVERSITY

———oo;◦;oo———

NEW YORK ∴ CINCINNATI ∴ CHICAGO
AMERICAN BOOK COMPANY

COPYRIGHT, 1899, BY
H. A. GUERBER.

STORY OF THE GREAT REPUBLIC.

W. P. 2

PREFACE.

———o∘⊙∘o———

THIS volume is intended as an historical reader, as an elementary text-book in the history of our country from the framing of the Constitution to the present day, or as an introduction or supplement to any of the excellent text-books on United States history now in use.

Although complete in itself, and hence quite independent, it is nevertheless a sequel to "The Story of the Thirteen Colonies," for it takes up the thread of the narrative at the point where it was dropped in that book, and carries it on unbroken to the present date.

No pains have been spared to interest children in the history of their country, to explain its gradual development, to teach them to love, honor, and emulate our heroes, and to make them so familiar with the lives and sayings of famous Americans that they will have no difficulty in understanding the full meaning of the numerous historical allusions so frequently found in the newspapers and elsewhere.

While a special effort has been made to cultivate a spirit of fairness and charity in dealing with every phase of our history, the writer's main object has been to make good men and women of the rising generation, as well as loyal Americans.

As in "The Story of the Thirteen Colonies," the pronunciation of difficult proper names is indicated in the text, and also, more fully, in the carefully marked index.

HINTS FOR TEACHERS.

In addition to its use as a reader, this book is of such a character that its stories can serve as themes for daily exercises in dictation and composition.

Also, such play-work as short and lively memory matches (on the plan of a spelling match) is of great help. Stimulated by it, the pupils soon pride themselves on remembering most of the facts and names after reading the chapters only once or twice.

In these ways children acquire considerable historical knowledge without any actual study, a fact which is of great importance, as many children leave school before they are sufficiently advanced to enter a history class.

It is also suggested that each place mentioned in the lesson should be carefully located on maps, by such means as are indicated in the Hints for Teachers in "The Story of the Thirteen Colonies." The pupils will then make rapid and unconscious progress in geographical as well as historical knowledge.

CONTENTS.

—∘o✧ᴏ✧oo—

MAPS.

UNITED STATES

SCALE OF MILES

0 50 100   200   300   400   500

(10)

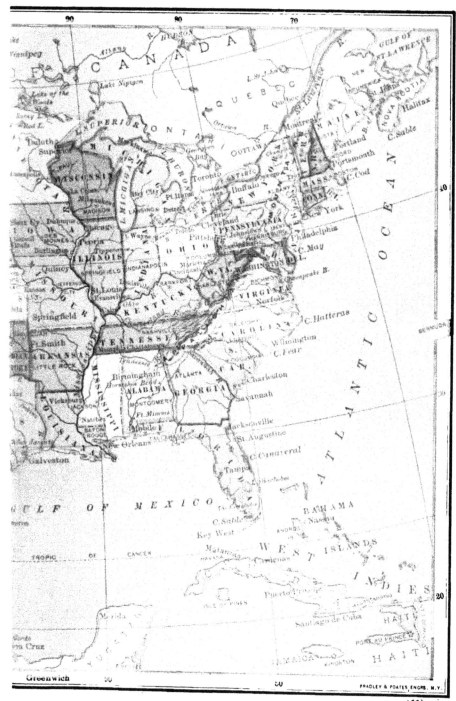

THE UNITED STATES
According to the Treaty
of 1783
SHOWING THE STATE CLAIMS

STORY OF THE GREAT REPUBLIC.

I. THE BEGINNING OF THE UNITED STATES.

THE birth of our great republic, the United States of America, took place on July 4, 1776; but although this event was joyfully hailed by patriotic Americans, it was some time before any of the foreign nations took public notice of the fact, or sent her their congratulations.

France was the first to stretch out a friendly hand to the United States, thus setting a good example which many other countries were glad to follow. These tokens of good will were gratefully received, for our poor country had a very hard time of it in the beginning, and spent the first few years of her life in constant warfare.

The mother country—also known as Bri-tan'ni-a, or Great Britain—wanted to keep the American colonies under her harsh rule, and when they revolted, she took up arms to force them back into a state of blind obedience. It was these thirteen revolted colonies which, banded together, decided to form the new and independent nation which in poetry is often called Co-lum'bi-a.

Now, Miss Columbia had inherited from her mother a

13

great love of liberty. She therefore insisted upon managing her own affairs; and when Britannia tried to prevent her from doing so, she fearlessly waged the Revolutionary War.

After about eight years of warfare, seeing that nothing else could be done with this high-spirited chip of the old block, Britannia finally consented to let her have her own way. This permission, very grudgingly granted, formed the second treaty of Păr'is, which was agreed to in 1783.

One of the commissioners who signed this treaty was Benjamin Franklin. He is one of our greatest men, and his name can also be seen on the Declaration of Independence, and on our first treaty of friendship with France.

Franklin had been working for years to secure this treaty from Great Britain, and as soon as it was concluded he begged permission to return to Phil-a-del'phi-a. Our Continental Congress—the body of men which had governed the United States ever since the Declaration of Independence—granted this request; but, knowing they must have another minister to represent our country in France, they sent out Thomas Jef'fer-son.

He, too, was a patriot, and the writer, as well as one of the signers, of the Declaration of Independence. Jefferson knew how dearly the French loved Dr. Franklin, and how much good this wise man had done by winning strong friends abroad for his struggling country. Therefore, when some one asked him if he had been sent to take Franklin's place, he quickly and modestly answered: " I succeed, but no one can replace him."

At the same time Congress also chose another patriot, the famous John Ad'ams, to be our minister in England. On arriving there, he was well received by King George III.,

Thomas Jefferson.

(15)

who said: "Sir, I will be very free with you. I was the last man in the kingdom to consent to the independence of America; but now it is granted, I shall be the last man in the kingdom to sanction the violation of it."

This was a fine thing for the king to say, and it showed the right spirit. Unfortunately, however, George III. had been cruel and unkind to the Americans for many years, and he soon proved rude to the very man to whom he had made this speech. At first our people naturally resented it, but they soon found out that the poor monarch was much more to be pitied than blamed.

This king, it seems, had had slight attacks of madness several times before, and he now became quite insane. The last ten years of his life were very sad, for he lost his sight as well as his reason, and used to grope his way around his palace with big tears coursing down his wrinkled cheeks.

Many persons now think that if this unhappy king had not partly lost his mind, and been ill advised by bad ministers, he would have acted differently toward the thirteen colonies. This is very likely, for George III. was at heart a good and well-meaning man, although rather stupid and very headstrong.

II. FRANKLIN'S RETURN.

AS soon as Franklin received permission from Congress to leave his post in Paris, he eagerly set out for America. There were no steamships in those days, and during the long journey passengers used to beguile the time by telling stories and playing games, much as they do now during far less tedious trips.

Although already quite old, Franklin was so merry, learned, and witty that his stories were always greatly appreciated by all who heard them. He had studied and traveled so much that his mind was like a rich store-house, and as he was kind-hearted, he probably spent his leisure hours in telling his fellow-travelers about the country toward which they were sailing as fast as they could.

While walking up and down the deck, sitting in the shade of the big sails, or in the uncomfortable cabin dur-ing the long evenings, he may have wondered aloud—as many persons do—at the boldness of Columbus in steer-ing on and on across the At-lan'tic, thus showing the way to the many vessels which have crossed the ocean since then.

He may also have described the different steps whereby America—the land of the redskins, of dense forests, and broad plains—in less than three centuries had become the home of a new and thriving nation. He may have begun his account by telling how the Spaniards who followed Columbus to the New World had confined their atten-tion mostly to the West In'dies, Flor'i-da, Mex'i-co, and South America; and how, later, the French entered the St. Law'rence and made settlements along its banks; the English planted colonies at James'town, in Vir-gin'i-a, and about Mas-sa-chu'setts Bay; and the Dutch took posses-sion of the Hudson valley.

Next, Franklin may have dwelt upon the many hard-ships endured by the early settlers, before land could be cleared, farms and cities laid out, and the Indians driven from their hunting and fishing grounds on the coast. After explaining how the English had won from the Dutch the country around the Hudson and Del'a-ware rivers, he prob-

Flags of New England (the Colonies East of New York).

ably told how they had made the other settlements, until there were thirteen English colonies occupying all the coast between No'va Sco'tia and Florida : —

namely, New Hamp'shire, Massachusetts, Rhode Island, Con-nect'i-cut, New York, New Jersey, Penn-syl-va'ni-a, Delaware, Ma'ry-land, Virginia, North Car-o-li'na, South Carolina, and Geor'gi-a.

Then he probably talked of the quarrels between these English colonies and the French settlers in the St. Lawrence valley, or Can'a-da, as it was called. Both parties claimed nearly all the interior of North America; they therefore soon came to blows, and as the Indians helped the French, these conflicts are known in history as the French and Indian wars. The first one broke out in 1689, seven years after Franklin's father arrived in America, and good Dr. Franklin himself took an active part in the fourth and last. When it had ended in the victory of the British, he wrote a very clever pamphlet advising Great Britain to keep Canada; and when the first treaty of Paris was signed, in 1763,—twenty years before the second,—all the land north of the thirteen colonies, and west as far as the Mis-sis-sip'pi River, was given to the British. The French at the same time gave all their lands west of that river to Spain, and withdrew entirely from our continent.

When Franklin's listeners inquired what had caused the Revolutionary War, which was just ended, he perhaps told them how, already in the thirteenth century, liberty-loving Englishmen forced their king to grant them the Great Charter. This was a new set of laws, giving them the right to be represented in the Par'lia-ment, or congress, which fixed the taxes and made the laws. This right, which Englishmen had enjoyed for five hundred years, was also claimed by their descendants in America; and each colony elected an assembly to help make its laws and lay its taxes, though the govern-ors of most of the colonies were appointed by the king. When King

Flags used in the Revolutionary War.

George III. and the British Parliament insisted on impos-ing taxes on the colonists without the consent of their assemblies, they openly rebelled, because it was an attempt to deprive them of rights inherited from their ancestors.

As Franklin had taken part in this rebellion, had seen the king, had sat in Congress, and had spoken with most of the great men of his time on both sides of the ocean, his account of the war must have been of thrilling interest. The name of his friend George Washington, commander in chief of the Continental Army, and the savior of his country, must often have been upon his lips. Some of his hearers, coming to build new homes in America, may never have heard it before, but, as you will soon see, they were to learn much more about him.

Franklin, however, often told them funny stories, too, and perhaps he even mentioned one of his childhood which has given rise to an expression we often hear. As you may like to know just how the good man talked, here is the story as he once wrote it:

"When I was a little boy, I remember, one cold winter's morning, I was accosted by a smiling man with an ax on his shoulder. 'My pretty boy,' said he, 'has your father a grindstone?' 'Yes, sir,' said I. 'You are a fine little fellow,' said he; 'will you let me grind my ax on it?' Pleased with the compliment of 'fine little fellow,' 'Oh, yes, sir,' I answered; 'it is down in the shop.' 'And will you, my man,' said he, patting me on the head, 'get me a little hot water?' How could I refuse? I ran, and soon brought a kettleful. 'How old are you, and what's your name?' continued he, without waiting for a reply. 'I am sure you are one of the finest lads that I have ever seen. Will you just turn a few minutes for me?'

"Tickled with the flattery, like a little fool, I went to work; and bitterly did I rue the day. It was a new ax, and I toiled and tugged till I was almost tired to death.

The school bell rang, and I could not get away; my hands were blistered, and the ax was not half ground. At length, however, it was sharpened; and the man turned to me with, ' Now, you little rascal, you've played truant; scud to school, or you'll rue it! ' ' Alas!' thought I, ' it is hard enough to turn a grindstone this cold day; but now to be called a little rascal is too much.'

" It sank deep in my mind; and often have I thought of it since. When I see a merchant over polite to his cus- tomers,—begging them to take a little brandy, and throw- ing his goods on the counter,—thinks I, ' That man has an ax to grind.' When I see a man flattering the people, making great professions of attachment to liberty, who is in private life a tyrant, methinks, ' Look out, good people! that fellow would set you turning grindstones.' "

—oo;o;oo—

III. TROUBLES AFTER THE WAR.

ON arriving in America, Dr. Franklin received a warm welcome from all his fellow-citizens, who were very proud of what he had done for them abroad. But although he had come home intending to rest, he soon found plenty of work awaiting him.

The Revolutionary War had cost the Americans a great deal; now that it was ended, one of their first duties was to find some way of repaying all the money they had bor- rowed.

Ever since the royal governors had fled or had been driven away in 1775 or 1776, the thirteen different states

STO. OF GT. REP.—2

had ruled themselves. Although near neighbors, they were not always on the best of terms, but often seemed rather inclined to quarrel with one another.

When the colonies were first planted in America, some of them were granted strips of land running "from sea to sea." Of course, this was before any one knew just how broad our continent is; and although none of the colonies claimed from sea to sea in the eighteenth century, many of them still said they owned land as far as the Mississippi River.

As the charters had often been carelessly made, it happened that the same lands were granted to two or three colonies, which fact gave rise to many quarrels. But after several years of talking about the matter, New York, Virginia, Massachusetts, and Connecticut finally consented to do as Congress wished, and give up their claims to the land northwest of the O-hi'o River.

This region was then called the Northwest Territory. It was given up, on condition that Congress should sell part of it to pay the interest on the national debt, and divide the rest among the soldiers instead of giving them money. Besides, it was afterwards arranged that this territory should finally be cut up into three or five new states, each of which could join the Union as soon as it had sixty thousand inhabitants.

Until that time, the Northwest Territory was to be ruled by one governor and several judges, all chosen by Congress. This body now began to give land to such soldiers as were willing to accept it instead of money, and before long many emigrants were on their way to Ohio, where they founded Ma-ri-et'ta, in 1788, and Cin-

cin-na'ti soon after. Many large tracts of land in the South were distributed in the same way; and thus it came to pass that, at the end of the Revolutionary War, the famous general Nathanael Greene received a large plantation from the state of Georgia.

As you can see from the map on page 12, North Carolina, South Carolina, and Georgia once owned western lands too; but one by one these tracts were given up to Congress, to form territories like the Northwest Territory.

In 1781, several years before Congress took possession of the western lands, the states had all signed "Articles of Confederation," a system of federal government proposed in 1776. But as this system did not give Congress power to impose taxes, make trade laws, secure money enough to pay government expenses, or make people obey the laws, it did not work well. For several years, therefore, different experiments were tried, but in spite of all efforts things went on from bad to worse.

Congress had promised at the treaty of Paris that all debts should be paid, and that all the Tories, or friends of the king, in America should be protected. But the British soon complained that they could not collect their money, and it was plain that the Tories were badly treated, for in two years more than a hundred thousand left our country to settle in Canada, Florida, or Ber-mu'da.

The British, who had left New York two months after the treaty was signed, kept possession of Os-we'go, De-troit', and Mack'i-naw in the Northwest until the promises made should be kept. Their presence there made the people restless and unhappy, for they secretly urged the Indians to rise up against the Americans.

Besides, there were money troubles everywhere, for the states were so deeply in debt that they were obliged to lay heavy taxes on the people. These taxes were such a burden that in some places the people actually rebelled and made riots.

The most serious of all these outbreaks was in Massachusetts, where Shays, an old Revolutionary soldier, led a

Shays's Rebellion.

force of about two thousand men against Worcester (woos'-ter) and Spring'field. Although this revolt—known in history as Shays's Rebellion—was put down in 1787, it helped to show the necessity for better laws. These had to be made soon, if the thirteen states were to remain united, and not form thirteen small republics, which would be sure to quarrel.

In 1786, five of the states suggested that a meeting or convention of all the confederacy be held, to change the Articles of Confederation in such a way as to suit everybody and secure a better government. Congress agreed to this plan, and each state was asked to send delegates to the Constitutional Convention.

———oo:o:oo———

IV. THE CONSTITUTION.

THE Constitutional Convention met in Independence Hall, in Philadelphia, in 1787. All the states sent delegates except Rhode Island, and among these, one man, the beloved Washington, was chosen by every one present to act as president. As it seemed best that the public should hear only the final result of the meetings, the convention held secret sessions. It was soon found impossible to revise the Articles of Confederation in a satisfactory way, so it was decided to make a new constitution, or set of general laws. They were to be laws which all the states should obey, but which would still leave them the right to settle minor matters to suit themselves.

Although all the members wished to do their best, opinions were so very different that for four months there was a great deal of quarreling in the convention. Indeed, it often seemed as if the members never would agree; and, seeing how heated some of the delegates became, the aged

Franklin once suggested that it would be well to begin every session with a prayer for wisdom and divine guidance.

Washington, too, often tried to pour oil on the troubled waters; but sometimes even he grew frightened, and once he said: "It is too probable that no plan we propose will be adopted. Perhaps another conflict is to be sustained. If, to please the people, we offer what we ourselves disapprove, how can we afterwards defend our work? Let us raise a standard to which the wise and honest can repair; the event is in the hand of God."

After four months' discussion, and after all parties had given up some of their ideas and wishes to please the rest, the present Constitution of the United States was drawn up. It was called the "new roof," because it was to serve as a shelter in time of storm for all the states who chose to take refuge under it.

This Constitution provided that the lawmaking part of the government should be carried on by a new Congress, consisting of two houses. One was to be called the House of Rep-re-sent'a-tives. The men forming it were to be elected by the people, who at first had a representative for every thirty thousand inhabitants, though they now have only one for about six times as many people. But it was then agreed that as there were many slaves in the South who could not vote, the Southerners should consider five slaves equal to three white men in taking the census, or counting the population. At the same time, to please the men of the South, the North agreed that Congress should not forbid the importing of slaves until 1808.

The other house of Congress was called the Senate,

The Present House of Representatives.

where each state, large or small, was to send two members, called senators.

After a new law had been talked over and voted for in both houses, it was to be sent to the President for him to sign. If the President did not wish to sign the law he was not obliged to do so, and if he vetoed it,—that is, if he said, "I forbid it,"—the law was to be sent back to Congress. There it was to be talked over again, the votes of the houses taken once more, and if, on counting, it was found that two thirds of each house still thought the law was best for the country, it was to be put in force without the President's consent.

As Congress thus had the right to make the laws, it was to be called the lawmaking or legislative part of the government. Now you know it is not enough to make laws: you must have somebody to see that they are obeyed, or to execute them. The Constitution said that this part of the work was to be done by another part of the government, to be called the executive.

Several persons cannot well give orders at once, so it was thought best that one man should be the executive. This man was to be called the President. He was to be chosen every four years by electors, each state having as many electors as it had senators and representatives in Congress. The duty of the President was to see that the laws made by Congress were properly carried out, and to call out the soldiers in case of war. A Vice President was also to be chosen in the same way as the President. His duty was to be head or president of the Senate, and to take the President's place if the latter died.

The makers of the Constitution knew that there would surely be disputes between states, which ordinary state

The Present Senate Chamber.

courts could not settle; so they further decided that there should be a third part to the government. This was to be the judiciary, or justice-dealing part, composed of judges chosen by the President. These United States judges were to form a Supreme Court, where all such cases could be tried, and they were also to settle all disputes concerning the laws of the nation.

Each state was still to govern itself in home matters, but treaties with other countries, questions of trade, war, etc., were to be settled by the United States government. Thus, you see, it had the right to coin money, keep the post office, tax the people, and see that the nation was ruled in the very best way.

The Constitution thus made did not quite suit everybody; but most of the members of the Constitutional Convention felt like Washington, who once said that it was the best Constitution which could be obtained at that epoch; and all knew that unless it was accepted the thirteen states would fall apart. That, you see, would have been very bad; for while they could hold their own when they were united, they were too small and weak to stand alone.

James Mad'i-son had taken a large share in all this work. He had made many speeches, taken notes, tried to coax the members to agree, and had labored so hard to suit everybody that he is generally called the " Father of the Constitution." This important paper, the " title deed of American liberty," begins with the words : "We, the people of the United States, in order to form a more perfect union, establish justice, insure domestic tranquillity, provide for the common defense, promote the general welfare, and secure the blessings of liberty to ourselves and our posterity, do ordain and establish this Constitution for the United States of America."

The Constitution having been drawn up, read, and signed by the members of the convention, it was sent to the Continental Congress at New York, which forwarded

The Room where the Constitutional Convention met.

copies to each state. It was provided that when nine or more states approved of it, the new Constitution should go into effect for those states.

The disputes had been so bitter in the Constitutional Convention that it had often seemed as if no agreement would ever be reached. So when Franklin came forward to sign the Constitution, he quaintly said, pointing to the back of Washington's chair, upon which was carved a sun:

" In the vicissitudes [changes] of hope and fear, I was not able to tell whether it was rising or setting. Now I know that it is the rising sun." Franklin was right. The sun was rising for our dear country, and we hope it will go on growing brighter and brighter for many a year yet to come.

All the delegates present, except three, signed the Constitution, which was accepted by Delaware, Pennsylvania, New Jersey, Georgia, Connecticut, and Maryland just as it stood. Massachusetts, South Carolina, New Hampshire, Virginia, and New York accepted it, but at the same time proposed a few additions called " amendments." Thus, in August, 1788, all the states had adopted it except Rhode Island and North Carolina, which, however, joined the Union soon after.

When so many states agreed to the Constitution, there were great rejoicings everywhere. Bonfires, illuminations, and processions were seen in all large cities, and many fine speeches were made. In one procession there was a big float, representing the Constitution as the " Ship of State." It rested upon a platform where Alexander Ham'il-ton's name was written in huge letters, for he too had had a great share in making it, and in persuading the people of his state to accept it.

V. THE FIRST PRESIDENT.

THE new Constitution having been accepted by enough states, the Continental Congress decided that its rule should end, and the new Constitution go into force, on the 4th of March, 1789. Having arranged for the beginning of the new government, the Continental Congress, after ruling our country nearly fifteen years, ceased to exist.

As had been decided, the electors chosen by each state met in February, to vote for our first President. Each man wrote Washington's name at the top of his ballot, and thus the " Father of his Country " was chosen first President of the United States of America. Now, it had been settled in the Constitution that the man who received the next largest number of votes should be Vice President. But while all were agreed that Washington was the best man in the country, and voted for him, the second name was not the same on every paper. Still, when the votes were sent to Congress and counted, it was found that John Adams had received more than any one else, and he became our first Vice President.

As soon as the election was over, the news was carried by a horseman to Mount Vernon, where Washington was busy farming. Although several attempts had been made to reward him for his services, he had steadily refused all pay. When the state of Virginia wished to honor its greatest citizen, it made him a present of some bonds. But, true to his principles, Washington would not accept any reward. Still, finding it would hurt the Virginians' feelings if he entirely refused their gift, he suggested that the money be used to found the university which now bears his name and that of Robert E. Lee, the great Southern general.

Washington had hoped he would never have to leave his beautiful home again, but when he heard that he was elected President, he quickly and unselfishly prepared to go and serve his country in a new way.

All along the road to New York he was welcomed by bell-ringing, speeches, receptions, etc., the people all trying to show their love and respect for the man who had brought them safely through the Revolutionary War. When he came to Trenton Bridge, where he had once won a great victory, thirteen young girls, all dressed in white, strewed flowers under his horse's feet. Over his head were great green arches, bearing mottoes, one of which said that Washington had watched over the mothers, and

At Trenton.

would therefore take good care of the daughters. Here, too, a band played music written in Washington's honor, and called the "President's March."

As there were no ferries in those days such as we have now, Washington was rowed across to New York in a barge, which was manned by thirteen sailors in fine new red, white, and blue uniforms.

Owing to the slow means of travel, Congress had assembled on the 6th of April, instead of on the 4th of March, as had first been planned; and Washington's inauguration did not take place till the 30th of April. For this solemn ceremony, Washington was clad in garments every thread of which had been grown and made in America. To give all the people a chance to see him, Washington stood on the balcony of Federal Hall, New York, on the very spot where his statue now stands, on Wall Street.

Federal Hall, New York.

Laying his hand upon a Bible, which has been carefully preserved, he then publicly took this oath: "I do solemnly swear that I will faithfully execute the office of President of the United States, and will to the best of my ability preserve, protect, and defend the Constitution of the United States."

As you see, this is a very solemn promise, and it was no easy task that Washington had thus undertaken. The Congress was all new, President and Vice President were new, and there was no one there to tell them what they were to do. The United States was then, it is true, only a third-rate country (of no more importance than Bel'gi-um or Denmark is now), but the men at the head of the government had to behave in such a way that every one would learn to respect it. Besides, as there were then no other republics in the world which could serve as models, except Swit'zer-land, it was hard for them to know just how a republic should act.

Nevertheless, Washington proved calm, firm, and just, as ever, and order was soon brought out of chaos. Washington, who was addressed as " Mr. President," chose Jefferson, Hamilton, Knox, and Randolph to help him govern, and they formed what is now called the Cabinet. He also selected judges, making John Jay the first Chief Justice of the Supreme Court, and sent ministers to the principal countries in Europe.

To make sure that the people, who had been accustomed to the pomp of royal governors, should not fail in respect for their new government, Washington, who was always very dignified, generally rode out in a carriage drawn by six

Washington's Coach.

Irving R. Wiles, Artist.

A Ball in Washington's Time.

(36)

horses, and escorted by powdered and liveried servants. He also gave stately dinner parties and balls, which latter he generally opened himself by dancing a minuet. Besides that, he held receptions, to which every one could come. He did this because all men have equal rights in a republic, and, being the representative of the poor as well as of the rich, he said both had the same right to visit him.

Congress was very busy for several years, for the money affairs of the United States were in a bad condition. Some of the members said that our country would never be able to pay all the money it owed. But it was finally decided that not only the debts of the Continental Congress should be paid, but also the state war debts. This was a large sum, amounting to about seventy-five million dollars; but Congress promised to pay it, saying it would be as dishonest for a country to refuse to pay every penny owed, as for a private person to do so. Congress also put a tariff upon goods brought from abroad; arranged, in obedience to the Constitution, that a census should be taken every ten years; and decided that the United States should have a national bank, and a mint to coin the money used in the country.

Hamilton had a great deal to do with arranging money matters; and he suggested that instead of using the English money table, we should adopt the dollar as the unit of money. This unit was then divided into hundredth parts, or cents, coins which were first used by our government in 1793. In fact, Hamilton's ideas proved so good that the great orator Webster once said in speaking of him: " He touched the dead corpse of public credit, and it sprang upon its feet."

VI. WASHINGTON'S TROUBLES.

THE Continental soldiers who received land in the
Northwest Territory had from the first quarreled
with the Indians. As the latter had sworn that no white
man should ever plant corn on the Ohio, settlers were
obliged to float down the river in well-armed boats, and
till the ground with their guns always within reach.

But, in spite of these drawbacks, the land was rapidly
becoming cultivated. Hoping to check the white men, or
drive them away, the Indians now began to murder them,
stealing upon them when they least expected such unwel-
come visits. When Washington heard of this, he sent General St. Clair with an army to attack them. Although
warned to be wary with such foes, St. Clair proved over-

St. Clair's Defeat.

confident, and his little army was surprised and slaughtered. The news of this disaster was a great blow to Washington, but he quickly took measures to punish the Indians, and sent General Anthony Wayne into the Northwest Territory to take St. Clair's place.

The Indians found " Mad Anthony " so alert that they soon declared he never slept. But although their principal chief advised them not to risk a battle, they insisted upon doing so. They were defeated on the Mau-mee' (1794), and were pursued many miles. Then their fields and houses (for these Indians owned real houses) were laid waste and burned, to teach them never to attack the settlers again.

This done, Wayne made the Indian chiefs sign a treaty, whereby they gave up much of the land north of the Ohio, and when they had obeyed, he frightened them by solemnly warning them that if they ever broke it he would rise up out of his grave to fight them. Although Indian troubles were really most severe in the North, they were very bad, too, in the South, and it has been said that no less than fifteen hundred men, women, and children were murdered in Ken-tuck'y alone, during this period.

As if Indian raids were not enough to trouble the country, a rebellion soon arose in western Pennsylvania, because the people did not want to pay the tax laid upon whisky. They said they could not sell their grain, and that they had to make whisky out of it or lose it. When told they must obey the government, they grew so defiant that troops had to be sent out against them. Indeed, it was only when forced to do so that they laid down their arms, and the Whisky Rebellion came to an end (1794).

As it is quite impossible to please everybody, many people found fault with all that the new government said or did. Before long, Washington himself was greatly abused, and a few rebels and politicians even began to call him the "stepfather of his country." Then, as if the troubles at home were not enough to worry him, Washington also had troubles from abroad.

In 1789, the French, who had long been dissatisfied with their government, rose up against the good but somewhat stupid Louis XVI. After some changes, they decided to set up a republic, like the Americans. To get rid of their king they finally beheaded him (1793), more in punishment for the sins of his fathers than for his own. The famous General La-fā-yette', who had fought in our War for Independence, took part in this revolution also, knowing that the French people had good cause to complain of their government; and when they tore down the great state prison, La Bastille (bas-teel'), he sent one of its huge keys to his friend Washington.

But the French did not know how to make the best of the power they had seized. Before long, they made such bad use of it that much innocent blood was shed and people grew indignant at their cruelty. The English, who had always hated and had often fought against the French, soon took advantage of this sad state of affairs to begin a new war.

When the Americans heard of this, some cried that, as the French had helped us, we ought to help them. But others, cooler and wiser, with Washington at their head, said that it would be far better for the United States not to have anything to do with European quarrels. As

George Washington. (41)

people began to side everywhere for or against this opinion, they were soon divided into two parties. The one led
by Washington was called the Fed'er-al-ist party, while
the men who favored the French were known as Re-
pub'li-cans. But these two parties also differed on questions concerning our own government.

Genet (zheh-nā'), a Frenchman, shortly after came to
America to ask help. He felt so sure it would be granted
that, without waiting for permission from either President
or Congress, he began buying vessels and fitting them out
to attack the British navy. He had no right to do this,
and Washington immediately bade him cease, saying that
the United States meant to keep neutral—that is to say,
not to side with either country. Genet, however, paid no
attention to Washington's orders, and, as he was not behaving as a minister should, our President forced France
to recall him.

At that same time, Great Britain complained louder
than ever that her subjects could not collect the money
due to them in America, and began to try to hinder our
commerce. To prevent this, Washington sent John Jay to
London, to sign a treaty which bears his name. By it
the British promised to give up the forts in the Northwest.
This treaty was the best which could then be obtained,
but it greatly displeased many Americans, who not only
blamed Washington and the Senate for agreeing to it
(1795), but burned Jay in effigy, to show their anger.

They were better pleased, however, with a treaty made
that same year with Spain. It settled the boundaries between Florida and the United States, and gave the Americans permission to sail up and down the Mississippi as

much as they liked, without paying either duty or toll to Spain. This was a great advantage, for the farmers along the Ohio could now float their produce down to New Or'le-ans, where they were sure of a good market.

A third treaty was signed with Al-giers', in Africa, where many of our countrymen had been kept prisoners by pirates. All the Americans thus held were set free for $1,000,000, and our ships were allowed to cruise in the Med-i-ter-ra'ne-an, on condition that we paid the pirates a certain sum every year, just as other countries then did.

But there were many people who did not approve of this treaty either, and they were so ready to criticise everything Washington said or did, that he once sadly said—what many a President must have felt since: "I'd rather be in my grave than President."

---oo;oo;oo----

VII. A WONDERFUL INVENTION.

THE country was in such a bad state, toward the end of Washington's first term, that he saw there was as yet little chance of his going back to Mount Vernon to rest. Besides, his friends insisted that as he had so often sacrificed his own wishes for the good of his country, he really could not desert her now, at such a time of need. Thus it came to pass that Washington served as President for two terms, or from 1789 to 1797, although he would rather have lived quietly at home.

During these eight years he lived first in New York and then in Philadelphia, for, although Congress had decided that the future capital of the United States should be on the Po-tŏ'mac, it was not to be ready until 1800. Still, in 1793 Washington went there to lay the corner stone of the Capitol, the future home of Congress, in the city which bears his honored name.

The City of Washington in Early Days.

It was during the President's second term that streets were laid out in Washington, in the midst of swamps and forests. At first, the Capitol, and the White House, or the home of the President, stood nearly alone in this " city in the woods," but soon other buildings rose like magic around them, and now Washington is justly considered one of the most beautiful cities in the world. It occupies the small District of Columbia, which is governed by Congress.

Many very interesting events happened in America

while Washington was President. For instance, in 1791 and 1792, two new states, Ver-mont' and Kentucky, were admitted to the Union, and the American flag was adorned with two new stripes and two more stars. In 1796, Ten-nes-see' was also admitted, but our flag kept fifteen stars and fifteen stripes for many years. When several more states had joined the Union, Congress decided that it was impossible to keep adding stripes. It was therefore settled that the flag should always have thirteen stripes, to represent the thirteen colonies, and one star for each state.

At about this time, General Greene's widow was once journeying southward, to return to the plantation her husband had received from Georgia. On board the ship she met Eli Whitney, a young Yale graduate, who was on his way to teach in a planter's family in Georgia.

Eli Whitney had always been eager to learn all about machinery. Even when a mere child, he carefully took his father's watch apart, and put it together again, while the rest of the family were at church. This was done so cleverly that the watch went on running as well as before, and no one would have known it had been taken to pieces, had not the lad confessed it.

When he grew older, Whitney made many useful inventions, and, as his father could not afford to send him to college, he began making nails, and thus earned enough money to study at Yale. Once, while there, he borrowed a carpenter's tools to make some handy contrivance. The man, watching his deft fingers, cried: "There was one good mechanic spoiled when you came to college!"

On landing in Sa-van'nah, Whitney was greatly disap-

The rest, after great suffering, landed at some Southern port, and were taken to a slave market, where they were sold at auction just as if they had been sheep, or articles of

A Cotton Field.

furniture. Both men and women were forced to work in the cotton fields, and if they did not do as much work as their master or his overseer expected, they were sometimes whipped.

VIII. DEATH OF WASHINGTON.

WASHINGTON served two terms, and although people were very anxious to elect him a third time, he refused so positively to serve again that they had to let him withdraw. The two parties which had arisen in our country both wanted the presidency, but John Adams, of the Federalist party, succeeded Washington, for he had three votes more than Thomas Jefferson, his Vice President, who was favored by the Republican party.

It was during Adams's rule that the government officers left Philadelphia and went to settle in their new quarters at Washington. We are told that both Capitol and White House then stood in a sort of wilderness. Besides, there were so few visitors, and life was so simple, that the lights in the White House were always out before ten, and that Mrs. Adams used what is now the famous East Room to dry clothes in whenever it rained.

The Present East Room.

The people in favor of helping France had wished for some time to drag the United States into war with Great Britain, so Congress now passed two laws to prevent anything of that sort. These laws were called the Alien and Sedition acts. The first said that the President might send any foreigner, or alien, out of the country, if he thought the man was trying to harm it, and that a stranger could become an American citizen only after living in the United States nine years. The Sedition Act decreed that if any newspaper editor or other man publicly spoke ill of Congress or President, he should be fined or imprisoned. This law roused the anger of the people, for they said that as all Americans were free and equal, they had a right to say whatever they pleased.

Still, in spite of objections, both laws were passed, for just then trouble with France was worse than ever. In fact, the French were so angry with the United States for not helping them, that they captured more than a hundred American vessels, refused to show due respect to our flag, and said that they would not receive our envoys unless they were paid a large sum of money as a bribe.

The American envoys were too good patriots, and too noble men, to listen to such talk. It is said that one of them, Charles C. Pinck'ney, proudly answered that his country would give " millions for defense, but not one cent for tribute." When John Adams, the " Colossus of Independence," heard of this answer he declared that Pinckney was right, and, to show the people how unjustly the French were acting, he published the letters Pinckney had received. They were called the " X. Y. Z. Letters," for the writers, being too ashamed to use their own names, had signed them by those initials.

Although the Americans knew they were not strong enough to fight France then, they nevertheless echoed Pinckney's answer, for they felt ready to give every cent they had to uphold the nation's honor. As it now seemed as if the United States would soon be engaged in war, Congress asked Washington to resume his old place as general in chief. However anxious to rest, Washington could not refuse, but he begged permission to choose the generals he wished to help him, and to remain quietly at home until actual war began. Still, although he staid at Mount Vernon, Washington was now very active in getting ready, for he well knew and wisely said that "to be prepared for war is one of the most effectual means of preserving peace."

War had already begun on the sea, however, and our small navy was doing wonders, when a sudden change of government in France put an end to all hostilities. The United States had no cause to quarrel with the new government, so the war between our country and France ceased before it reached our shores. It was during this war scare that Joseph Hop'kin-son wrote the words of "Hail Columbia," setting them to the famous "President's March," composed for Washington's inauguration. Since then this song has been sung by millions of our countrymen, for it is one of our national airs.

All the preparations made for the war cost so much money that heavier taxes had to be laid upon the people. This made them so angry that a few of them rebelled. Led by Friēs, they made a riot, which was quickly put down by President Adams, who firmly insisted that the laws of the country should be obeyed.

During Adams's presidency an event occurred which brought sorrow to every American heart. Although Washington was only sixty-seven years old, and seemed well and hearty, he caught a severe cold by riding in the snow and rain, and sitting down to dinner afterwards in his wet clothes. At first, he thought it was only a sore throat, and doctored himself with molasses and vinegar, but when he grew worse a physician was hastily called. It was too late, however. After the doctor had done all he could, Washington quietly thanked him, and said: "I die hard, but I am not afraid to die." Nor did he need to be afraid, for as he had always done the best he could, his conscience was at rest.

Surrounded by his wife, his doctor, his secretary, and a few faithful friends and servants, Washington gave his final orders and arranged for his burial at Mount Vernon. Then, whispering, "It is well!" he quietly breathed his last (1799).

The news of Washington's death struck every·heart with dismay. Congress broke up in silence, but, on assembling again the next day, it decided that the nation should wear mourning for thirty days to honor the great man who was, as Chief Justice Marshall said, "First in war, first in peace, and first in the hearts of his countrymen."

The United States was not alone, however, in showing Washington due respect. Times had so changed that the British admiral made the sixty men-of-war off the English coast fly their flags at half-mast, for the very man whom his country had once wished to hang. In France, Na-po'le-on Bo'na-parte ordered public mourning for ten days; for Washington's name was known and honored everywhere.

America's greatest man was, as he had wished, laid to

rest at Mount Vernon, and since then countless thousands of his fellow-citizens and many strangers have visited his tomb. Very near it, in the beautiful grounds which sur-

Washington's Tomb at Mount Vernon.

round the house, there are many trees he planted with his own hands. Inside of his home, the room where he died is just as he left it.

In his will, Washington remembered his slaves. Some of them were set free then, while the rest were to cease being slaves only at the death of Mrs. Washington. His estate was left to some of his relatives, who in 1859 sold it to the ladies of the Mount Vernon Association. These women decided that the home of Washington ought to

STO. OF GT. REP.—4

A Room in Washington's House at Mount Vernon.

remain as nearly as possible as he left it, and raised the money to buy it. Since then, it has been kept up for the benefit of all who care to visit it.

There are many relics of Washington at Mount Vernon, as well as some of his wife. Among the former you can see the chest containing the tableware he used during the Revolutionary War, some of his clothes, and the big key Lafayette sent him. Among the latter are pieces of the gowns once worn by Mrs. Washington, and the heel of one of her slippers, made of pure silver.

Of course, every one wants to know just how Washington looked and what he did. So painters and sculptors, poets and historians, have all tried to give us some idea of the man whom " Providence left childless that his country might call him Father."

The best pictures of Washington are said to be copied

from a bust made by the Frenchman Houdon (oo-dawN′), in 1785. We are told that this artist went to Mount Ver-non-to take a plaster cast of Washington's face. Just as he began operations, Mrs. Washington came into the room. She seemed so horrified when she saw what he was doing, that although Houdon had warned Washington to keep quite still, the latter could not help smiling. It is said that his efforts to get his face straight again, while the plaster flowed down over his cheeks, caused the deep lines on either side of his mouth which are so noticeable to-day in the Houdon bust.

———oo◦◦◦oo———

IX. THE UNITED STATES BUYS LAND.

THE third President of our country was Thomas Jefferson, author of the Declaration of Independence, and of the Act of Religious Freedom in Virginia. A good and honest man, the "Sage of Mon-ti-cel′lo" always kept the resolution made at the age of twenty-six, when elected a burgess: "Never to engage while in public office in any kind of enterprise for the improvement of my fortune, nor to wear any other character than that of farmer."

It was Jefferson who suggested our national motto, "E pluribus unum" [one composed of many], but, though one of the most learned and accomplished of all our Presidents, he was very plain and unassuming. Indeed, the story goes that at the time of his inauguration (1801), he rode alone to the Capitol, tied his horse to a picket fence, went in, took his oath as President, made a fifteen-minute speech, and rode off again as quietly as he had come.

Jefferson arrives at the Capitol.

This pleased the plain people, who showed their approval by sending the President a huge cheese, weighing more than a thousand pounds. It reached him on New Year's day, and was placed in the East Room in the White House, where all the callers could read the inscription: "The greatest cheese in America, for the greatest man in America."

As Jefferson never would hold stately receptions like those of Washington and Adams, and insisted upon doing everything simply, expenses were greatly reduced, and part of the national debt was paid. Jefferson's election, however, had not been a quiet one, for both he and Aaron

Burr received the same number of electoral votes. As there was then no way of telling which was elected President and which Vice President under these circumstances, the election was left to the House of Representatives, which chose Jefferson. But, to prevent any such doubt in the future, a new clause, or amendment, was added to the Constitution. This says that the electors shall cast separate votes for President and for Vice President.

Many interesting events took place under Jefferson's rule. For instance, our country doubled its size in a very strange way. At the end of the French and Indian wars, France had given New Orleans and all her land west of the Mississippi to Spain. The Spaniards, after owning Lou-i-si-ä'na, as this great colony was called, for thirty-seven years, made a secret treaty giving it back to France. As it was very important that the Americans should be able to sail as much as they pleased up and down the Mississippi, and sell their produce in New Orleans, Jefferson thought it might be well to buy that city. He therefore sent a man to France to see if it could be done.

Now, it happened just at this time that Napoleon needed money to make war against his enemies the British. Besides, he could not spare any of his troops to occupy Louisiana, and he feared that the British would secure it. He therefore suddenly proposed to sell all Louisiana for the sum of fifteen million dollars, or about two and a half cents an acre; and the offer was accepted.

Napoleon, on signing the papers, gleefully remarked that he had now given England a rival, which, he added, " will sooner or later humble her pride." At first, Jefferson thought that under the Constitution our government had no right to acquire so much land; but, seeing what a fine bargain it was, he stretched his authority " until it cracked," to secure all Louisiana. Congress agreed with him, and the fifteen millions were duly paid.

In those days, no one knew anything about most of the country on the west side of the Mississippi, where only a few hunters and trappers had gone. Indeed, people so little suspected how quickly it would be settled that, at the time of the purchase, in 1803, some Americans said we would probably not send a settler across the Mississippi for a hundred years!

But Jefferson had long wished to have this part of our country explored, and even before the purchase was completed, he urged Congress to send out an exploring party under his secretary, Meriwether Lewis, and William Clark. Congress consented, so these two men and their followers left St. Louis, then a mere village (1804), and went up the Mis-sou'ri to the " Gate of the Rocky Mountains." They passed through what is now called Yel'low-stone Park, saw the many natural curiosities there, and tried to make friends with the Indians wherever they went. With much trouble, they crossed the mountains, where they carved their names upon a high rock. Then, although their supply of food was very scanty, they journeyed bravely on, until they reached the Columbia River.

Floating down this stream, the forty-six men composing the expedition reached the Pa-cif'ic Ocean, in 1805. It is said they were thus the first white men who crossed our country to the Pacific since Cabeza de Vaca (cah-bā'sah dā vah'cah) had done so, more than two and a half centuries before. But the Columbia River had already been

Scene in Yellowstone Park.

visited by an American in 1792, for Captain Gray had then sailed into its mouth, giving it the name borne by his ship. It seems that this seaman went there to get furs, intending to exchange them for tea in China, and to bring the latter cargo back to Boston. It was because the valley of the Columbia was first explored by Gray, Lewis, and Clark, who were all three loyal Americans, that it was later claimed by the United States when Great Britain tried to take it.

After spending the winter at the mouth of the Columbia, where he and his men lived principally upon elk and salmon, Lewis and Clark made their way over the Rockies to St. Louis, which they reached after an absence of two years and four months. During that time they had learned a great deal about the geography of the western part of our country, and the report they made showed President and Congress what a rich and beautiful country it really is.

Still, at that time people knew very little about any but the eastern part, and even the source of the Mississippi had never been visited. Hoping to find out where it was, Congress sent Zebulon Pike to look for it. He traced a stream, which he wrongly took for the beginning of the " Father of Waters," in a hard journey of more than eight months. Then, in 1806, he started on a new expedition up the Missouri. Crossing to the Arkansas (ar'kan-saw) River, he saw the peak now bearing his name, and in looking for the Red River came to the Rio Grande (re'o grahn'dā).

This proved a long, painful, and heroic journey. The snow lay upon the ground several feet deep; the explorers often lacked food, and, losing their way in the trackless mountains, they would have perished of cold and hunger, had it not been for the instinct of their horses and mules. Even when Pike and his party reached the Rio Grande, their troubles were not over, for they fell into the hands of the Spaniards. Taken as spies to Santa Fé (sahn'tah fā'), they proved that it was all a mistake, and, being set free, returned home.

Pike, Lewis, and Clark spoke so warmly of the fine hunting grounds they had seen that John Jacob As'tor, a fur trader in New York, decided to found a trading post on the Pacific. He therefore sent out a party, which crossed the continent and built a fort called As-to'ri-a, at the mouth of the Columbia River. The adventures of this party were described by Washington Irving, an American author. He gives a charming account of the long journey across the plains, of the buffalo hunting, and of many encounters with the Indians, besides telling us about the life at Astoria, the first American settlement on the Pacific coast.

X. OUR WAR AGAINST AFRICAN PIRATES.

THE purchase of Louisiana, and the explorations of Pike, Lewis, and Clark, were not the only important and interesting events during Jefferson's two terms as President of the United States. He also had to make war against the pirates living on the northern coast of Africa and belonging to the Bar'ba-ry States, or Algiers, Tu'nis, Trip'o-li, and Mo-roc'co.

For many years these pirates had attacked any vessel they met in the Mediterranean. Generally it was only to demand a certain sum of money, but if the captain either could not or would not pay it, they often sank the vessel after robbing it, or towed it into one of their harbors, where they sold the crew into captivity.

The people of northern Africa were Mus'sul-mans, and for that reason hated all Christians. Captive sailors were therefore often treated with the greatest cruelty. European countries, wishing to trade in the Mediterranean, had learned to fear these pirates so greatly that they actually paid the Barbary rulers large sums for leaving their ships alone. As we have seen, our government followed their example in the treaty made with Algiers in 1795.

In 1800, one of our brave naval officers, William Bain'-bridge, was sent to carry the agreed tribute to the dey of Algiers. While he was in the harbor, directly under the guns of the fortress, the dey suddenly ordered him to carry an ambassador to Con-stan-ti-no'ple, flying the Al-ge-rine' flag at his masthead. Bainbridge refused, saying that the Americans were not the dey's slaves. But the pirate haughtily answered: "You pay me tribute, by which you become my slaves, and therefore I have a right to order you as I think proper."

As the guns of the fort were pointed straight at him, and resistance would bring about the destruction of his ship and slavery for his crew, Bainbridge had no choice but to obey. But as soon as he was out of gunshot, and long before he had lost sight of Algiers, he ordered the dey's flag hauled down and again hoisted our stars and stripes.

Of course, Bainbridge was very indignant at the way his country had been treated, and complained to the sultan at Constantinople. The sultan did not approve of what the dey had done, and gave Bainbridge full power to force the dey to give up all his American prisoners without asking any ransom in exchange. While still in Constantinople, Bainbridge wrote home, saying: "I hope I shall never again be sent to Algiers with tribute unless I am authorized to deliver it from the mouth of our cannon."

The insulting and treacherous behavior of Algiers and the other Barbary States roused the anger of our countrymen. But Jefferson once remarked that what had happened proved the truth of Franklin's famous words: "If you make yourself a sheep, the wolves will eat you," and declared that no more tribute should be paid.

In the meantime, the ruler or bashaw of Tripoli, hearing that Algiers received tribute from America, wanted some too. So, in 1800, he demanded money, threatening war unless it was paid. The United States, instead of sending it, merely waited until the bashaw declared war, and then sent a squardon to the Mediterranean. On the way thither,

it captured a Tri-pol'i-tan pirate ship, and, appearing off
Tripoli, began to blockade the port, to the bashaw's dismay. As our navy was very weak, and the Tripolitan
harbor was defended by one hundred and fifteen guns,
nineteen gunboats, and about twenty-five thousand soldiers, it could not do more, and the war dragged on some
time without any great event.

But in 1803 the *Philadelphia*, under Captain Bainbridge, while pursuing a Tripolitan gunboat, suddenly ran
upon a rock not marked upon any chart. The American
seamen frantically tried to get her off; then, seeing it was
in vain, they made an attempt to scuttle their ship. But, in
spite of their efforts, the *Philadelphia* was seized by the
enemy, who towed her into the harbor of Tripoli, intending
to change her into a pirate ship.

Bainbridge and all his men were made prisoners, and
kept in Tripoli, where they were treated very unkindly for
many months. But, although a prisoner, Bainbridge managed to send a letter to Prĕ'ble, another American officer,
who was then cruising about the Mediterranean.

In this letter, Bainbridge told the Americans what the
pirates were doing to the *Philadelphia*, and suggested
that our men should rescue or destroy her rather than see
her put to so shameful a use. Preble talked the matter
over with his officers, and they decided that it would be
impossible to rescue the ship with their small force.
Among these officers was Stephen. De-cā'tur, who was
such a patriot that when asked to give a toast at a public
dinner he proudly cried: " Our country! In her inter-
course with foreign nations may she always be in the right;
but our country, right or wrong!"

This young man bravely offered to steal into the harbor and destroy the ship. His offer was discussed, then accepted, and a boat which had recently been captured was chosen for the expedition. It was loaded with powder and all kinds of things which would burn quickly. Then most of the seventy heroes who volunteered to take part in the dangerous work went below, to remain hidden until their help was needed.

Decatur, and the few men needed to sail the ship, dressed like Mediterranean seamen, and in that disguise entered the harbor of Tripoli at nightfall without arousing any suspicions. Little by little, they brought their boat close up to the *Philadelphia*. Pretending they had lost their anchor in a storm, they asked and received permission to moor their boat to the frigate, so as to make it safe for the night.

When all this was done, Decatur gave a signal, and the Americans, rushing out of their hiding places, scrambled up over the sides of the *Philadelphia*. There they had a short but fierce fight with the Tripolitans, who, in their terror of these bold Americans, finally jumped overboard and swam ashore.

The powder was now brought from the vessel to the frigate, which was speedily set afire in many places. Then the Americans rushed back to their boat, and, cutting it loose, began to make their way out of the harbor. As they sailed away they beheld the *Philadelphia* wreathed in flames, and heard her heated guns go off one after another with a loud and solemn boom. These sounds were also heard by the Americans in their prison, and you may be sure they were proud of the daring of their friends.

Harry Fenn, Artist.

Burning of the Philadelphia.

(65)

The Tripolitans, in the meantime, were stiff with amazement at seeing the vessel destroyed in their port, directly under their big guns; and before they thought of avenging themselves it was too late. Owing to their terror, Decatur got safely back to our fleet, where he gladly reported the complete success of his undertaking, which had not cost the life of a single man.

This deed, which the great English admiral, Nelson, called "the most bold and daring act of the age," was soon followed by an attempt to bombard the city. Then there were five naval battles, in one of which Decatur narrowly escaped death at the hands of a Tripolitan pirate. But, although our vessels managed to do considerable harm to the enemy's navy, the war threatened to run on.

----oo$o$oo----

XI. DEATH OF SOMERS.

KNOWING that the Tripolitans were short of powder, Richard Som'ers, an intimate friend of Decatur's, next suggested a plan to destroy the Tripolitan shipping by means of a floating mine. This idea was warmly welcomed, and great stores of powder, shot, and iron were placed on board Decatur's boat, the *Intrepid*. Then Somers solemnly warned the few men who were to go with him that he would blow up the boat, and all on board, rather than let the powder fall into the enemy's hands.

In spite of this warning, many brave men volunteered, and one boy, rather than miss the honor of sharing the danger of the picked crew, hid himself on board the floating mine. At dusk, the *Intrepid*, manned by thirteen American heroes, entered the harbor of Tripoli.

Meanwhile, the other Americans anxiously watched and listened to find out what would happen. When it was quite dark, and while they were hanging over the railing of the ships, they suddenly saw a little light flit about, as if carried by some one who was moving rapidly.

A moment later there was a dazzling flash, which lighted up the whole harbor. It was quickly followed by a loud explosion, which shook all the houses in Tripoli and the vessels both in and out of the harbor. That was all; and although the Americans peered anxiously into the darkness, waiting for the return of their men, they never came back.

On the next day, thirteen blackened bodies were washed up on shore, but no one has ever known exactly what happened. Some say the explosion was an accident, but others declare that Somers, seeing he was discovered before he could fulfill his object, blew up the vessel with his own hand. His heroic deed has always been greatly admired, and a monument has been erected in his honor on the western side of the Capitol at Washington.

Somers's attempt to set fire to their ships, lack of ammunition, and the fact that there was some trouble in the city, finally induced the Tripolitans to make a treaty of peace with the Americans in 1805. All through the war our navy had behaved so well that the pope declared that the United States, although only thirty years old, had done more in two years to put an end to piracy than all the European states together in nearly three centuries.

During the next seven years American shipping was left alone; but after the War of 1812, about which you will soon hear, the Barbary pirates, thinking the British had destroyed our navy, again began to attack our ships. They also ordered the American consul to leave Algiers, and he saved himself and family from slavery only by paying the dey twenty-seven thousand dollars.

Once more the dey demanded tribute of our country, and as it was not paid as he wished, he declared war upon the United States in 1815. In reply to this declaration, Decatur, the hero of the war with Tripoli, was again sent to the Mediterranean. He boldly forced his way into the bay of Algiers, where he threatened to shell the town if the dey did not surrender all his prisoners, pay for the damage he had done to American shipping, give up all future claim to tribute, and come in person on board the American flagship to sign a treaty.

The dey tried for a while to get better terms, even hinting that he would gladly accept a tribute of powder instead of money. But although Decatur had only four sloops, four brigs, and one schooner wherewith to meet the pirates' strong navy, he firmly answered: "If you insist upon receiving powder as a tribute, you must expect to receive balls with it."

This threat proved enough. The dey was forced to yield, and, coming aboard the flagship, he surrendered his prisoners and signed a treaty in 1815. To end the trouble with the Barbary pirates once for all, Decatur next visited Tunis and Tripoli, where, in less than two months' time, he forced the rulers to release their prisoners and promise never to harm Americans again. By this time the pirates had learned not to trifle any more with our country, nor have they dared to touch any of our ships since then.

XII. THE FIRST STEAMBOAT.

OUR greatest trouble during Jefferson's rule was brought about by the war between France and Great Britain. The British did not want the French to have any food from abroad, and, hoping to starve them, said that no vessels should be allowed to enter French ports. The French, to take their revenge, then promptly decreed that no vessels should enter British ports. To make sure these orders should be obeyed, French ships stopped all American vessels to ask where they were going. The British did the same, and, moreover, seized any men on board who were born in England, for they said: "Once an Englishman, always an Englishman."

This, as you know, is not our way of looking at things. Americans declared that they had a right to trade with any country they pleased, and that a foreigner who had lived a certain number of years in the United States became a citizen of the country, if he chose to be so. Several quarrels on this subject had already arisen, when the British frigate *Leopard* suddenly chased and fired upon the American frigate *Ches'a-peake.*

The American vessel, unprepared for war, was forced to strike her colors, after three men had been killed and eighteen wounded. Then the British boarded the vessel and carried off three American sailors, saying they were deserters from the British navy. This insult, added to many others,—for the British had seized about four hundred American ships and six thousand American sailors, —made Jefferson justly angry.

Still, he decided not to declare war, for we had only twelve war ships to oppose to Britain's thousand. Our President, therefore, merely ordered all British vessels to leave American waters, and by his advice Congress forbade our ships visiting any foreign port. This law was called the "embargo," but most people preferred to spell that word backward, and said it was the "O grab me" Act.

It put an end to commerce, and thereby caused such a loss to our people that it had to be repealed at the end of about a year. Instead, a law was passed allowing our ships to trade with every country except Great Britain and France. As we had depended upon the French and British for goods not made in our country, manufactories were now started to supply them, and thus our land developed new industries.

Two great events happened in 1807. One was the downfall of Aaron Burr, the handsome and talented American who was Vice President during Jefferson's first term,

The Duel between Burr and Hamilton.

and lacked but one vote of being President in his stead. But Burr was, unfortunately, a man of no principle. He quarreled with Hamilton, and killed him in a duel, although Hamilton discharged his pistol in the air rather than injure Burr. As people ceased to approve of him after this duel, Burr made use of his talents to win rich friends. With their aid, he tried to seize New Orleans, intending to make it the capital of a kingdom of Louisiana. But his plans were discovered, and he was caught and tried for treason.

Many people knew that Burr was guilty, but though his friends were ruined by him, no real proofs of his guilt were secured, and he was set free. Still, the rest of his life was spent in poverty and disgrace; for while a few persons still believed in him, the greater part of the nation respected him as little as Benedict Arnold, for he, too, had betrayed his country.

The other event of 1807 was the completion of Fulton's steamboat. The United States was growing so fast that a quicker and easier way of traveling had become very necessary. Fulton and others had already been working at this invention more than twenty years. In spite of many failures, they kept on, until Fulton finally built the *Cler-mont'*. It was advertised to sail up the Hudson River, and, as it was a great curiosity, a big crowd collected to see it start. Nearly all the spectators made fun of it, declaring it would never go, and when it did set out they wonderingly cried: "She moves! she moves!"

Not only did the boat move, but it went up to Albany in thirty-two hours—a rate of speed which seemed so great then that people could hardly believe it either possible or safe. Still, before long Fulton's boat made regular trips up and down the stream. For a short time it was the only successful steamboat in our country, but two years later others were plying along the Delaware and Rar'it-an rivers and on Lake Champlain (sham-plān').

Clermont.

In 1811, the first steamboat went from Pittsburg to New Orleans, creating a great sensation all along its way. Although vessels without sails or oars were a surprise to all, they especially amazed the negroes and Indians. Indeed, we are told that when the first steamboat was seen on Lake Mich'i-gan, the savages called it "Walk in the Water." Some of them, too, actually believed a joker who told them it was drawn by a team of trained sturgeons!

XIII. THE GERRYMANDER.

IN 1808 the time came for a new presidential election; but as Jefferson, like Washington, refused to serve a third term, another man had to be chosen. Of course, different candidates were suggested by the two principal political parties, which, as you know, were then called Federalists and Republicans.

Then there was, as there always is, a time of great excitement, until it was decided that James Madison was to be the fourth President of the United States. He had been, as you may remember, so active in the Constitutional Convention that he had earned the title of " Father of the Constitution." Besides that, he had served his country in many other ways, and had been secretary of state under Jefferson.

A quiet and courteous man, he was so fond of peace that his enemies once said " he could not be kicked into a fight." Still, in spite of the genial nature which won the hearts of all who knew him, Madison soon showed that when war could no longer be avoided, he could be trusted to uphold the honor of the nation. It was on account of his firmness, as well as of his gentleness, that Madison was reëlected and allowed to serve as President a second term.

At about this time, Elbridge Ḡer'ry, governor of Massachusetts, helped in changing the voting districts of his state in such a way as to make sure that most of the state senators would continue to be Republicans. To do this, some of the Federalist districts were cut in two and added to others, where Republican voters were found in large numbers.

The map of one of these newly arranged districts was hung up in the office of a newspaper editor, and the changed parts were brightly colored, to call people's attention to what had been done. One day, an American painter, Gilbert Stuart, came into this office. He saw the map, and laughed at the queer shape of the new district. Being an artist, he quickly saw that it looked like a monster, and, seizing a pencil, he added a head, wings, claws, and a tail.

Turning to the editor, he then exclaimed: "There, that will do for a salamander!" The editor, who disliked Gerry, and knew the unfair change was his work, quickly answered, "Salamander! Call it *Gerrymander!*" This queer word struck people's fancy, and ever since then gerrymandering has been used to express any change in district boundaries which is made to help one party unfairly. As for the picture, copies of it were sent everywhere, and when the voters saw what had been done, and heard that Gerry had allowed

Gerrymander.

it, they ceased to respect him as much as before. Although one of the signers of the Declaration of Independence, and once Vice President of the United States, Gerry is now best known for this one unjust deed.

It was during President Madison's first term that war broke out. Ever since the beginning of the Revolutionary War, the British had secretly excited the Indians against the Americans. This was easy to do, because the Indians were already angry at the rapid advance of the settlers. In 1800, so many Americans had gone to live in the Northwest Territory that it was cut in two. Three years later, one part of it became the state of Ohio, while the rest was called In-di-an'a Territory. Although the white men had paid the Indians for part of this land, the red men would not give it up. They were encouraged

in behaving so by the British, and, led by their chief, Te-
cum'seh, they prepared for war. But the governor of
Indiana Territory was William Henry Har'ri-son, son of

Battle of Tippecanoe.

one of the signers of the Declaration of Independence.
He was very brave, and, meeting the Indians at Tip-pe-
ca-noe', in 1811, he won a great victory over them.

---o○⫷☀⫸○○---

XIV. THE WAR OF 1812.

THE people in the West agreed with those along
the seaboard, in 1812, that it was now time to prove
to Great Britain that they would no longer submit patiently to insult and unfairness. So, after all means had
been vainly tried to bring about an honorable peace, the
" War Congress " directed Madison to begin fighting.

As this struggle began and ended while Madison was President, you will often hear it called " Mr. Madison's War;" and because its object was to win commercial freedom for our country, it is also known as the "Second War of Independence." When it began, three armies were sent out to invade Canada, and punish the British agents there, who had bribed the Indians to rebel. These three armies were to attack Canada at different points; but the first, under Governor Hull of Michigan, soon retreated to Detroit. There, instead of defending the place bravely, Hull surrendered without firing a shot. But this surrender made his soldiers so angry that he was never allowed to command again. It has since been said, however, that Hull yielded only because he fancied the British force larger, and feared lest the Indians with them would kill all their prisoners.

General Harrison, who took Hull's place, started to recover Detroit, but on the way thither part of his troops were conquered by a large force of British and Indians on the Raisin River. Here the Indians were allowed to kill and scalp their prisoners of war. This act of cruelty so angered the Americans that the cry: "Remember the Raisin!" was ever after the signal for desperate fighting on their part. The British not only held Detroit, but, becoming masters of all Michigan, soon pushed on into northern Ohio. But there they met patriots who would not yield, and who managed to defend Forts Mĕigs and Ste'phen-son against forces three times larger than their own.

In the meantime, the two other armies were just as unlucky; for while one was beaten at Queens'town, the other did not dare obey orders and venture across the frontier.

Still, while these mishaps were taking place on land, our little navy was doing wonders at sea. Fighting pirates in the Mediterranean had been good training for our sailors, and the vessels which the British seamen scornfully called " fir-built things with a bit of striped bunting at their masthead " were soon to show the enemy what they could do.

The most famous American frigate at that time was the *Constitution*, which came out safely from so many hard fights that she earned the nickname of " Old Ironsides." When war began, the *Constitution* had just come home. In her first cruise she fell in with a British squadron, and as she could not face several ships at once she tried to get away.

Now, you know sailboats depend upon the wind, and when there is none, they remain almost in the same spot. The wind having suddenly gone down, the American frigate and British fleet lay close together. The American officer was Captain Isaac Hull, a nephew of the man who surrendered to the British at Detroit. He was a very clever seaman, and, hoping to save his ship, he launched her small boats and had her towed along by his sailors. The British could not at first discover how the *Constitution* was handled, but as soon as they saw how it was done, they followed Hull's example. The pursuit went on so for about twenty-four hours; then a storm arose, and, taking advantage of it, the *Constitution* escaped.

A few months later, the *Constitution* left Boston to go in search of the *Guerrière* (gâr-ryâr), a British vessel whose captain had boasted that " a few broadsides from England's wooden walls would drive the paltry striped bunting from the ocean." After capturing several merchant ships, Hull met the *Guerrière*.

His men were so eager to begin fighting that he had some trouble in keeping them quiet until they got very close to the enemy. Then Hull cried: "Now, boys,

Constitution and Guerrière.

pour it into them!" The men obeyed with such spirit that fifteen minutes later the *Guerrière* was nearly disabled. But the *Constitution* was by that time afire, for the British officer Da'cres had been fighting with great courage, too.

The two ships tried to get close enough to board each other, but the sea was too rough to permit their doing so. Hull, having put out the fire on his ship, sent a cannon ball which broke the mainmast of the *Guerrière* and left it quite helpless. He then sent one of his officers to the British frigate to ask if it was ready to surrender.

The American officer, addressing Captain Dacres, said: "Commodore Hull's compliments, and he wishes to know if you have struck your flag." The British officer, who hated to confess he was beaten, would not at first give a direct answer; but when the officer threatened to resume the battle, he slowly said: "Well, I don't know; our mizzenmast is gone, our mainmast is gone, so, upon the whole, you may say we *have* struck our flag."

Not only was his ship helpless and riddled with cannon balls, but about seventy of his men were killed or wounded. The Americans took possession of the ship, and finding it was too much damaged to be of any use, they removed all their prisoners to the *Constitution*. Then the *Guerrière* was set afire and blown up.

Captain Hull, who had won such a brilliant victory, was a very stout man. As was the fashion of the time, he wore a tight pair of breeches. We are told that in the excitement of the battle he made a quick motion, which split them from top to bottom. But, in spite of that uncomfortable accident, he staid on deck until the *Guerrière* surrendered, before going below to change his garments.

The naval victory won by Hull made his name known throughout our whole country. It is because he was such a hero in the War of 1812 that his tomb in Laurel Hill Cemetery, in Philadelphia, is still often visited.

This same Captain Hull was a very generous man; he proved it by giving up the *Constitution*, so that his brother officers could have a chance to win honors with it too. Captain Bainbridge, who next commanded it, soon after won a great victory over the *Java*, another British frigate, which was also destroyed.

The *Constitution* was in many a fight all through the War of 1812, and afterwards in the Mediterranean. It won so many victories that all Americans felt proud of it. Many poems have been written about it, and the most famous of all is by Oliver Wendell Holmes. He wrote it when our government first talked of taking the old and almost useless war ship to pieces. When the Americans read this poem, they all felt that it would be a shame to lay a finger upon the vessel, and made such an outcry that it was kept as a schoolship.

XV. "DON'T GIVE UP THE SHIP."

SEVERAL other naval battles took place during the War of 1812. One of the most famous of these was a duel between Captain James Lawrence's ship, the *Chesapeake*, and the British frigate *Shannon*. The *Chesapeake* had just come back from the Cape Verde Islands, and had lost a mast in a storm. The crew, numbering many foreign sailors, was therefore sure the ship was "unlucky;" but when the British captain sent Lawrence a challenge to come out and fight, he sailed out of Boston harbor without delay.

Lawrence was very brave, and had taken part in many a fight since he had helped Decatur destroy the *Philadelphia* in the harbor of Tripoli; besides, he had sunk the British vessel, the *Peacock*, only a short time before. His ship soon met the English frigate, and the battle began shortly before nightfall. Twelve minutes later the *Chesapeake* was unmanageable, but Lawrence called his

"Don't give up the Ship."

men to board the enemy. They did not obey very quickly, and before the order could be repeated, Lawrence was mortally wounded by a musket ball. As his men carried him below, he cried: "Tell the men to fire faster, and not to give up the ship; fight her till she sinks."

In spite of these brave words, Lawrence's ship had to surrender, but his heroic cry has never been forgotten; and whenever people seem discouraged or ready to give up trying, we still urge them on by Lawrence's cry: "Don't give up the ship."

The captive *Chesapeake* was taken to Hal'i-fax, where Lawrence and his brave officer Ludlow both breathed their last. But their remains were finally brought to New York, where they rest under the same monument in Trinity churchyard.

Although the British navy was so much larger than ours, it had suffered so much in encounters with our vessels that this first victory caused extravagant joy in England. Captain Broke of the *Shannon* was loaded with honors, and the people of his native county, Suffolk, gave him a beautiful silver plate, in the center of which the two vessels are shown.

Not long after the death of Lawrence, Oliver H. Perry, a young naval officer on Lake E'rie, sailed out to meet a British squadron with his nine small and roughly built vessels. Perry, who had never been in a real naval battle before, finding himself face to face with one of Nelson's officers, determined to do his best. As the enemy began fighting, he boldly unfurled a blue flag, upon which was written, in big white letters, Lawrence's famous words, "Don't give up the ship."

This was the signal for the Americans to begin. With a wild cheer they joined in the fight, serving their guns with great energy, until their principal vessel, the *Lawrence*, was completely disabled. But although the *Lawrence* could not go on fighting, Perry was not yet ready to stop. He left the shattered vessel, with four seamen and his young brother, and in spite of a rain of cannon balls, carried his flag to another ship. Then, instead of surrendering, as the enemy expected, he continued the famous battle of

Perry leaving the Lawrence.

Lake Erie with such energy that eight minutes later the enemy's flagship struck her colors, and Perry was master of the inland sea.

Hoping to cheer his countrymen, he quickly wrote this message on the back of an old letter, the only paper at hand: " We have met the enemy, and they are ours—two ships, two brigs, one schooner, and one sloop." At nine o'clock that same evening he came back in triumph to the harbor he had left that morning, and ever since then his name has been famous. It is because he won such a great victory that all Americans honor him, and that two monuments have been erected for him, one in Cleve'land, Ohio, and the other in Newport, Rhode Island.

Thanks to the victory of Lake Erie, Perry could take Harrison's soldiers over into Canada. Here they fought the battle of the Thames (temz), beating the British and Indians, and killing the dreaded Tecumseh. This chief, as you may remember, was the principal leader of the Indians, so when he fell they were ready to give up the struggle.

Before dying in Canada, however, Tecumseh had gone south to stir up the Creek Indians in Al-a-ba′ma. As they did not seem inclined to rebel, they made Tecumseh very angry. He finally cried: " Your blood is white. You have taken my red sticks and my talk, but you do not mean to fight. I know the reason; you do not believe the Great Spirit has sent me. You shall believe it! I will leave directly and go straight to Detroit. When I get there, I will stamp my foot upon the ground and shake down every house in Toock-a-batch′a!" The Indians, somewhat awed by this threat, counted the days after his departure, and when an earthquake took place one night shortly after, they rushed wildly out of their dwellings, crying: " Tecumseh is at Detroit; we feel the stamp of his foot!"

After this, and the appearance of a comet which also terrified them, they no longer dared disobey Tecumseh's orders, and, rising up, they murdered the garrison at Fort Mimms. To punish them for this cruel massacre of men, women, and children, General Jackson soon after met and defeated the Creeks at Horseshoe Bend. So many savages were slain in this battle that the rest were glad to lay down their arms and beg for peace.

In 1813, a British fleet began ravaging our coast, landing here and there to do damage. Thus they set fire to towns and shipping, robbed churches, and behaved everywhere with great cruelty. But although the enemy rav-

aged the Southern coast, they spared New England, because they thought the Northern states might yet offer to
rejoin England.

Disappointed in this, the next year they ravaged the
coast both north and south, until commerce came to a
standstill. The Americans, perceiving that their beacons
served only as guides to the British, ceased to light them
every night as before.

A British force landed in Scit'u-ate, Massachusetts,
intending to set fire to the shipping. All the men were
away, but we are told that two quick-witted girls managed
to frighten off the enemy by seizing a fife and drum, and
hiding behind a sand bank. There they cleverly beat the
drum and played the fife, beginning very softly and then
playing louder and louder. The British, fancying that a
large force was coming, beat a hasty retreat before this
" army of two."

During the War of 1812, an inspector of army supplies
at Troy marked all the boxes and bales with the initials
of the contractors and the letters " U. S." Of course the
latter meant that the goods belonged to the United States
government. But as the inspector was known as " Uncle
Sam " by every one in town, and as he took a great interest in the army, a joker said that he always put his own
initials on every parcel to let the Troy soldiers know he
had not forgotten them and was sending them food and
clothing.

The Troy soldiers repeated this joke until it was known
by all the army, and the men got in the habit of calling
the government " Uncle Sam " instead of " United States."
This custom soon spread beyond the army, and gave rise

to the funny picture which you will often see, dressed in garments cut after the fashion of 1812, but striped and starred like our national flag. Thus, while in poetry and art our country is generally personified by Columbia or Liberty, in politics and prose it is more often represented as " Uncle Sam."

XVI. THE STAR-SPANGLED BANNER.

TWO exciting engagements took place in the North, in 1814. One was the battle of Lun'dys Lane, or Ni-ag'a-ra, so near the falls of that name that the roar of the water rose above the din of battle. Here, one of the offi-cers under General Scott pointed out a battery to Colonel Miller, asking him if he could take it. The young officer modestly said : "I'll try, sir," and, march-ing fearlessly on, tried to such good

Lundys Lane.

purpose that the battery was taken, and a victory won soon after. Still, as the Brit-ish recovered possession of the battlefield on the next day, both nations claim the vic-tory at Lundys Lane.

Another American force, under Mac-don'ough, encountered the British on Lake Champlain. We are told that the first shot fired by the British in this battle broke a chicken coop on one of the American vessels. A rooster, thus freed from his cage, flew out, and, perching on the rigging, flapped his wings, crowing defiantly. The American sailors, delighted with the rooster's spirit, laughed and cheered, saying that they too meant to crow over their foes. They went into battle with such vigor after this little episode that they soon won a brilliant victory.

But while our forces were thus winning laurels in the North, a great misfortune had happened farther south. The British fleet, sailing up Chesapeake Bay, landed soldiers, who suddenly appeared near Washington and defeated the raw American troops at Bla'dens-burg. Hearing of this, and knowing the British would soon be masters of the capital, the people fled.

Beautiful Dolly Madison, the President's wife, alone retained enough presence of mind to carry off the Declaration of Independence and a fine portrait of Washington. But she escaped only at the last minute, leaving her dinner table all decked for a party she intended to give that evening.

The British, marching into the deserted city, swarmed into the Capitol, and, after breaking all the windows, seized torches and set fire to the "harbor of the democrats." Next, they went to the White House, where they gayly ate the dinner prepared for the President's guests. When their hunger had been satisfied, the soldiers rambled all over the house, sacking and ruining everything, and finally setting fire to the building.

Indeed, they destroyed all the public buildings except

the Patent Office. They spared this place only because the man in charge convinced them that it held the records and models of inventions which had been made for the benefit of all mankind, and not for the Americans alone:

The burning of the public buildings at Washington was not approved of by the greater part of the English people, although their government praised the commanders Ross and Cockburn for what they had done. Indeed, it ordered that the former should have a monument in West'-min-ster Abbey, where the best and greatest Englishmen are laid at rest.

It is said that the British thus destroyed our costly buildings to avenge the burning of New'ark, a village in Canada. Others claim that they did it because York (To-ron'to) had been taken and ruined by the Americans some time before. However this may be, the fact remains that many priceless relics were thus lost, together with many important state papers.

Not content with burning Washington, the British next attacked Bal'ti-more, where they shelled Fort McHenry for more than twenty-four hours. When their ships first drew near the fort, some Americans came on board with a flag of truce, to arrange for an exchange of prisoners. But fearing that these men would betray their plans, the British held them, and it was from the enemy's vessels that they saw the whole battle.

One of these Americans, the poet and patriot Francis S. Key, stood there, anxiously watching his country's flag, to see whether the fort would surrender. But although hidden by smoke from time to time, the flag waved proudly on all day, and when the sun rose on the morrow it still greeted his delighted eyes. This sight filled Key's heart with such joy and pride that he then and there wrote the words of one of our most famous national songs, "The Star-Spangled Banner."

The British, seeing their cannon had had no effect upon Fort McHenry, finally sailed away, allowing the Americans to go back to land. The song which Key had composed was printed without delay, and before long it was sung everywhere. Now it is familiar to every citizen of the United States, and is sung on every national festival.

Although a treaty of peace was being arranged with Great Britain, a British army under General Pak'en-ham now set out to seize New Orleans and Louisiana. But when this officer landed near the mouth of the Mississippi, he found General Jackson there ready to meet him. And when a British officer loudly boasted that he would eat his Christmas dinner in New Orleans, Jackson coolly said: "Perhaps so; but I shall have the honor of presiding at that dinner." Thus, you see, Jackson expected to take him prisoner.

The American troops, fewer in numbers than the British army, stood behind a rampart made of cotton bales and mud, waiting for the enemy. Shortly before the battle a young officer asked Jackson: "May I go to town to-day?" The general quietly answered: "Of course you *may* go; but *ought* you to go?" This reminder of duty was enough, and the young man went back to his post to fight. At the first shots, the cotton in the ramparts caught fire, so the Americans had to tumble over their cotton walls, and await their foes behind little heaps of mud four or five feet high.

The British now advanced in admirable order. As they drew near, Jackson rode slowly along his line, encouraging his men and saying: "Stand to your guns. Don't waste your ammunition. See that every shot

Battle of New Orleans.

tells." The Americans, therefore, took careful aim, and when Jackson cried, "Give it to them, boys! Let us finish the business to-day," their firing proved so deadly that whole rows of dead soldiers lay upon the ground.

Still, the enemy marched steadily on, encouraged by the loud music of a little drummer boy perched up in a tree, but they were driven back again and again. The hot fire of the Americans slew Pakenham and many officers, and killed or wounded about a fifth of the British army, while the American loss was trifling. But had there been an Atlantic cable in those days, this battle of New Orleans (January, 1815) need never have been fought, for peace had been signed in Europe a few days before it took place. Henry Clay expected to go to England as ambassador, and when he heard how bravely our men had fought at New Orleans he joyfully cried: "Now I can go to England without mortification."

The news of the treaty of Ghent (1814) reached Washington just nine days after the tidings of the victory at New Orleans. Although no mention was made of boarding ships, seizing sailors, or exciting the Indians, the war and treaty put an end to most of those things.

In the War of 1812 the United States won the right to trade as it pleased, and proved to England that its rights had to be respected, and that our men were as brave on land as on sea. But the war cost many lives on both sides, and greatly increased our national debt, which, in 1816, when our Union counted nineteen states, amounted to about one hundred and twenty-seven million dollars.

XVII. CLINTON'S "BIG DITCH."

MADISON was succeeded, in 1817, by President James Mon-roe', who took his oath on the ruins of the Capitol. As he gazed at the foundations, which were quite unharmed, he said that they reminded him of the Union, which was as firm as ever, in spite of all that had happened.

The war being over, a period of peace and prosperity set in for our country. Instead of fighting, people devoted all their energies to tilling the soil, working in the new manufactories, and building towns and roads. War having ceased in Europe also, people in America no longer sided for or against the French or the British, and all quarrels on that subject were so entirely forgotten that this period of time has been called the " era of good feeling."

Monroe did not have nearly so many cares as the Presidents who came before him, and had leisure to travel. He therefore decided to make a tour of the Eastern and Northern states, so as to inspect forts and harbors, and see how the people were thriving in different parts of the country. As he had taken part in the Revolutionary War, still wore his uniform, and was a general favorite, he was warmly received everywhere, and the signs of industry and prosperity which he saw on all sides greatly pleased him.

The United States, having been cut off from commerce with Europe for some time, had learned to depend more upon itself. Cotton and woolen mills had been built, discoveries of coal had given a new start to the iron trade, and American wits were hard at work over many new inventions. Among other things, matches now took the place of flint and steel, and when people wanted to light a fire in a hurry, they no longer needed to run into a neighbor's house for hot coals.

New roads were made in many directions, bridges were built over rivers and brooks, and the National Pike or Cum'ber-land Road made traveling easy between the

Potomac and Ohio rivers. Stagecoaches now ran regularly between the principal cities, and steamboats began to appear on all the large lakes and rivers.

Along the roads and down the rivers an endless stream of boats and wagons was going westward, where land could be bought so cheap that many emigrants hastened thither to secure farms. People declared that water ways binding together lakes and rivers would be a great improvement,

Clinton begins the Erie Canal.

so Governor Clinton of New York (1817) dug the first shovelful of dirt for a canal which was to connect Lake Erie and the Hudson.

As the work had all to be done by hand, people made great fun of Clinton's "big ditch," declaring it would never be finished. But Clinton's men went calmly on, and after eight years of patient toil his canal was ready. Starting from Buffalo with a party of friends, Clinton sailed all along the new canal to Al'ba-ny, and thence to New York by the Hudson. When he left Buffalo, a salute was fired, and cannons, stationed all along the road every few miles, boomed forth the great piece of news one after another, thus telegraphing it to New York in about eighty minutes.

It took Clinton much longer than that, however, to reach the ocean, for canal travel is very slow. Besides, he had to stop and listen to many speeches on his way. When he finally reached New York Bay, he solemnly poured a keg of Lake Erie water into the Atlantic, to celebrate "the marriage of Lake Erie and the ocean," which were now connected by an unbroken water way. This was a grand day for New York city, and the people cheered until they were hoarse, for they could now send merchandise to the Western farmers, and receive their produce in exchange, for about one tenth of the sum it had cost before.

An Old Stagecoach.

During Monroe's two terms as President, another great change took place. As there were places where steamboats could not go, and as stages seemed too slow, people began to talk of building passenger railroads. For more than two hundred years the English had used roughly built railroads to carry coal and other heavy materials short distances. In the year 1804 the first steam railroad was built in England, but it was a very imperfect one, the speed being only five miles an hour.

A short railroad to carry earth for grading streets had been built in Boston in 1807, where the cars were drawn by horses or mules. This was the first attempt at a railway in America, although one of our citizens had said in 1804: "The time will come when a steam carriage will set out from Washington in the morning, the passengers will breakfast at Baltimore, dine at Philadelphia, and sup at New York."

This prophecy seemed very wild to the people who heard it, but it soon came true. Now railroad travel

An Early Passenger Train.

is much faster than it was at first, so that one can easily breakfast in Washington, and still have half a day to spend in New York. Besides, people no longer need to stop for their meals, as the trains are provided with comfortable dining cars.

Soon after this prediction, the inventor John Stevens began making experiments with steam railroads, and in 1826 he built a small model road at Ho'bo-ken, in New Jersey. This attempt was laughed at just like the steamboat and canal, but people soon ceased to make fun when they saw how useful it would be. In fact, during the next five years orders were given for the building of several passenger and freight railroads, although the cars on them were at first to be drawn by horses instead of steam engines.

The most joyful event during Monroe's time was a visit

from the Marquis de Lafayette, who was well known to all because he had come over from France to America to help Washington resist Great Britain during the Revolutionary War. After fighting bravely till our independence was won, Lafayette had gone back to France to struggle for freedom there, and had been a prisoner in Austria for five years. Now, however, he was again free, so in 1824 our Congress invited him to make this country a visit.

As the whole nation longed to honor its guest, his visit was a long series of banquets and festivities of all kinds. People gave him so warm a welcome that his tour through the twenty-four states was like a long triumphal march.

Such was the anxiety to meet him, shake his hand, or win some token of his regard, that people constantly crowded around him. We are even told that a foolish lady, hearing he had kissed a little girl, gushingly cried: " If Lafayette had kissed me, I would never have washed my face again!" Since she was so silly, it was very fortunate that Lafayette did not kiss her, was it not?

Lafayette visited all the principal cities in our country, laid the corner stone of the Bunker Hill Monument, heard Daniel Webster's famous speech on that occasion, and finally made a pilgrimage to the tomb of his friend at Mount Vernon. There he entered the vault alone, kissed the marble coffin, and doubtless thought how happy he would have been could he only have gazed once more on the strong, good face of his fatherly friend.

On all sides Lafayette beheld great changes, for instead of the three million inhabitants of Revolutionary times, our country now had ten million. Besides, our wealth and territory had greatly increased, and, instead of occupying only a small strip along the Atlantic, the United States stretched from that ocean to the Rocky Mountains. Lafayette not only received many honors, but Congress gave him $200,000 and a fine tract of land in reward for his services to the nation.

When his visit was finished, and he wanted to return to France, he was sent home on a new man-of-war, which in his honor was called the *Bran'dy-wine*, because in the Revolutionary War he had been wounded in the battle of that name. When Lafayette died he was buried in a little cemetery near Paris, where Americans often go to visit the grave of the man who was Washington's dearest friend.

Lafayette's Statue at Washington.

It is because he was Washington's friend, and because he was brave, honest, and noble, that every one admires him. As he helped us in our time of greatest need, Americans have always wished to do him honor, and that is the reason why you will often see pictures and statues representing him.

XVIII. MORE LAND BOUGHT.

MONROE was so good a man that Jefferson once said in speaking of him: " If his soul were turned inside out, not a spot would be found on it." Still, you must not imagine that he was a weak man. Before his time as President was ended, he had to show that, while he was gentle and genial, he could also be very firm.

The Creek Indians, whom Tecumseh had roused to war, had been driven into Florida by Jackson. But they fancied that as they had made war to please the British, the latter would arrange, in the treaty of Ghent, that their lands in Alabama should be given back to them. Great Britain did nothing of the kind, however, and when the Creeks saw that they had been forgotten, they came over the border to take their lands by force.

The Creeks and their allies, the Sem'i-noles, murdered some white settlers, so Monroe sent troops southward to bring them to order. The leader of this force, General Jackson, was such a hard fighter that he soon drove the Indians back into Florida. There, finding the Spaniards had helped them, he burned a few small towns, and killed two English traders, who had also helped the Indians.

This might have made trouble, for the United States was just then trying to agree with Great Britain about our frontiers. Still, the work went smoothly on, until part of the northern boundary of the United States (that is, of the Louisiana purchase) was fixed as the 49th parallel of latitude, from the Lake of the Woods to the top of the Rocky Mountains. It was also decided that the Or'e-gon·

country, then a large tract of wild woodland reaching from these mountains to the Pacific, should be jointly occupied by Americans and British for the next ten years.

The following year, the United States made a treaty with Spain, which, for the sum of five millions, sold us East and West Florida (1819). Then our eastern sea-coast extended from the St. Croix (croy) River, in Maine, all along the Atlantic Ocean and the Gulf of Mexico to the Sabine (sa-been') River. The same treaty decided that the boundary between Mexico and our country should be formed by parts of the Sabine, Red, and Arkansas rivers, and the 42d parallel to the Pacific Ocean.

Spain was very glad to secure five million dollars just then, because the South American colonies had revolted and ceased to supply her with funds. Some of the principal European kings were so afraid that their states would soon follow the example of South America and set up republics too, that they made an agreement to help each other, and even to force the South American republics to submit again to Spain.

When Monroe heard of this agreement, or Holy Alliance, he said that, while the United States did not mean to meddle in European quarrels, we should no longer allow any European power to meddle in American affairs. The American continent was for Americans only, and no part of it could ever be seized by any one else.

When the Holy Alliance heard of this statement, which is known in our history as the " Monroe Doctrine " (1823), it no longer dared carry out its plans; for Great Britain sided with us against it. The Emperor of Russia, who had been trying to secure more land along the Pacific coast, felt so sure that the Monroe Doctrine would be upheld, that he consented to sign a treaty, whereby he promised never to claim anything on this continent but A-las'ka, or Russian America, as it was then called.

The United States had changed greatly during these years. Before the Revolution, negro slaves had been owned in all the states. As slaves were not needed in the North, where every one worked, and as many people thought that the colored race had as much right as the white to be free, one Northern state after another abolished or put an end to slavery within its limits.

But it was different in the South. The climate there was so warm, and often so moist, that it was thought negroes only could thrive as laborers. The planters, therefore, bought many slaves to cultivate their rice, cotton, indigo, sugar, and tobacco plantations. As white men refused to work side by side with the slaves, the latter soon came to form the whole working class in the South.

When the Constitution was signed, both slave and free states formed part of our Union, so it was settled that the western land north of the Ohio should be cut up into free states, while that south of the river should form slave states.

When Jefferson bought the Louisiana territory, both parties wanted to have their own way in the new land. But as the people at New Orleans were slaveholders, the first state formed, called Louisiana, asked and was allowed to come into the Union as a slave state, in 1812.

Later on, when our Union consisted of eleven free and eleven slave states, Missouri asked to join the Union as a slave state, too. To please both parties, and end quarrels in Congress which every day became more bitter, it was finally agreed that Maine should be separated from Massachusetts and come into the Union as a free state, while Missouri entered as a slave state. But, at the same time, it was also decided that in all the rest of the Louisiana territory north of the parallel 36° 30', slavery should never be allowed. This law is called the "Missouri Compromise" (1820), and was favored by Henry Clay, a great Southern orator.

While the Missouri Compromise did not exactly suit any one, it stopped serious trouble on the subject of slavery for about thirty years. Still, the Southerners thought they had been unfairly treated, and they found fault with Clay for supporting the Compromise. Indeed, some were so angry that they even refused to vote for him when he became a candidate for the presidency. Of course this was a disappointment for him, but he rightly felt that his nickname of the "Great Pa-cif'i-ca-tor" (peacemaker) was far nobler than any other, and once said: "I would rather be right than be President."

XIX. JACKSON STORIES.

THE sixth President was John Quincy Adams, son of Washington's successor. He was a good and learned man, but his election had to be decided by the House of Representatives, as neither he nor any of his three rivals received a majority of the electoral votes.

STO. OF GT. REP. —7

During his term, in 1826, on the fiftieth anniversary of independence, while joyful bells proclaimed the nation's "Jubilee," two old men quietly passed away. They had been friends, then rivals and foes, but were now at peace. In spite of suffering, both were conscious of the day, of which one of them, John Adams of Massachusetts, had said, in 1776, that it "ought to be solemnized with pomp and parade, with shows, games, sports, guns, bells, bonfires, and illuminations, from one end of this continent to the other, from this time forward forevermore."

Ever since then he had always helped to celebrate the glorious anniversary, and, thinking of his old friend, he now murmured: "Thomas Jefferson still survives." But

Monticello, Jefferson's Home.

Adams was mistaken. A few moments before, Thomas Jefferson had passed away at Monticello, in Virginia, his last words being: "This is the fourth day of July."

It was during John Quincy Adams's rule that the Erie Canal was opened, and work was begun on the Baltimore and Ohio Railroad. A great crowd assembled to witness the ceremony of breaking ground for it, and when John Carroll of Carrollton took up the first sod, he solemnly said: "I consider this among the most important acts of my life, second only to that of signing the Declaration of Independence."

Among the bystanders were educated men, who foresaw what an advantage railroads would be to our country. But there were ignorant ones also, who doubtless shook their heads and asked foolish questions. Indeed, we are told that a farmer in England once scornfully asked Stephenson, the inventor of the locomotive, what would happen were a cow to get in front of it? To the farmer's amazement, the engineer simply answered, "Well, it would be very bad for the cow!"

Every state now wanted roads, railroads, and canals, and there was much discussion as to whether the states or the national government should pay for all these improvements. Besides questions of roads and canals, new political questions also arose, and people began to say that those who helped a man to become President ought to receive some reward for their efforts. The reward they wanted was some government position, and this forced each new President to turn out officeholders appointed by the President before him, or else displease his friends.

Although this had been done very little hitherto, General Jackson's friends worked so hard to have him elected seventh President of the United States that he put about two thousand of them in office. When some one objected to this, one of these friends, named Marcy, carelessly said, "To the victors belong the spoils," little thinking that words thus spoken in jest would soon become proverbial.

The party to which Jackson belonged was the Republican, but his followers now changed the name to Dem-o-crat'ic, the name by which this party is still known.

Andrew Jackson, unlike the Presidents before him, came of a poor family, and had little education. When only fourteen he began to fight the British, and was taken prisoner by them. We are told that they once beat him most cruelly because he proudly refused to black their boots and act as their servant.

During his captivity, he took the smallpox, and shortly after recovering his liberty he lost his mother, who had procured his release and nursed him back to health. Left thus alone in the world, Jackson studied law for a little while, but he was too active to care much for books. A story says that his spelling especially was very bad. Early in his military career, it is said, he greatly puzzled one of the officers by putting the letters " O. K." on certain papers he had to examine. The officer finally asked him what these letters stood for, and Jackson scornfully answered: "Why, *all correct*, of course." This same story is also told of an Indian chief; and while it may not be any more true of him than of Jackson, you will often see these two letters used in this way.

As Jackson was very hot-tempered, he got into many quarrels. But he was loyal to his friends, and very quick-witted, as the following anecdotes prove.

We are told that once, during the races, a quarrel suddenly arose among the guests at a public dinner in Vir-

ginia. Seeing that one of his friends at the other end
of the room was in danger, Jackson promptly sprang
upon the table, and striding along, in the midst of glasses
and decanters, shouted to his friend that he was coming.

As he said this, he thrust his hand behind him into his
coat pocket, and loudly clicked the lid of his snuffbox.
The guests, thinking he had a pistol in his pocket, scat-
tered in great haste, frantically crying: "Don't shoot!
Don't shoot!" This terror enabled Jackson to reach his
friend, and made the rest of the guests forget the quarrel.

Jackson and the Wagoners.

Roads in those days were quite unsafe. Once, when
Jackson was driving along, he is said to have been way-

laid by wagoners, who, wishing to have some fun, pointed a pistol at him and bade him dance. With great presence of mind, Jackson gravely assured them he could not dance except in slippers, and when the men bade him get them out of his trunk, he had it taken down from the carriage and obediently opened it. But, instead of slippers, he took out a pair of pistols. Pointing these straight at the wagoners, he ordered them, in an awful voice, to dance themselves; and they capered frantically up and down the road until he allowed them to rest.

XX. JACKSON'S PRESIDENCY.

JACKSON was President two terms. About this time, Congress passed a law laying a high tariff, or duty, on goods brought from abroad, for the purpose of giving an advantage to home manufacturers. This law pleased the people in the North, because they manufactured many things, and wanted the Americans to buy from them rather than from European merchants. But in the South, where there were no manufactories then, people were angry, because they said that Northern goods were not so fine as the European, and that they already paid enough for all that came from abroad.

The result was that, in 1832, South Carolina said the law should be null, or of no force, in her limits. She claimed that, according to the Constitution, Congress had no right to make it, and announced that she would rather leave the Union than pay the tariff. Now, some members of Congress said that this question ought to be decided by the Supreme Court, and not by the states, and that a state, having once joined the Union, could not leave it without the consent of the rest of the states; but others, and among them the eloquent Southerners, Calhoun (căl-hoon') and Hayne, insisted that each state had the right to annul any law it considered unconstitutional, and even to leave the Union.

South Carolina was of the latter opinion, but Jackson was not, and we are told that when he heard the "Nullification Act" had been passed by South Carolina, he flew into a great rage, dashed his corncob pipe on the floor, and cried: "By the Eternal! I'll fix 'em! Send for General Scott."

General Scott was then promptly sent to Charles'ton to see that the tariff law should be obeyed. Still, the two opinions on state rights were so strongly rooted that neither party could convince the other. It was therefore finally agreed that while the tariff should be collected at all the ports of the country to please the North, it should be lowered little by little so as to please the South.

In settling this question, however, several famous speeches were made, among them one by Daniel Webster, who said that the Constitution was greater than any state, being "made for the people, made by the people, and answerable to the people." On that occasion also he spoke of "Liberty and Union, now and forever, one and inseparable," a phrase which became the watchword of a great part of the country. This was Jackson's feeling also, so at a dinner party he once gave the toast: "Our Federal Union: it must be preserved."

President Jackson, or "Old Hickory," as his soldiers called him, was very fond of having his own way; and while he had many devoted friends, he also had some bitter enemies. As he did not call meetings of his regular Cabinet, but instead listened to the advice of a few other men, these were scornfully called, by his enemies, the "kitchen cabinet."

It was probably by advice of the "kitchen cabinet" that Jackson decided not to continue the United States Bank, but to send the money to different states, to be placed in what were called "pet banks." This change caused some trouble, for people borrowed that money and used it in rash ways, hoping to get rich very fast.

Jackson had two Indian wars to carry on while he was President. One was the Black Hawk War (1832), in Il-li-nois' and Wis-con'sin, where the Indians, after selling their lands, obstinately refused to give them up to the settlers. The other was the Florida or Seminole War which began in 1835. The Seminole Indians had been beaten by Jackson himself some time before, and after the purchase of Florida they had consented to give up their land and go to the other side of the Mississippi.

Still, when the time came for them to move, their chief, Os-ce-o'la, would not go, and defiantly drove his knife into a table, saying: "The only treaty I will execute is with this." His influence was so great that the Seminoles rose up in arms and began to massacre all the whites. They surprised and killed one officer at dinner, and surrounded another in Wa-hoo' Swamp, where he was slain with more than a hundred men.

The Seminoles next retreated into the Ev'er-glades,

where several battles took place. Finally they were beaten at Lake O-ke-cho'bee. Osceola, having been treacherously seized in the meantime under a flag of truce, was imprisoned in Fort Moultrie (moo'try), near Charleston, where he died and was buried. The Indians, however, continued fighting, but were finally forced to submit. Many of them were then removed to the Indian Territory, so that the white people in Florida, Georgia, and Alabama need no longer dread their presence.

During this Seminole War, which lasted until the year 1842, there was one engagement in which all the officers but one were soon killed. Bravely heading what was left of his troop, this young man cried: " Follow me! I'm the only officer left, boys; but we'll all do the best we can." Doing his best he bravely died, but if his last words serve as a motto for every American boy and girl, our country will become greater than ever.

XXI. NEW INVENTIONS.

WHILE Jackson was President, he called upon France to give the five millions she had agreed to pay for damages caused to American ships. This the French did not wish to do, and if England had not interfered there might perhaps have been war.

A story of the time, however, claims that war nearly resulted simply because the French ambassador sent to discuss this question of money with the President knew so little English, and Jackson, on his part, did not know a

word of French. After exchanging the usual greetings,
we are told that the ambassador began in halting speech :
" Mr. President, France demands dat dis matter be ar-

Jackson and the French Ambassador.

ranged." Jackson, hearing the word " demands," sprang
to his feet with clenched fists, crying : " France *demands!*
Let me tell you, sir, that France has no right to demand
anything from the United States!"

The Frenchman, who thought that " demand " meant
" ask " in English as well as in French, gazed at the President in utter amazement, and had not a third person hastened to explain matters, the interview might have had
a stormy close. But when the President heard that the
ambassador meant that France was anxious to have the
matter closed, he sat down again quietly, saying : " Oh! if

France *asks* anything, I am, of course, always ready to grant it if I can."

It had seemed, for some time past, as if every year some new and important change was taking place. The discovery of coal and the building of canals and railroads were great improvements; besides, steamboats now ran along all the principal rivers, and had even begun to cross the Atlantic. In 1839, the express business began in a small way, and before long goods could be sent quickly from one place to another with little trouble.

One of the greatest improvements, however, was brought about by the McCor'mick reaper, which was patented about ten years before it came into much use. Until then, the broad acres of the West had not paid well, for farmers could not get hands enough to cultivate the fields where wheat grew so well. Of course, they could do their plowing and sowing little by little; but when harvest time came, the grain had to be cut quickly if they did not wish to lose most of their crop. With the reaper, one man could do the work of many; and farmers soon found that they could send their grain by canal, river, or train to the principal ports, and thence to Europe, where breadstuffs were scarcer than in America.

Women's work, too, had grown far easier than in colonial or Revolutionary times. Spinning and weaving were now done by machine in large mills; cooking was made simpler by the discovery of coal and gas and the invention of friction matches; and even sewing and knitting took far less time since they could be done by machinery. The Patent Office was so busy registering all the new inventions made, that it had to have a large force of clerks.

Countless other discoveries were soon to make life still easier and pleasanter. For instance, a few years later, a man named Good'year, after many experiments, found how to "vulcanize" rubber, thus preventing it from melting in summer and freezing or breaking in winter. Before long, clothes, shoes, diving dresses, and countless other articles were made of rubber, which is so useful in many ways that we could hardly get along without it.

The country had been growing so rapidly, and so many improvements had been made, that when Jackson left the White House he said: "I leave this great people prosperous and happy." But the prosperity of our twenty-six states was to suffer a severe check, for no sooner had Martin Van Bu'ren become President than the panic of 1837 began. You see, people had tried to become rich too fast, too much paper money had been issued, and when suddenly called on to pay their debts, so many business houses failed that many men were out of work. In New York, where the merchants had already lost heavily by the great fire of 1835, there was such distress that "bread riots" took place among the hungry people.

Then, too, the Ca-na'di-ans revolted against Great Britain, and, as many Americans remembered the War of 1812 and still hated the British, they wished to help the rebels. Neither Jackson nor Van Buren would allow this, however, and General Scott was sent to guard the frontier and prevent our citizens from taking any part in the war.

In spite of this, a few Americans managed to disobey. They even put arms on board a vessel in the Niagara River, to ship them to Canada. But the British, warned in time, seized the vessel, set it on fire, and, cutting it adrift, saw it poise a moment at the head of the Niagara Falls, and then plunge down into the abyss!

The money troubles during Van Buren's rule were thought by many people to be his fault; so when the time came for a new election, General William Henry Harrison was chosen President in his stead. He had governed the Northwest Territory, had fought in the War of 1812, and on account of his victory over the Indians was known as "Old Tippecanoe."

A good and honest man, the chief fault his enemies could find with him was that he had lived in a log cabin instead of a palace, and had drunk hard cider instead of champagne. His friends, however, admired him all the more on this account, and carried little log cabins in all their parades, using "hard cider" as a rallying cry. They also liked the candidate for Vice President, and the rhyme "Tippecanoe and Tyler too," was soon heard on all sides.

After meetings and parades without end, Harrison was duly elected, and his friends began to crowd around him clamoring for government places. Wishing to please them all, Harrison worked so hard that one month after his inauguration (1841) he died. His last words were: "The principles of the government, I wish them carried out. I ask nothing more."

XXII. WHITMAN'S RIDE.

HARRISON being dead, John Tyler had to take his place. During his one term, Florida, the twenty-seventh state, was added to the Union. Although our country was already very large, the time was near when it was going to be even larger still.

It seems that, during Jackson's rule, a party of Indians traveled from Oregon to St. Louis, in quest of the " white man's Bible." They had heard of it from some traders, and the stories seemed so wonderful that they had journeyed many miles to get the book and some one to read and explain it to them.

It happened, however, that the people whom they asked for it were too busy or indifferent to pay much attention to this request from savages. Still, they kindly fed and clothed the Indians, and gave them many presents. After three of the messengers had died of fatigue and disappointment, the last sadly went home to tell his people that no one would listen to his prayer. The story of the long journey taken by these Indians, and of their pitiful requests, was told in the East, where it touched the hearts of many people.

Emigrant and Prairie Schooner.

Before long four missionaries were sent out to Oregon, to tell the Indians about the " white man's book."

Two of these men set out with young brides, and journeyed slowly all the way across our continent. They traveled the greater part of the way in an emigrant wagon, or " prairie schooner," and, coming to the foot of the Rockies, were the first to take a wagon over those mountains. When they reached the Oregon country, which Americans and British still occupied in common, they found that the latter were trying to get sole possession of the land. Still, the Americans claimed that Oregon should belong to them, not only because Captain Gray first sailed into the Columbia River, but because Lewis and Clark explored it from the mountains to the sea, and Astor built the first trading post there.

After living at Wal-la-wal'la five years, one of the American missionaries, Dr. Marcus Whitman, heard that the British were about to send many settlers into the Oregon country, and then claim it as theirs, on the ground that there were more English than Americans living there. This news was told at a British trading post, where it was received with loud hurrahs, for the British thought they had got the best of the Americans at last.

Now, Dr. Whitman knew that the United States was then settling boundaries with Great Britain. He thought that if he could only get to Washington in time to tell the President and Senate what a beautiful and rich country Oregon really was, and how easily emigrants could reach it, they would not be willing to give it up without making an effort to keep it. Riding back to his farm in hot haste, he therefore told his wife and friends that he was going to start for Washington, and shortly after set out for a five months' ride. It was autumn when Dr. Whitman left home, and as he knew the season would not allow him to pass over the mountains by the way he had come, he journeyed farther south.

Through blinding snow and deep drifts, across frozen streams, and over mountains so steep and rough that it seemed almost impossible to climb them at all, Whitman made his way. After thrilling adventures with wolves and bears, and many hairbreadth escapes, he reached Great Salt Lake, then Santa Fé, and, following the trail from there, came to St. Louis. Thence it was easy to reach Washington, where he told both President and Congress all about Oregon, and offered to lead a train of emigrants into that territory.

By the Ash'bur-ton treaty, which had just been signed with Great Britain, the boundary between Maine and New Bruns'wick had been settled. But, fortunately, nothing had been said about Oregon. The news of Whitman's daring ride, and of his desire to people Oregon with Americans, rapidly spread all over the country. Before long, many pioneers were ready to accompany him, and when he began his return journey two hundred emigrant wagons followed him across the plains and over the mountains.

Although the British made sundry attempts to stop them, they were followed by so many others that, three years after Whitman's famous ride, no less than twelve thousand Americans had passed into Oregon. Our countrymen thus proved so much more numerous than the English that they soon claimed the whole territory, asking that the boundary be drawn at the parallel of 54° 40'. The British, however, did not wish to give up so much land. So, before long, a quarrel arose, and the Americans began to cry that they would fight Great Britain unless it consented to what they wished.

Many people justly considered that this was a very foolish way of acting, and Webster made one of his fine speeches to show both parties that it would be wiser to settle the dispute in another way. After a great deal of talk, and many threats about " fifty-four forty or fight," the United States finally thought best to accept the 49th parallel as its northern boundary from the Rocky Mountains to the Pacific Ocean (1846).

———oɔʓɞʓoo———

XXIII. THE MORMONS.

EACH state in our Union is allowed to govern itself by any set of laws it pleases, provided these laws do not conflict with the Constitution of the United States, which all are equally bound to obey.

In 1841 the people of Rhode Island were not satisfied with their state constitution, because, among other things which they did not like, it said only property owners could vote. It was therefore agreed that a new constitution or set of laws should be made, and when that was done the people chose Thomas W. Dorr for governor.

But the old governor, Samuel W. King, refused to give up his place to Dorr, and said the new constitution should not be obeyed, because it had not been adopted by vote of the property owners. As Governor Dorr and his party would not listen to this, and tried to seize the state arms, there was some trouble in Rhode Island. Although Dorr himself was caught and put in prison, the "Dorr Rebellion," as it is called, went on until the property owners adopted a new and better constitution.

At about the same time the tenants of some great landholders in New York also revolted, saying they would not pay rent. But when they threatened to make serious trouble, troops were sent to put an end to what is known as the Hel'der-berg War. The soldiers were called out, because, although people in the United States are free, they are not allowed to disobey the laws made by the greatest number.

Minds were very active at this time, and many people talked of their theories of life. You will not be surprised, therefore, to hear that a Scotchman, Robert O'wen, said that all men ought to live exactly alike. He declared there should be no rich or poor people, and that all kinds of work should earn the same pay. Thinking this could be managed, he bought land in several states, and started what were known as "Owenite communities." But although his ideas sounded very well, the people soon grew tired of living all alike and having everything in common. The Owenite communities therefore broke up, after having lasted only a few years.

Another man, named Joseph Smith, claimed, in 1827, to have been helped by an angel to find the "Book of Mor'mon," which is an account of a people chosen by God to live in America, many hundreds of years ago. The book was said to have been written on golden plates, in a language which could be read only by means of two precious stones, called U'rim and Thum'mim.

Smith printed this book in English in 1830, claiming that Christians should accept it in addition to the Bible. Many people believed his teaching, and considered him a prophet; so they went to live with him first in Ohio, then in Missouri, and lastly at Nau-voo', in Illinois. Here they built a town, and began a fine temple, but as the people around them did not like them or their teachings, trouble soon arose. Smith was killed, and his people were next led by Brigham Young, a man they greatly respected. He said that a man could have several wives, but as polygamy (having more than one wife) is not allowed in any part of our country, he had to take his people first to Council Bluffs, and from there to U'tah,

Scene in Utah.

which then belonged to Mexico. It was only after the Mexican War that Utah became a territory in our country.

This journey across the plains was both long and tedious, but the Mormons, who believed they were led by a special order from God, went bravely on. They divided their forces and marched and camped like the Israelites in the days of Moses, for they said they, too, were going in search of a Promised Land. When they finally beheld the Utah basin from the top of the surrounding mountains they greeted it as their future home with loud songs of praise.

Before long, they began to send out missionaries, and Mormonism, the religion taught by Smith, was preached everywhere, until converts from every state and from every country in Europe went to live in Utah. There they built Salt Lake City, and erected a huge tem-

Mormon Temple, Salt Lake City.

ple, which is said to seat more people than any other church in the world.

The Mormons felt the deepest veneration for their leader, Brigham Young, who died in 1877. Later, however, they gave up the polygamy he had preached, so that Utah could join our Union. They are very numerous, and have been so active and thrifty that their state, which was once a desert, is now very fertile. It is, besides, so attractive in scenery that many travelers visit it.

Many other changes had been taking place in our country. For instance, as people became rich, they grew more kind-hearted, and longed to help those who were poorer than they. Newspapers were now seen in nearly every home, and in reading of all the sad things which are always happening, the people who had the means sought to remedy them by building hospitals and asylums for orphans, for the deaf and dumb, for the blind, the idiotic, and the insane. There, many of these unfortunates were taught by clever means, so that they, too, could become good and useful citizens, of whom our country could be justly proud. Other well-meaning people visited the prisons, and when they saw how cruelly the criminals were treated, they talked and worked until new and better laws were made, and until prisoners were kept in clean and healthful places. Little by little, too, classes and shops were started in the prisons, so the people could learn better ways. The fact that they knew a trade well helped many prisoners to find work when their term of imprisonment was ended, and many of them have greatly repented of their past, and by hard and honest work have since won the respect of all who know them.

XXIV. THE FIRST TELEGRAPH.

THERE was one institution in our country which many people had long felt should be stopped. This was slavery. Even in 1688 the Quakers declared it was wrong, and made the first petition to have it ended. This opinion spread little by little, until, as you know, laws were made in several states, stopping or abolishing slavery.

People now began to say that in a Christian country, and especially in a republic where "all men are created equal," it was very unjust and even sinful to allow one class of human beings to be bought and sold, and treated like cattle. Those who talked thus and said slavery must stop were called "abolitionists." To gain more influence and bring others to share their views, they soon formed what were known as "abolition societies."

The people in New England were in general against slavery, and, as many of the clever men and women of the day were abolitionists, they began to write and talk against slavery as much as they could. Now, it happened that clever people were just then very numerous in our country, and among them were our brightest literary stars, men whose names should be familiar to every good American.

There were, for instance, our famous poets, Bryant, Poe, Whit'ti-er, Longfellow, and Low'ell; our novelists, Cooper and Hawthorne; our essayists, Irving, Em'er-son, and Holmes; our historians, Prescott, Bancroft, Motley, and Parkman; the great naturalists Au'du-bon and Agas-siz (ag'a-see); and countless other men who had the welfare of our country at heart.

Noah Webster, a great student, had worked hard for more than twenty years to make a big dictionary. He also wrote primers and a spelling book; and, instead of writing words just as they pleased, Americans learned to spell alike. They were so glad to do so that they considered it great fun to have young and old take part in "spelling bees," or "spelling matches." Webster's dic-

A Spelling Match.

tionary thus proved a great help to literature, and every one admired and respected the man who made it, and of whom it has been said: "He taught millions to read, but not one to sin."

There were, as we have seen, more and better newspapers. Some were written by men who were strong abolitionists, so they were called antislavery papers. The first and most famous of all these editors was a man named

William Lloyd Gar'ri-son, who, although poor, devoted all his time and money to a paper wherein he tried to convince people that slavery is wrong. These papers were sent everywhere; but the people in the South soon learned to hate them so bitterly that a law was made forbidding such papers to be sent in the Southern mails.

Among other interesting inventions of this time was the making of the first photographs, or da-guerre'o-types. Then there was also the discovery that a patient could be put to sleep, so that he need not feel pain, while doctors performed an operation. But the greatest change in our country, and, indeed, in the whole world, was brought about at this time by the invention of the electric telegraph, by Samuel Morse.

You have heard, have you not, how Benjamin Franklin made his electrical experiments? Well, once when Morse was on his way to America, a passenger on the same ship told him that an electric current could be sent along a wire. Morse immediately thought that if such was the case, an electric current could be used to convey messages, and during that long sea trip he worked out the system which still bears his name.

Although poor, he spent every cent he had in making experiments. Then, when his plans were all ready, he laid them before Congress, and, after many discouraging delays, he was finally given thirty thousand dollars to build the first telegraph line in the United States. This was between Baltimore and Washington, and Ezra Cornell, founder of Cornell University, invented the machine to lay the wires.

But, after the greater part of the money had been spent

in vain efforts to make underground wires work, Morse hung them on poles, and the first official message was sent over the line in 1844, by the young lady who had brought Morse the welcome news that Congress had given him thirty thousand dollars. She telegraphed the words: "What hath God wrought!" Two days later a message was sent from Baltimore to Washington, to announce that Polk was to run for President, but some people refused to believe it until the news reached them in the usual way.

Since then telegraph lines have been built in every direction. Wires run now underground as well as above it, and a way has also been found to lay them in the sea.

XXV. THE MEXICAN WAR.

WE have seen how Oregon became a part of our country. It was settled mostly by people opposed to slavery, so that it came in as free soil. But the Southerners had already asked that Tex'as be allowed to join the Union as slave soil. Many people wished thus to keep the balance even.

Now, you must know that Texas had grown very tired of Mexico's harsh rule. So Stephen Austin and Samuel Hoū'ston, two Americans who had received large grants of land in Texas, encouraged the people to revolt and form a republic of their own. They did so, and when the Mexicans tried to force them to obey, they won their freedom at the battle of San Ja-cin'to (1836).

The most exciting event during this war was the siege of the Alamo (ah′lah-mo), a large building in the town of San An-to′ni-o. Here about one hundred and fifty Texans held an army of more than four thousand Mexicans at bay, until all but seven of the men in the fort were killed. When the Mexicans finally forced their way into the place, they cruelly killed these men, too, although they begged for quarter. Among the dead was the great Kentucky hunter and pioneer, Davy Crockett, whose motto, "Be sure you are right, then go ahead," you will often hear quoted. The Mexicans' lack of mercy made the Texans so angry that after this event they used the words, "Remember the Alamo!" as a battle cry.

Eight years later, Texas asked permission to join the United States. This pleased the Southern people, for although Texas had been free soil according to Mexican law, slavery was permitted in the "Lone Star Republic" when it gained its independence.

Just before Tyler finished his four years' term, therefore, Congress decided to admit Texas (1845); but as a dispute soon arose about its southern boundary, the eleventh President, James K. Polk, found himself with a war on his hands. Many good Americans say that Texas had no right to claim the land between the Nueces (nwā′sĕs) River and the Rio Grande, and that this was an unfair and needless war, but others claim that it was for the best.

The new President began his term by sending General Zachary Taylor down to Texas to occupy the disputed strip of land. There he was met by the Mexicans, who attacked the American troops. A skirmish took place, blood was shed, and soon after war was declared. Instead of waiting until more troops could join him, Taylor pressed on, and, meeting the Mexicans at Pa'lo Al'to and Re-sa'ca de la Pal'ma, near the mouth of the Rio Grande, he defeated them both times, in spite of their superior numbers.

The Mexicans having fled over the Rio Grande, Taylor pursued them, took Mat-a-mo'ros, and began to besiege Mon-te-rey'. This place, too, was carried, though defended by a garrison of about ten thousand men. In the meantime, two other armies had been sent out; so the Mexicans were obliged to defend themselves not only against Taylor in the north, but also against General Scott, who took his army by sea to Vera Cruz (vä'rah croos), and marched thence across country toward the city of Mexico. The third American army, under Colonel Stephen W. Kearny (car'ny), was directed toward New Mexico and Cal-i-for'ni-a, both of which belonged to Mexico at that time, and included all the land from the Pacific Ocean to Texas and the Rocky Mountains, up to the parallel of $42°$.

After the siege of Monterey, the Mexican general, Santa Anna, tried to crush the Americans, under Taylor, in a mountain pass at Bue'na Vis'ta (1847). But Taylor was a very good general, and as cool as he was brave. Sitting sidewise on his horse, he calmly directed the troops, paying no heed to the bullets raining around him. We are told that one of his officers suggested that his white steed made such a fine target for the enemy that he had better withdraw; but Taylor quietly patted "Whitey," and said: "The old fellow missed the fun at Monterey; he must have his share this time." A little later, a Mexican brought a message from his army, and, seeing Taylor sitting there, wonderingly asked what he was waiting for.

Taylor at Buena Vista.

"Oh," said Taylor, coolly, " I am waiting for Santa Anna to surrender."

Taylor's men, following his example, were just as cool as he. One of them was sent over to the Mexican camp with a message, and Santa Anna told him that he would treat General Taylor well if the latter would only surrender. The officer, looking straight at him, is said to have proudly answered: " General Taylor never surrenders." This remark so delighted the Americans that they quoted it very freely during the Mexican War, and even long after.

The battle of Buena Vista lasted all day, and toward evening Bragg's artillery came up to help our troops. They poured their shot upon the Mexicans, who, in spite of all their courage, began to give way. When Taylor saw this, he is reported to have cried: "A little more grape, Captain Bragg!" In obedience to this order, a few more rounds were fired, and the Mexicans, unable to face the shot any longer, turned and fled.

While Taylor was holding the ground he had won, Santa Anna hurried off to meet and stop General Scott, on the road Cor'tez had traveled when he came to conquer Mexico, more than three centuries before. Scott's advance was one continual fight; but although he lost many men from wounds and disease, he won several battles.

The principal engagements took place at Cer'ro Gor'do, not far from the coast, and at Contreras (con-trä'rahs), Churubusco (choo-roo-boos'co), and Cha-pul-te-pec', near the city of Mexico. In this campaign our troops did wonders, for they had to climb tall mountains and scale high walls before they could march in triumph into the capital of Mexico (1847).

Taylor and Scott were not the only ones to win laurels during this war, for Kearny, after leaving Fort Lĕav'enworth, went on to take Santa Fé and all New Mexico. He next intended to conquer California, but when he got there he found the work nearly done, and could only help win the struggle against the Mexicans. This was because Captain Fré-mont', who was surveying there, had taken command of the American settlers as soon as the Mexicans tried to turn them out. Helped by Commodore Stockton, who was on the Pacific coast at the same time, this small force beat the Mexicans. Next, the Americans decided that California should be called the "Bear State Republic," and govern itself until it could join the United States.

XXVI. THE SLAVERY QUARREL.

JOHN C. FRÉMONT is one of our national heroes and pioneers. Besides conquering California, he is noted for his explorations, which he had been carrying on for more than five years. His guide and friend was the

Frémont the Explorer.

famous trapper, Kit Carson, whose name is now borne by a prosperous city in Ne-va′da. Once when Frémont crossed the Rocky Mountains, he carved his name on a bowl-der more than thirteen thousand feet above the sea, on Frémont Peak.

People had long believed that the wide tract of land just east of the Rocky Mountains, which was called the "Great American Desert" on old maps, was entirely barren. But Frémont, the "Path-finder," discovered that the greater part could be cultivated or used as pasture land.

Frémont had also explored a vast tract of land in northern Mexico, which the United States wished to own. So, when the treaty of Gua-da-lu′pe Hi-dal′go was signed, in 1848, it was agreed that Mexico should give up all claim to Texas as far south as the Rio Grande, and also to New Mexico and what was then called Upper California,—including all the land between the Gila (he'la) River and the parallel of 42°,—in exchange for fifteen million dollars.

There was, however, soon after this some slight trouble about the boundary, so James Gads'den was sent to sign a new treaty. He bought for the United States another strip of land, south of the Gila River, for ten million dollars (1853). Because he did this, and signed the treaty, that strip of land is known as the " Gadsden Purchase."

The war with Mexico was, according to Northern views, unfair, and it seemed doubly so because Mexico just then was weak and poor. In speaking of it later on, General Grant, who took part in it, said it was " one of the most unjust wars ever waged by a stronger against a weaker nation." Many other people did not approve of it, either, and when they heard how much money the war cost, some remarked that if Texas were spelled properly it would read " Taxes."

Meanwhile, the old quarrel about the slavery question raged worse than ever. When President Polk, in 1846, asked for money to pay Mexico, a man named Wil'mot proposed that it should be granted only on condition that the territory bought with it should be free soil. This is what is known as the " Wilmot Proviso," and it gave rise to endless disputes, not only in Congress, but all through the country.

The quarrel between the slavery and antislavery parties, which had begun so long before, was to go on much longer, and many eloquent speeches for and against slavery were made in the House during the following years. Among the many able speakers of that time there was John Quincy Adams, who was now over eighty, and was known as the

" Old Man Eloquent." Hearing the wrangling over this vexed question, he once said, with great sadness: " Slavery is in all probability the wedge which will split up this Union."

Still, John Quincy Adams did not live long enough to see his words come true, for he died soon after in Congress, crying: " This is the last of earth; I am content" (1848). As he had served his country faithfully for many years as minister, President, and in Congress, he had a public funeral, and Daniel Webster was asked to make a speech about him.

This Daniel Webster is one of the greatest orators of our country. He had already made famous speeches for the laying of the corner stone of the Bunker Hill Monument, and in praise of John Adams and Thomas Jefferson. Since then, he had spoken in many parts of the country, and he had now reached the highest point of his fame.

As he is one of the great men of our country, it will interest you to hear a few anecdotes about him.

XXVII. DANIEL WEBSTER'S YOUTH.

DANIEL WEBSTER'S father lived in central New Hampshire, at the time when miles of uninhabited forests lay between him and the nearest settlement in Canada. He took part in the French and Indian War, and when the Revolution began went to serve at Boston. He also took part in the famous fight at Ben'ning-ton, and the night after Arnold's flight from West Point

Washington chose him to mount guard over his tent, saying: "Captain Webster, I believe I can trust you."

As a child, Daniel Webster was very delicate. Hoping to do him good, his mother once took him to the sea-shore, making the long journey on one of the old farm horses, with her sick boy in her arms.

Although not strong enough to work on the farm like his eleven brothers and sisters, Daniel learned to read before he was five, and went to the village school, where he was the brightest pupil. His memory was so good that when the schoolmaster once offered a jackknife as a prize to the scholar who learned the most Bible verses, he

Daniel Webster recites Bible Verses.

recited chapter after chapter. Indeed, the teacher cried "enough," and gave him his reward long before he had said all he knew!

Daniel Webster was so fond of reading that he borrowed all the books he could, and learned them by heart. Besides, he carefully saved up his few pennies to buy a handkerchief on which was printed the Constitution of the United States, and committed that to memory, too. When told to watch the saw in his father's mill, he used to set it going, and read while the work went slowly on, instead of playing or fishing, as did most boys of his age.

When Daniel had learned all the village schoolmaster could teach him, his father made a great effort, and sent him first to Ex'e-ter Academy and then to Dart'moŭth College. He studied hard in both places, for he knew he must make the best of his opportunities.

Daniel was, besides, very quick-witted. Once, when he and an older brother were out driving together, they found the road completely blocked by a heavily laden cart. Ezekiel, who was large and strong, fancied they would have to wait until the teamster came back with men to help him; but Daniel cried: "Come, we can start this team. You put your shoulder to the hind wheel, and I will mount the near horse." Ezekiel obeyed, and the team, thus encouraged, drew the load up to the top of the hill, where the road was wide enough to let the Websters drive past. They were almost out of sight when the teamster came back with the help he no longer needed.

Like most New England country people of that time, the Websters made their own garments from the wool of their sheep. Once, on his way to college, the sleigh in which Daniel was riding broke through the ice while they were crossing a stream, and the young man was drenched To keep from freezing, he ran behind the sleigh until he came to a farmhouse, where he went to bed so that his clothes could be dried. On undressing, he was at first greatly alarmed to find his body dark blue; but after a while he discovered, as he quaintly said, that "the contents of my mother's dye pot were left on my body instead of my clothes."

Daniel was very kind and brotherly, and taught school for a while to help Ezekiel through college. Then he began to study law, although an old farmer had advised him to become a conjurer, saying he could earn a great deal of money by telling people where to find the things they had lost, or by telling fortunes.

His family was so poor that it seemed at one time as if he would have to give up his studies to accept a position offered him. But the lawyer with whom he was studying said: "Go on and finish your studies. You are poor enough, but there are worse evils than poverty. Live on no man's favor; what bread you do eat, let it be the bread of independence. Pursue your profession, make yourself useful to your friends and a little formidable to your enemies, and you have nothing to fear."

Daniel Webster took this advice, finished his studies, and went to Ports'mouth to practice law. Although far from rich, he was generous. One night, while walking home very late, he saw a poor woman steal the boards he had laid down in front of his house as a walk. He followed her home, and seeing that she was in great need, sent her a load of wood the next day.

XXVIII. WEBSTER'S SPEECHES.

ONCE a blacksmith came to Daniel Webster with a very difficult case. Webster had to study hard to get it right, and was even forced to spend fifty dollars for the books he had to consult. He won the case, and, knowing the man was poor, charged him only fifteen dollars. This good deed was not to remain unrewarded, however. A few years later Aaron Burr, Vice President of the United States, consulted Webster about a case like the black-smith's. Thanks to the careful preparation he had made for that case, and to his wonderful memory, Webster this time earned a large fee in a few minutes.

A teamster who had known him as a dark-eyed, brown-skinned farmer's boy was disgusted to find he had been engaged to defend him. But after Daniel had made one of his grand speeches, and thus won the case, the man's friends slyly asked what he thought of Webster now. "Think!" cried the teamster, warmly; "why, I think he is an angel sent down from heaven to save me from ruin, and my wife and children from misery."

As time went on, Webster rose ever higher in his pro-fession, until he was elected to Congress, where his careful study of the Constitution was a great help to him. Be-sides being a lawyer, he was also a good statesman, and one of the most eloquent men the world has ever seen. His first public speech was a Fourth of July oration, de-livered when he was only eighteen; but after that he made many famous speeches besides those already mentioned. One of his finest historical speeches was made at Plym'-

oüth, to celebrate the two hundredth anniversary of the
landing of the Pilgrim Fathers, and his greatest political
speech was his answer to Hayne, while in the Senate.

When this last-named speech was over, knowing Webster could never do any better, one of his admirers said:
"Mr. Webster, I think you had better die now, and rest
your fame on that speech." But Governor Hayne quickly
said: "You ought not to die; a man who can make such
speeches as that ought never to die."

This was very generous on Hayne's part, for Webster's
speech had surpassed his own. The next time they met,
when Webster asked him how he felt, Hayne again
showed that he owed his rival no grudge by answering,
with a merry smile, "None the better for you, sir."

Webster not only helped to make the Ashburton
treaty, but wrote such a clever letter to England that,
although the British had still claimed the right to search
American ships, they no longer dared do so except in the
way the law allowed.

Webster, like his father, was an ardent patriot, and
when the quarrels on the slavery question grew so bitter
that it seemed as if the words of John Quincy Adams
must soon come true, he made a great effort to preserve
the Union. He fancied this could best be done if the
Northern people yielded to the Southerners on some points,
and he therefore made a speech in Congress on the 7th of
March, 1850, which greatly disappointed his antislavery
friends.

Because they did not like the views expressed in that
speech, they began to abuse him, and when he wanted to
be nominated for President most of them would not even

consider him. This was a great disappointment to Webster, who sadly withdrew to private life. Soon after this he became ill, and being thrown from his carriage, he

Webster's Country House at Marshfield, Mass.

grew rapidly worse until he died. As the churcn bells tolled out his age, the people around his country house at Marshfield looked at one another, and solemnly said: "It must be that Daniel Webster is dead. The pride of our nation is fallen."

Webster's famous speeches have been printed, and if you want to read some of the most soul-stirring and patriotic words an American orator ever spoke, you must turn to the speech which he made in Congress to answer Hayne. Because Webster is one of our greatest orators you will often see his portrait. A fine statue of him has been erected in Central Park, New York, and on its pedestal you can read what are probably the finest words he ever spoke: "Liberty and Union, now and forever, one and inseparable."

———oo○●○oo———

XXIX. EARLY TIMES IN CALIFORNIA.

THE land taken from Mexico included, as we have seen, our present state of California. This new section was still little known, although more than three hundred years had passed since the Spaniards first visited it. They named it California because a fabulous story of the time claimed that there was a rich province of that name near India. As people then fancied that India could not be very far away from this part of America, the Spaniards considered this name most appropriate for the newly discovered region.

Some time later California was visited by Sir Francis Drake in the course of his famous journey around the world. He renamed it New Al'bi-on, and is said to have discovered San Fran-cis'co Bay and the one bearing his name, near by. We are even told that he landed on the shores of Drake Bay to refit his vessel, and that he made such friends with the Indians that they begged him to stay with them and be their king.

Drake was followed, early in the seventeenth century, by a Spaniard who not only discovered the bays of San Diego (de-a'go) and Monterey, but claimed the whole region for his sovereign. Nevertheless, for nearly a century and a half after that no lasting settlement was made in California. But at the end of that time some Franciscan friars came from Mexico to preach the gospel to the Indians.

These good men built churches and a score of mission stations in some of the most charming "garden spots" in California. Here they preached to such good purpose

Spanish Mission in California.

that at the end of about fifty years—in 1820—there were nearly thirty thousand Christian Indians. Indeed, the natives felt such awe for the priests that they obeyed them at a word, and worked so hard that the missions soon became very rich.

The Spanish had hitherto been the only white men in California, with the exception of a few trappers and traders.

The trappers roamed about the pathless woods and wild mountains, while the traders, who were mainly New Englanders, sailed up and down the coast, landing from time to time to exchange calicoes and groceries for the hides which the herders had to sell.

Sometimes these traders carried the hides to China and exchanged them for tea, but as a rule they went home again and sold their cargoes in Boston or New York. The two-year journey around the Horn was not only long, but often very tedious, for ships were often becalmed, or driven out of their course by unfavorable winds.

Still, both traders and trappers told such wonderful stories of the land they had visited in the far West, that a number of adventurers longed to go there. But the journey across the plains, through the deserts, and over the mountains, was so long and painful that only the bravest and strongest dared undertake it.

These men generally followed the road pointed out by the trappers, who often served as guides for the travelers, and beguiled the way by their many stories. Some of these were quite true, but others were told in fun to see if people would really believe them.

For instance, James Bridges, a famous trapper, used to tell of an awful snowstorm in the Great Salt Lake valley which lasted seventy days and stopped only when there were seventy feet of snow on the ground. He said that vast herds of buffaloes perished from the cold, and that their meat was kept fresh by the snow in which they were buried. When spring came, and the snow melted, he tumbled the frozen buffaloes into Great Salt Lake, where the water was so briny that it pickled all the meat perfectly. Thus, he had food enough to last several years for himself and for a whole tribe of Ute Indians. Of course this story was pure nonsense, but it shows what kind of stories some of these backwoodsmen told.

———o○⟩⟨○○———

XXX. THE DISCOVERY OF EL DORADO.

CALIFORNIA was so sparsely peopled, in the first half of the nineteenth century, that the Russians tried to get a foothold in it by building a trading station, and several adventurers settled in the places which best suited their fancy.

One of these men was a Swiss, John Sutter, who had been a soldier, and wanted to plant a Swiss colony in California, on the Sac-ra-men'to River. He was very successful in his ventures, and soon owned large herds of cattle, sheep, and horses. Besides, his farm was thriving, and most of the Western travelers, including Frémont, visited him in the course of their journeys.

Shortly before peace was made with Mexico, and the land really purchased by the United States, a man working for Sutter saw some shiny gravel in a mill race which he was digging. The man picked up a few of these small shiny lumps, and carried them to his employer, who, examining them carefully, saw that they were pure gold.

He tried to keep his discovery a secret, but it soon leaked out. When it became known, every white man dropped his work as a herder, lumberman, or trapper, and began to dig for gold, or to wash the mud and gravel at

Sutter's Mill, where Gold was discovered.

the bottom of the streams, where sometimes as much as forty dollars' worth of gold dust was found in a panful. A few, more lucky than their companions, found larger lumps, and thus became rich in a few minutes.

The news of the wonderful discovery spread like wildfire, passed over the mountains, reached the nearest telegraph station, and thence flashed all over the country, creating the wildest excitement. On all sides one heard of nothing else, and people remembered how the Indians had told the Spaniards, more than three hundred years before, that there was a land of gold in the West. The Spaniards had vainly sought this " El Do-ra'do," as they called it, which had now been discovered by chance.

As soon as the newspapers began to describe how easily a fortune could be made in California by a few days of digging, hosts of men started westward. But the journey was long and dangerous, no matter what road one took to get there. Some went by sea, sailing around Cape Horn. Others sailed to As'pin-wall, and made their way as best they could across the unhealthful Isthmus of Pan-a-ma', waiting on the Pacific coast until some vessel came along to carry them the rest of the way.

Both of these roads were, however, costly as well as tedious, so the majority of the gold seekers set out, on foot, in ox carts, and on horseback, across the plains. Such was the rush for the gold fields in California that before long one could see hundreds of emigrant wagons, and trains of mules, horses, and men afoot, crossing the plains. Of course, there were by this time several ways of getting to California overland, but the most traveled of all the roads was the old Santa Fé trail.

As long as people were on the grass-covered prairies traveling was quite easy, but after a time they came to the desert places and alkali plains, where the fine dust choked both men and beasts. Water was so scarce that many of the animals died of thirst on the way ; and as no one stopped to bury them, the road was soon strewn with whitening bones.

XXXI. THE RUSH TO CALIFORNIA.

IN spite of dangers, suffering, and hardships of all kinds, men kept hurrying on to California, where many of them refused to do anything but dig for gold. It was in January, 1848, that the first gold was found in Captain

Sutter's mill race. San Francisco was then but a tiny settlement. But before long ship after ship came into the harbor, laden with gold seekers. In 1849 the " gold fever " attacked even the officers and crews of these vessels, which were forsaken in the harbor while the seamen went to seek their fortunes also.

So many people came thus to California that in less than a year San Francisco became a large and prosperous city. Many of the inhabitants were mere adventurers, some of them were criminals, but others were men who came there for love of excitement or in hopes of getting rich in an honest way. Seeing that the bad men thought they could do anything they pleased in a city where there was as yet only a weak government, the better class banded themselves together, and in 1851 formed what was known as the Vigilance Committee. This was a body of men who kept watch over the people, and who promptly punished all who did wrong.

Most of the men who came over to California in 1849 called themselves the " forty-niners." At first they kept order with their pistols, and executed justice by lynch law. But they soon saw that it would be better for California to have good laws, and the proper officers to see that they were carried out.

The most important forty-niners, therefore, assembled at Monterey to draw up a constitution, and then asked permission to join the Union as a free state. This was granted, and California, which had been for a short time the Great Bear Republic, became in 1850 the " Golden State." During the next five years it grew rapidly, until its population increased fourfold. Besides, many interesting discoveries were made by men in search of gold, and before long several other metals and borax and asphalt were found in considerable quantities.

In 1851, while tracking some Indian thieves, a band of white men came by accident into the Yo-sem'i-te Valley,

Yosemite Valley.

which is about one hundred and fifty miles from San Francisco. This is one of the most wonderful places in the world, for the narrow valley is hemmed in by huge straight cliffs two and three thousand feet high.

In one place the Yosemite Creek falls down over the face of a cliff twenty-six hundred feet high, forming three cascades, the highest of which falls more than fifteen hundred feet. Here, too, is the Bridal Veil Fall, whose waters are dashed into fine spray as they fall. Besides wonderful mountains, tall peaks, strange rocks, carpets of bright-hued flowers, and countless charming views, this region also has some of the California big trees, which are the largest in the world.

A few miles south of the Yosemite Valley there is a grove of about six hundred of these trees. A few have been cut down, and by patiently counting their rings people have found out that some of the giant trees are more than twenty-five hundred years old. One of them is so large that a four-horse stagecoach with all its passengers can drive through a hole cut in the trunk, and there is still so much wood left on either side that the tree grows on, and does not seem to have suffered in the least.

A Big Tree.

In 1864, thirteen years after the discovery of this grove and the Yosemite Valley, Congress decided that these wonderful curiosities should remain untouched. Since then the Yosemite has been a state park, and although every one is allowed to go in it and admire its matchless scenery, no one is allowed to cut down trees, blast rocks, or build roads or houses there without the permission of those who keep guard over it for the benefit of the nation.

XXXII. THE UNDERGROUND RAILROAD.

IN 1849 General Zachary Taylor became twelfth
President of the United States. He had served in
the War of 1812, and had won many friends by his victories in Mexico. All who fought there with him admired
him greatly, and affectionately called him "Old Rough
and Ready."

But, the year after his inauguration, Taylor died, and
Vice President Millard Fillmore took his place. He was
able and honest, and had been a workman, school-teacher,
and lawyer before he became a politician.

Several interesting things happened while Fillmore was
President. For instance, it was then that the first measures were taken to build a railroad from the Mississippi
to the Pacific Ocean. This road was to make the journey so short and easy that there would be no more need
of crossing the continent in emigrant wagons.

Besides, Fillmore soon saw that it would be a fine thing
if the Americans living in California could trade with Japan.
In those days, however, the Emperor of Japan feared
strangers and would not allow any foreign vessels to come
into his ports, except a few Dutch ships. Hoping to make
him change his mind, and to get him to sign a treaty
which would open his ports for American trade, President
Fillmore sent him a letter and several presents, among
which were mechanical inventions which had never been
seen in Japan before.

As there was then no postal service between the United
States and Japan, this letter was given to Commodore

Perry, the brother of the hero of Lake Erie. Although told to be very friendly with the Japanese, he was sent out with seven war ships, so that he could hold his own if attacked. Perry delivered his letter, and after long delays finally got the Emperor of Japan to make a trade treaty with the United States.

The main trouble at home during Fillmore's rule was the old quarrel between the slavery and antislavery parties. For a time it had slumbered, but the fact that California wished to join the Union as a free state, started it up again with new fury. Men got excited over it, and the Capitol rang with the speeches of Calhoun, Clay, Seward, and Webster. The quarrel raged until Clay, the "peacemaker," finally suggested the bills forming what is known as the "Compromise of 1850."

Each party again gave up something to please the other, deciding that California should be a free state, but that Utah and New Mexico should form territories where slavery would be allowed or forbidden, just as the people settling there wished. Besides, to satisfy the Texans, who said that part of New Mexico belonged to them, ten million dollars was given in exchange for it. Clay's bill for settling all these questions was called the "Omnibus Bill."

The Compromise of 1850 also decided that slaves should no longer be bought and sold in the District of Columbia, although members of Congress and others might still keep their slave servants.

A law had long been in existence which, in accordance with the Constitution, allowed slaveholders to go into free states to claim their runaway slaves. But instead of helping the owners, the Northern people often hid the negroes who besought their aid, and helped them to escape. They did this because they believed that slavery was wrong and that it was better to break such a law than to keep it.

A Fugitive Slave.

To stop this practice, a new fugitive-slave act was included in the Compromise of 1850; but before long it made a great deal of trouble. Slaves who had run away many years before were now seized in the North and brought back by force to their masters. The poor negroes, who had thought themselves safe, naturally made a loud outcry when caught, and so roused the pity of people in the North that they several times rescued them from their captors.

As slaves were no longer safe in any part of our country, kind-hearted people who thought more of their suffering than of obeying the law, now sent them into Canada. But, not daring to oppose the law openly, they forwarded them secretly from place to place, hidden under loads of hay, packed in barrels, or done up in queer-shaped parcels. These were passed on from one person to another, who thus formed what was known as the " underground railroad."

Of course, the sight of slave catchers in the Northern towns made people talk and write more than ever against slavery. All agreed that the trouble had begun in 1619, when the first negroes were sold in Virginia, and that it had steadily grown worse. Many people in the South also thought slavery an evil, but they added that their negroes were so ignorant and helpless that they had to be treated like children, for they would starve if left to themselves.

Still, there were also many others who insisted that it was only right that negroes should serve white men. These people were very angry when Northern papers were sent south, or when their slaves were taught to read, for they said any knowledge the colored people gained would only make them discontented with their lot.

XXXIII. THE FIRST WORLD'S FAIR.

WHEN the government was formed, slave property was recognized in the Constitution, and each state was left free to do as it chose about keeping slaves. But since then ideas had been changing. The appearance of slave catchers in the North, and the publication of a novel called " Uncle Tom's Cabin "—of which many thousands of copies were sold—created a great sensation.

This novel was written by Mrs. Harriet Beecher Stowe, while busy with her house and children. It told a great deal about slavery, made people laugh, and cry, and *think*, and showed so plainly what slavery might be under cruel masters that most of those who read it declared the slaves ought to be freed.

Now, no one had a right to force the Southern states to set the slaves free, except—some people said—the President, in time of war. But the Northerners thought it was bad enough to have slaves in the states which already existed. You know that when Missouri was admitted as a slave state, it was decided that all the rest of the Louisiana purchase, north of a line drawn west from the southern boundary of Missouri, should be free soil. But although people thought this Missouri Compromise would end all trouble about slavery, quarrels broke out again, as we have seen, over the lands acquired from Mexico.

After the Omnibus Bill had been passed (1850), people again thought the slavery question settled forever. But four years later Senator Stephen A. Doŭg'las proposed that two territories, Kan'sas and Ne-bras'ka, should be carved out of the old Louisiana purchase, and be admitted as states as soon as they had enough inhabitants. He added that these should be allowed to choose for themselves whether they would be free or slave states, although they lay north of the Missouri Compromise line.

This proposal made the antislavery men very angry, and they wrote and talked against it with all their might. Still, in spite of all their efforts, the Missouri Compromise was repealed, in 1854. The only way now left to prevent the new territories from becoming slave states was to send out as many settlers as possible who were against slavery; so the Northern people worked hard to do this.

On their part, the Southerners hastened into these lands with large bands of slaves. Thus it became a race, each party trying to send the most settlers. The two kinds of men—antislavery and proslavery—thus began farming side by side; but when they began to talk politics, they soon quarreled fiercely.

People rushed into the country so fast that before long there were men enough in the present state of Kansas to vote and decide whether it should be free or slave soil. The excitement, therefore, daily grew greater and greater, and as the Missouri people hoped it would be slave soil, there was some cheating about voting. Some Missouri men crossed the frontier to vote for slavery, and this fact helped to make trouble when the elections decided that it should be slave soil. For several years there were quarrels and fights between the two parties in the territory, and this time of violence, bloodshed, and border warfare won for that part of our country the name of "bleeding Kansas."

Fillmore, in the meantime, had been succeeded by Franklin Pierce, fourteenth President of the United States. Pierce had been a poor lad, but he managed to secure a good education. He then became a lawyer, and was so determined to succeed that when some people made fun of him, after a first failure, he firmly said: "I will try nine hundred and ninety-nine cases, if clients continue to trust me; and if I fail just as I have failed to-day, I will try the thousandth. I shall live to argue cases in this courthouse in a manner that will mortify neither myself nor my friends." As the young man proved as good as his word, it will not surprise you to hear that he did succeed.

All through Pierce's term of office, the quarrels between the slavery and antislavery parties continued. Charles Sumner, a senator from Massachusetts, once spoke so strongly against slavery that Preston Brooks, saying that he was insulting all Southerners, attacked him in the Senate chamber, and hit him such a cruel blow on the head that Sumner was ill for more than two years. But, although a few slavery men approved of what Brooks had done, and made him a present of a fine cane as a reward, most people believed that he

Brooks and Sumner.

had done wrong. It was not in Pierce's power, however, to put an end to the quarrel of those who were for or against slavery, although he made a good President.

The first summer of his term was an interesting time, for people in our country, wishing to follow an example set by England, held their first world's fair, or exhibition, in the Crystal Palace in New York. At first, people in Europe made fun of the idea of having a world's fair in

America, but it soon proved a great success. Not only were there exhibits from every foreign country, but our own was well represented. Indeed, when foreigners saw the McCormick reaper, and heard of the changes it had brought about, one of them declared the inventor had "done more for the cause of agriculture than any man living."

England and the United States were now on such friendly terms that when the English explorer, Sir John Franklin, was lost in the ice of the Arctic Sea, Dr. Kane,

Part of Kane's Expedition.

an American, went off in search of him.   Unfortunately, as was found out later, Franklin and all his companions were dead; but Kane made many interesting discoveries in the north.   To show their gratitude to the Americans for Kane's friendly deed, the English, finding the remains of one of his ships some time after, had a beautiful desk made out of it, and sent it to the White House, where it is reserved for the President's use.

It was under Pierce, too, that our fleet came home from Japan, where, as we have seen, a treaty was made which allowed our ships to trade there.   Ever since then, America has kept up a lively trade with Japan, where the people are learning civilized ways so rapidly that it is said they will soon overtake the most advanced countries.

XXXIV. JOHN BROWN'S RAID.

THE slavery question created such very strong and bitter feeling that the next election saw the rise of what is still called the Republican party, which soon included all those in favor of free soil.   The Democrats proving the stronger, however, James Buch-an'an, their candidate, became the fifteenth President of the United States.

As Buchanan was already sixty-six and unmarried, he is sometimes called the "Bachelor President."   Many had hoped that his election would put an end to all quarrels.   But he was neither firm nor tactful, and things had already reached such a state that it seemed as if no ıt the terrible events which were soon

ɔf Buchanan's term a dispute was settled
ked about in all parts of the country.
ᴎ his slave, Dred Scot, north.   After
and a free territory several years, this
ᴌs free, and when his master took him
ᴌd him, he appealed to the courts.
ʂ finally laid before the Supreme Court
ᴈs, which decided that a man's slaves
ᴌo matter where he happened to live.
.e free states heard this, they made a
great outcry, because, as they said, slaves could now be
held anywhere.

The people in the South, on the other hand, were
greatly pleased, for this was just what they wanted. The
result was that both parties felt all the more determined,
the one to stop the spread of slavery, the other to extend
it over the whole country.   Fiery speeches were again
made on both sides of the question, and people grew more
and more excited.

Now, one man who was against slavery was named
John Brown.   He was a religious man, but not very wise.
He went to settle in Kansas, where he spoke his mind so
freely that the slavery people there soon learned to hate
him.   In a fight at Os-a-wat'o-mie, John Brown was victorious, but lost one of his relatives.   This loss almost
crazed him, and made him all the more anxious to put an
end to slavery.   Indeed, he finally imagined that the Lord
had specially chosen him to do this work.

As he could not stay in Kansas, where a price had been

set upon his head, John Brown of Osawatomie went to Harpers Ferry, in Virginia, in 1859. There, with the help of a few well-meaning but very unwise persons in the North who supplied him with money, John Brown made a plan to free the slaves. As he knew they would need arms to resist capture, he and twenty followers seized the United States armory at Harpers Ferry. Then they seized and imprisoned a few slaveholders.

This was against the laws of both state and country. Before John Brown could escape, he was caught by our troops, tried for treason and murder, and hanged. " John Brown's

John Brown at Harpers Ferry.

Raid," as his expedition in Virginia is generally called, created a great excitement, for the Southern people did not realize at that time that it was merely the plan of a man half-crazed by suffering. Some Southerners fancied that all the abolitionists in the North were in league with John Brown, and as they had lived through the horrors of small negro revolts, they were naturally indignant.

In fact, most people in the North thought it very wrong of John Brown to take the law into his own hands or to try to free slaves by violence. They did long to see slavery ended, but they wanted it to be done by vote, and not by force. Besides, they knew, as well as the Southerners, that an uprising of the negroes was greatly to be dreaded, for the latter were so ignorant at that time, and so easily led, that they might have been urged on to commit the most horrible crimes.

John Brown's attempt only made slavery quarrels worse, and when the time came for a new election, four candidates were proposed. One of these men, Breck'in-ridge, was in favor of allowing slaves to be carried into all the territories, but another, Stephen A. Douglas, said that the new territories ought to be opened to slaveholders and free men, the settlers themselves deciding for or against slavery. The third man declared merely in favor of union and peace. The fourth, Abraham Lincoln, claimed that, while the laws of states should be respected, slavery ought not to spread any farther, because it was morally wrong.

Now, by the last census made, there were thirty-one million inhabitants in our country, only twelve million of which lived in slave states. You will therefore not be surprised to learn that Abraham Lincoln, the Republican candidate, was elected sixteenth President of the United States (1860).

Abraham Lincoln.

It was in 1861 that Kansas joined the Union as a free state, and the thirty-fourth star was added to our flag. In mentioning Old Glory, Senator Charles Sumner once spoke these words, which every American citizen should remember: "The stripes of alternate red and white proclaim the original union of thirteen states to maintain the Declaration of Independence. Its stars, white on a field of blue, proclaim the union of states constituting our national constellation, which receives a new star with every new state. These two signify union, past and present. The very colors have a language which was officially recognized by our fathers. White is for purity, red is for valor, blue is for justice."

XXXV. LINCOLN'S YOUTH.

BEFORE we go on to speak of the great events which took place after Lincoln's election, it will interest you to hear something about Lincoln, who, as you will see, was one of the most remarkable men that ever lived.

Born in a Kentucky log hut in 1809, Lincoln belonged to the poor white class; indeed, his father was so ignorant that he did not even know how to read. But, like most great men, Lincoln had a very good mother, who, although poor and far from learned, taught her boy all she could. She died soon after they had moved to Indiana, and when only nine years old the poor little fellow had to help his father dig her grave. He never forgot his mother's teachings, however, and many years later, when in the White

House, he said: "All that I am, or hope to be, I owe to my sainted mother."

The Lincoln family had but one book, a Bible, which Abraham used to read by the light of the pine knots he picked up, for they could not afford any other light. Instead of a slate, Lincoln had a piece of rough board, or an old fire shovel, and used a bit of charcoal or limestone as a pencil. He was eager to learn, and so persevering that he borrowed an old arithmetic, and not only worked out all the sums without any help, but copied it all so as to have a book of his own.

Obliged to work all day, Lincoln plowed, sowed, and reaped, and split rails to fence in his father's little farm.

Cabinet made by Lincoln.

The only way the farmers in that region could get money was by building flatboats and taking their produce to New Orleans. Lincoln soon did this too, and on reaching that city saw many strange new sights. For instance, he once went to the slave market, where, for the first time in his life, he saw human beings sold like cattle.

It made him feel so bad that we are told he then said, in regard to slavery: "If I can ever hit that thing, I'll hit it hard!"

Lincoln made several trips to New Orleans, and perceiving that flatboats were often caught in snags or tangles of branches in the Mississippi, he invented a kind of pole to lift them over such obstacles. The roughly whittled pattern of this invention can still be seen in the Patent Office at Washington, where it is shown as a curiosity.

When Lincoln became a young man, he was clerk in a small store in Illinois. He was so careful and upright in all his dealings while there, that he soon won the name of "Honest Abe." Indeed, we are told that after making a mistake in giving change, he once tramped several miles at night, after the store was closed, to give an old woman the few cents he still owed her. On another occasion, Lincoln found he had given short measure in tea to a customer, and could not rest until he had corrected his mistake.

Lincoln as Clerk.

While in charge of this country store, Lincoln was postmaster, too. But letters were so few that he carried them around in his hat. When any one called for mail, he quickly produced the small bundle, and, looking it over, found the right letter. Both store and post office came to an abrupt end; but Lincoln was so honest that when people came to him, several years later, to straighten out the post office accounts, he brought out an old stocking containing the little sum still due to the government. The money had lain there ever since; but although often penniless, Lincoln had never even borrowed a cent of it.

He was so anxious to study law that when some one offered to lend him Blackstone, he hastened to go and get the four heavy volumes, although he had to tramp twenty-one miles and back in the course of one night. Then he began to study, working so hard that before long he became a good lawyer and settled in Springfield.

Lincoln's Law-office Chair.

Lincoln was so clear-headed, so kind-hearted, so full of humor and tact, so unselfish and honest, that he won friends wherever he went. We are told that, when riding to court, he once saw that some little birds had fallen out of their nest. In spite of his companions' jeers, he got down from his horse and carefully put them back. When he again joined his friends, they asked why he had stopped, and began to make fun of him; but he quietly answered: "I could not have slept unless I had restored those little birds to their mother."

Lincoln was tall and ungainly, but his homely face was so strong and kind that every one trusted him. He was for several years a member of the Illinois legislature, and was once a member of Congress. Later on, when it came time to elect a senator for his state, some of his friends named him, while others named Stephen A. Douglas.

Both men were fine orators, and although Douglas was small, he was so strong in argument that he was called the "little giant." Douglas's speeches were very eloquent; but Lincoln's were so simple, so full of common sense and human sympathy, that they went straight to people's hearts. These two men had many a debate during this campaign, and although Lincoln failed to be elected, he won many good friends.

Lincoln never pretended to be either wise or clever, but his life motto was "to do his level best," and he manfully put it into practice. He did not like to hear all the quarreling that was going on, and always did all he could to stop it. But when he thought a thing right, he could be very firm; and once, after some ministers tried to convince him, by quoting Bible texts, that slavery was not wrong, he cried:

"I know there is a God, and that He hates injustice and slavery. I see the storm coming, and I know His hand is in it. If He has a place and work for me,—and I think He has,—I believe I am ready. I am nothing, but truth is everything. . . . Douglas don't care whether slavery is voted up or down; but God cares, and humanity cares, and I care, and with God's help I shall not fail. I may not see the end, but it will come, and I shall be vindicated [proved right], and these men will find that they have not read their Bibles aright."

When called upon to make his first speech as senatorial candidate, Lincoln said: "'A house divided against itself cannot stand.' I believe this government cannot endure permanently half slave and half free. I do not expect the house to fall, but I expect it will cease to be divided. It will become all one thing or all the other." This speech is so plain, yet so clever, that it has always been greatly admired. As we have seen, Lincoln had won many friends, so when the time came to elect a new President he was one of the candidates proposed.

During this campaign some of the opposite party tried to spoil Lincoln's chances by calling him a " rail splitter." But his friends promptly said *that* was nothing to be

ashamed of, and even carried rails in their processions. When asked whether he had really split the rails they thus paraded, Lincoln once smilingly said that he could not swear to the rails, although he had certainly split a great many just like them.

Lincoln's Broadax.

A few gentlemen from the East, seeing Lincoln's awkward figure, felt sure he would never do for President, but they changed their minds after hearing a speech he made in New York. All listened to it spellbound until he closed it with the noble words: "Let us have faith that right makes might, and in that faith let us to the end dare to do our duty as we understand it."

The campaign was an unusually exciting one, for the Southern states had vowed that if Lincoln was elected they would leave the Union. Every one, therefore, anxiously awaited the result of the election ; and when it finally became known that Lincoln was chosen, the long-gathering storm burst.

The time was now rapidly drawing near when our country was to be a prey to the saddest and bloodiest conflict in our history. War is a very sad thing, even when it has to be waged on outsiders; but a civil war, where friends, fellow-citizens, and even families are often divided, is the saddest thing in the world.

XXXVI. THE FIRST SHOT.

WITHOUT even waiting to see what Lincoln would do, the senators from South Carolina left their seats in Congress and went home. Next, a meeting was called in Secession Hall, in Charleston, South Carolina, where it was decided that South Carolina, the " Palmetto State," should separate, or secede, from the Union (December 20, 1860). The Southern people, you know, firmly believed that they had a perfect right to leave the Union whenever laws were made which they thought unfair.

They were so sure they were doing right that in less than two months six other states joined South Carolina in seceding from the Union. Then the seven states, South Carolina, Georgia, Alabama, Florida, Mississippi, Louisiana, and Texas, united to form a new republic, which was called the " Confederate States of America." Southerners said that this new republic was to have " slavery for its corner stone," and chose a well-known man, Jefferson Davis, for its President. At first Mont-gom'er-y was the capital of the Confederacy, which adopted a flag with three bars and seven stars instead of the stars and stripes. When this

(168)   **Jefferson Davis.**

became known in the North, and the people there realized that the new banner would be raised instead of the stars and stripes, they became so excited that Secretary Dix telegraphed to New Orleans: "If any person attempts to haul down the American flag, shoot him on the spot!"

The Confederates, or secessionists, next seized most of the Southern forts belonging to the United States, except Forts Pick'ens and Sum'ter, which the officers refused to surrender. They also fired upon a ship called the *Star of the West*, when it came into the Charleston harbor to bring supplies to the government troops at Fort Sumter. In fact, the Confederates showed themselves so determined not to let it come in that it had to turn around and go back.

The Southerners believed so thoroughly in state rights that, although many of them did not wish to secede, they felt it their duty to do so. Thus more than two hundred officers who had been in the United States service, and had won laurels in the Mexican War, now gave up their positions in the army and navy and returned home.

The action taken by the Southern states greatly bewildered President Buchanan, who looked on helplessly, and did nothing. He said that the Southern states had no right to secede, but added that he had no right to force them to stay in the Union. Everything was therefore left for Lincoln to settle, and people anxiously wondered what he would do.

A rumor had arisen that, even if elected, Lincoln should never be inaugurated. This made his friends so anxious for his safety that they persuaded him to travel secretly to

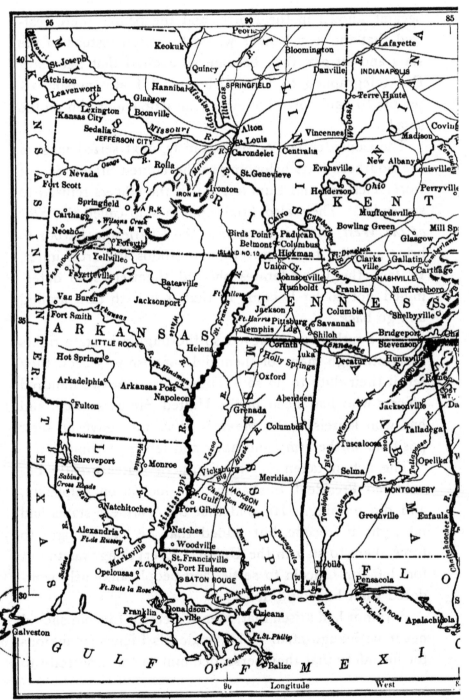

MAP TO ILLUSTRATE THE

WAR FOR THE UNION

SCALE OF MILES

0   100   200

BRADLEY & POATES, ENGRS., N.Y.

Washington.   There he was inaugurated, on M
1861.   After taking his solemn oath to "preser
tect, and defend the Constitution of the United
Lincoln made a grand speech, saying that, while
at any cost keep this oath, he had no intention v
of meddling with slavery in the states where it
existed.

He said that, in his opinion, no state could le
Union, declared that he would hold the forts still
ing to the Union, and firmly but kindly adde
your hands, my dissatisfied countrymen, and not
is the momentous issue of civil war.   The gove
will not assail you.   You can have no conflict without
being yourselves the aggressors."

For the first month after his inauguration, Lincoln was
so bothered by office seekers that he could not attend to
much else.   But by this time Major An'der-son, who
was holding Fort Sumter, was so short of food and supplies that Lincoln sent word to South Carolina that he
was going to send him help.   This message was given to
Jefferson Davis, who called a council to decide whether the
supply should be allowed to come in or not.

There were two opinions about this, even in the Confederate Cabinet, and after some one had spoken warmly
in favor of taking the fort by force, the secretary of state
gravely said: "The firing upon that fort will inaugurate
a civil war greater than any the world has yet seen. . . .
You will wantonly strike a hornet's nest which extends
from mountains to ocean, and legions now quiet will swarm
out and sting us to death."

In spite of this warning, Jefferson Davis finally decided

hat Sumter must be taken. He bade the Southern general, Beau're-gard, not to allow any supplies to pass in, and to fire

Fort Sumter.

upon the fort if it did not surrender. As Anderson firmly refused to yield to Beauregard's summons, the bombarding of Fort Sumter began on April 12, 1861.

At the end of about thirty hours the fort was a heap of smoking ruins, and as there was neither food nor ammunition left, Anderson was forced to haul down the Union flag and surrender. But he and his men were allowed to leave with their arms and colors, and the flag they thus saved was, as we shall see, again raised over Fort Sumter four years later.

Although there were none killed on either side in this battle of "seventy men against seven thousand," the firing on Fort Sumter acted like an electric shock upon the whole nation. Until then there had been two kinds of patriots in the North; but the fact that the flag had been fired upon put an end to all disputes, and the people rose like one man to defend it.

Lincoln, who had made no preparations for war, so as not to make the South angry and force matters, now called for seventy-five thousand men "to maintain the

honor, the integrity, and the existence of the Union."
These men were called for three months only, because
people then fancied that the war would be over in ninety
days at the utmost.

In fact, at this sad time both parties greatly misunder-
stood each other. Educated people in the North felt sure
the South would yield rather than see blood shed. But
educated people in the South felt equally certain that for
the sake of peace the North would yield, as had so often
happened before. Besides, there were ignorant Northerners who fancied that Southern people were "fire eaters,"
and could only talk ; while the same class in the South loudly
boasted that the Yankees " would back up against the
north pole rather than fight," and that " one Confederate
could whip five Yankees."

XXXVII. THE CALL TO ARMS.

LINCOLN'S call was answered with a promptness
which showed how ready Union men were to defend
their flag. Before thirty-six hours were over, troops
began to gather in Washington, which was considered the
most dangerous point, as it was so near the Southern states.
These Northern soldiers wore blue uniforms, and as they
came to defend the Union and uphold the federal government, they were called Unionists or Federals. As
many of them came from the New England states, they
were also often called Yankees. Southern troops, who
responded to Jefferson Davis's call just as promptly,

wore gray uniforms, and were called Confederates by their own people, and rebels or Johnnies by the Unionists.

Confederate.

In those days there were not nearly so many railroads as there are now. To reach Washington, troops from Pennsylvania and the East had to pass through Baltimore, where the two depots were at opposite ends of the town. Now, Maryland was a slave state, but so many people there were against slavery that it never joined the Confederacy.

Unionist.

While some Union troops were marching through the city on their way to Washington, on the eighty-sixth anniversary of the battle of Lex'ing-ton, they were first hooted at and then attacked by a mob of slavery men. The soldiers kept their temper and took the insults calmly, but before long several shots were heard. One of the soldiers, mortally wounded, swung around, saluted the flag, crying, "All hail the stars and stripes!" and then fell down dead.

The sight of three lifeless companions proved the "lighted match which set fire to the powder magazine," and the Union troops shot at the mob. Several persons in the crowd were killed or wounded, and the troops had to fight their way, as it were, out of the town. Because these Northern regiments suffered in passing through

Baltimore, the rest were taken by water to An-nap'o-lis and thence on to Washington.

The Southern people were very brave, and to show the North that they were not afraid, Jefferson Davis made a proclamation two days after Lincoln called for soldiers. In it he said he would give Confederate vessels leave to take or destroy Union vessels wherever they met them on the seas.

Now, you must know that war consists largely in giving tit for tat. So when Lincoln heard that Southern vessels were making ready to capture Northern vessels, he quickly ordered all the Southern ports closed, and forbade any ships to sail out of the harbors of the states which had seceded. To make sure that these orders would be obeyed, Northern vessels were sent to blockade the Southern ports. But, at that time, there were very few ships in the Union navy, and to keep guard over a coast line more than two thousand miles long a great many were needed.

Almost everything that could float was, therefore, called into service, and Southern vessels passing in and out could do so only by running past the Union blockade. This was dangerous work, for the Union vessels were armed with guns, and did their best to catch or sink the Southern vessels. Still, the blockade runners were very wary, and as their ships and sails were painted gray, they could not easily be seen, and they often managed to slip past. At first the blockade was not strict at all, but every day it became more severe. It had to be close to prevent the South from sending out cotton, sugar, or tobacco, because the money those products brought in served to buy new supplies for the Southern army.

When war broke out, several states were undecided which side to take, but before long they made up their minds, and Arkansas, Tennessee, North Carolina, and part of Virginia joined the Confederacy, which thus embraced eleven out of the thirty-four states. But the western part of Virginia later formed a separate state, called West Virginia, because the people living there wanted to remain in the Union.

Soon after Virginia joined the Confederacy, Richmond became the Confederate capital. The fact that Washing-

The Confederate Capitol at Richmond.

ton and Richmond lay so close together made the largest forces collect there, and while the cry in Washington was "On to Richmond!" in the Confederate army it was "On

to Washington!" As the Confederates held the Shen-an-
do'ah valley, and had long been preparing for war, it
seemed as if they could easily reach the Union capital;
and hence it became necessary to have troops enough to
defend it.

The Southerners were ready, as we have seen; and
while most of the white men fought in the army, their
plantations were worked by their slaves, who thus supplied
them with the food they needed. Hearing that war had
broken out, a few negroes came into the American lines,
asking to be set free. But the Northern people, mindful
of the fugitive slave law, would not at first allow them to
stay, and sent them back to their masters.

Still, when the Unionists saw that the slaves built most
of the fortifications, acted as teamsters, and served the
soldiers in many ways, General Benjamin F. Butler said
they ought to be seized as well as tools, ammunition, or
anything else which helped the enemy. Because such
things are called " contraband of war," slaves were classed
as such, also, and before long many of them came into the
Union lines, shouting, " I's contraband, massa, I's contraband! " knowing this would secure them good treatment.

XXXVIII. THE PRESIDENT'S DECISION.

ALTHOUGH quite unprepared for war, the North was
in many respects better off than the South. Not
only did it have many more inhabitants, but it owned
shipyards, machine shops, and manufactories of all kinds,

and could thus supply all its army's needs. This was not the case in the South, where, until then, the main occupation of the people had been agriculture.

By the time summer came on, General George B. McClel'lan was·at the head of a large force in control of West Virginia. Missouri, in the meantime, was almost all in the hands of Union forces, in spite of a Confederate victory won at Wilsons Creek, where the Federal General Lyon was killed. But, although the Confederates failed to secure Missouri and West Virginia, they had built forts so as to control the Mississippi, and still hoped to get Kentucky.

As Kentucky had not seceded from the Union, General U-lys'ses S. Grant was sent down there to defend it. Before long he managed to take Pa-du'cah, which was in the power of the Confederates. He seized it, although the Union troops at this time were not yet used to warfare. Indeed, they knew so little about discipline that when marching along they often broke ranks to pick blackberries.

After several small victories in West Virginia, a Union army under General McDow'ell marched southward to meet Beauregard at Ma-nas'sas, or Bull Run. Here the Confederates were first driven back; but they bravely rallied when one of their officers cried, pointing to another: "See, there's Jackson standing like a stone wall." This remark was so true that ever after this Southern general was known as "Stonewall Jackson."

The battle of Bull Run, where two untried armies found themselves face to face on a hot July day, resulted in complete victory for the Confederates, and in an awful defeat for the Federals. To its great surprise and dismay, the Union army was completely routed; but both sides learned a great deal by this fight. The Southerners were no longer quite so sure that one Confederate could whip five Yankees, and the Northern men had found that if they meant to save the Union they would have to work very hard.

General McClellan—the "Soldiers' Pride," or "Little Mac," as his men affectionately called him—now entirely replaced General Scott, who was too old to continue as general in chief. He began to drill the troops vigorously; but there was very little fighting at first, and for a time "all was quiet along the Potomac." The only engagement of any importance took place at Balls Bluff. Here some Union troops barely escaped, by sliding down a slippery bank more than one hundred feet high. Although their boats were waiting for them in the river beneath, many sank, and the battle of Balls Bluff, like Bull Run, proved a Confederate victory.

Still, the North was not idle, but was making a plan of war. Besides keeping up a strict blockade, the Union government wanted to take Richmond, to drive the Confederates out of Kentucky and Tennessee, and to become master of the Mississippi River, thus cutting the Confederacy in two.

In war time it is very easy to make plans, but it is not nearly so easy to carry them out, as you will see. In spite of the blockade, two Southern men, Mason and Sli-dell', went to Ha-van'a. Here they embarked upon the British vessel *Trent*, to go to England and ask help for the Confederate States. They had been sent on this mission by the Southerners, who thought that the English would side with them because so many factories in that country depended upon the Southern states for all their cotton.

Captain Wilkes, a Union captain, hearing of this, promptly boarded the British ship *Trent*, a thing he had no right to do, as we were not at war with Great Britain. He seized Mason and Slidell, and carried them off to a Union fort, where they were kept prisoners. When the "*Trent* affair" became known, both the Confederates and the British were justly angry, and the latter sent a firm letter demanding that the two captives be set free without delay.

Many people in the North had not stopped until then to think whether it was fair to seize these men or not, and when the letter came they wanted to refuse to give them up. But Lincoln was very cool, and quietly and sensibly said: "We fought Great Britain in 1812 for doing just what Captain Wilkes has done. We must give up the prisoners to England."

Then, in spite of the outcry raised by some Americans, he calmly went on to do what he considered right. Not only were the two men allowed to go to England, but an apology was sent by Lincoln to Queen Victoria. Still, this capture, and the fact that the Confederates bought and armed vessels in England, caused a great deal of bitter feeling between the two nations, and for a time it really seemed as if the United States would have war with Great Britain too.

A country claiming to be neutral has no right to sell ships or arms to nations at war. Unionists were justly indignant, therefore, when they heard that a fine vessel

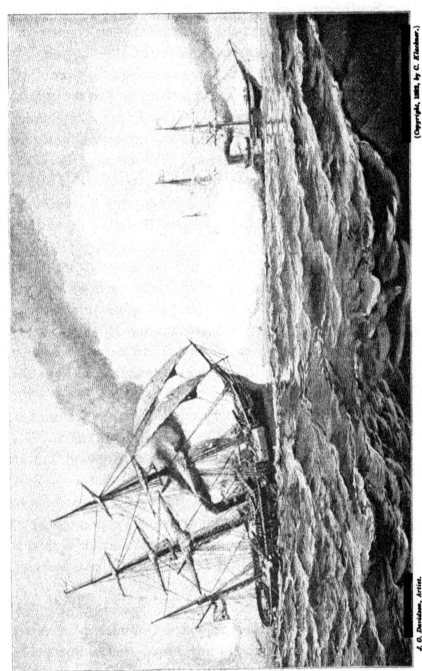

Alabama and Kearsarge.

J. O. Davidson, Artist.

(182)

called the *Alabama* had been sent out of British waters and handed over to the Confederate navy. After getting it all ready to fight, Captain Semmes (sĕmz) began to scour the seas in search of Northern vessels. He pursued and sank, captured, or burned many Northern ships, and it was not till 1864, after a hard fight, that the *Kear'sarge*, a Union frigate, finally succeeded in sinking this terrible foe, off the coast of France.

XXXIX. ADMIRAL FARRAGUT.

WHILE McClellan was drilling his troops so as to have them ready to take Richmond, other Union generals were trying to get possession of the Southern forts along the Cumberland, Tennessee, and Mississippi rivers. For instance, Commodore Foote and General Grant took Fort Henry (1862). Next, after three days' very hard fighting at Fort Don'el-son, General Buckner asked General Grant what terms he would make if the fort surrendered.

The Union general, who was a man of few words, promptly answered: "No terms except immediate and unconditional surrender can be accepted. I propose to move immediately upon your works."

When this short letter, which Buckner was not in a position to resent, became known in the North, some one exclaimed that Grant's initials, U. S., evidently stood for "Unconditional Surrender." This joking remark so pleased the public that the name was generally adopted, and you will often hear this Union general mentioned as

"Unconditional Surrender," instead of "Ulysses S.,"
Grant.

We are told that a Union officer had been accused of
not being loyal, simply because he was very quiet and inclined to be fair. When one of his friends asked why he
did not deny the accusation, he gently said: "Oh, never
mind; they'll take it back after my first battle." At Donelson, when called upon to take a battery, this same officer
called out: "No flinching now, my lads! Here—this is
the way; come on!" And he led his men so bravely that
his fellow-soldiers not only took back all they had said
against him, but declared that their triumph was due to his
good example.

The taking of Forts Henry and Donelson broke the
Confederate line in one place, and the Union army and
gunboats now went on southward, to win the victory of

Battle of Shiloh.

Shi'loh. Here nearly ten thousand men on each side were killed or injured, and the Southern General Albert S. Johnston received a mortal wound. He was one of the South's noblest men, and proved it to the very last by begging his surgeon to leave him and hurry off to help the Union soldiers, some of whom could yet be saved. In this battle, General William T. Sherman did such wonders that when Grant sent the news of the victory to Washington, he said: "I am indebted to General Sherman for the success of that battle."

The Union troops had already secured Nashville and Columbus, and, while the battle of Shiloh was being fought, they became masters of Island No. 10, and soon after of Fort Pillow and Mem'phis. Thus they won control of the Mississippi as far south as Vicks'burg, where large Confederate forces blocked their path. Hoping to regain lost ground, the Confederates, under General Bragg, now made a raid into Kentucky, but they were defeated at Per'ryville and twelve weeks later at Mur'frees-bor-o. While this raid was taking place, part of their army, left behind, was beaten at I-u'ka and Cor'inth.

Other Union troops had in the meantime won a victory at Pea Ridge in Arkansas, and by the end of the year they managed to drive the Confederates south of the Arkansas River. At the same time an attempt was made to secure the rest of the Mississippi, an undertaking which needed the efforts of both army and navy. So the fleet which the year before (1861) had taken the forts at Hat'ter-as Inlet in North Carolina, and Port Royal in South Carolina, was now ordered to the Gulf of Mexico.

The plan was that Commodore David G. Far'ra-gut and

General Butler should take New Orleans, and then sail up the Mississippi to meet the army under Grant, and the gunboats under Porter, at Vicksburg. But this was a very difficult undertaking, for the Confederates had Forts Jackson and St. Philip, on either side the river, about sixty miles below New Orleans, and between them there was a line of hulks, chained fast together, so as to form a very strong barrier.

The first thing was, if possible, to reduce these forts; so Farragut prepared to attack them. To protect his large fleet of wooden vessels, and make them ball-proof, he looped heavy chains all over their sides; for there were at this time only two ironclads in the whole fleet. Sailors were then so sure iron ships must sink that when one was asked to transfer his flag to an iron vessel, he angrily muttered that he did not want to go to the bottom " in a teakettle."

Besides these ships, Farragut also had a number of mortar boats anchored along the shore. They were so well hidden by leafy branches and long canes that they could not be located against the green banks. The bombarding of the two strongholds now began, and was kept up for six days and nights, during which time nearly seventeen thousand shells were hurled at the forts.

The noise of the bombardment was so deafening that it was heard forty miles away. Windows thirty miles away were shattered; birds flying near there were stunned, so that they fell to the ground as if shot; and fishes floated as if lifeless on top of the waters, into which so many cannon balls fell that it looked as if they were boiling hard. But, in spite of all this, the forts did not surrender.

Finally Farragut made up his mind to break the chain,

W. H. Overend, Artist.

An August Morning with Farragut.

sail boldly up the river between the forts, and then land forces so as to attack them on all sides. His plans being ready, a brave young officer volunteered to cut the chains which held the hulks together. As soon as he had done so, the hulks, driven by the current, drifted apart, and the Union fleet suddenly started upstream. The orders were to run the vessels as close to the shore as possible, so that shots from the forts would pass right over them.

In spite of a hot fire, the Union fleet, directed by Farragut, steamed safely past the forts, and destroyed the Confederate ships there. Troops being landed, the forts were forced to surrender to the double attack by land and sea.

Meanwhile, Farragut proceeded up the river to New Orleans. Large quantities of cotton had been stored there, and when the people heard that the Yankees were coming, they set fire to it, so it should not fall into their hands. They also burned their shipping, and when Farragut drew near the city, he saw a line of fire on the piers five miles long. Ever so much property was thus destroyed, for the cotton alone was worth more than $1,500,000. But the people of New Orleans could not prevent the landing of the Union troops, who joyfully hauled down the stars and bars, and hoisted the stars and stripes instead.

The Northern army now took control of affairs in New Orleans, where people felt very bitter toward it. It also secured the cities of Natch'ez and Bat'on Rouge (roozh), and thus gained control over all the lower part of the Mississippi. The Confederates, therefore, had only two important points left on the river, Port Hudson and Vicksburg, which were both situated on such high bluffs that they were above the reach of cannon balls hurled from the river.

XL. THE MONITOR AND THE MERRIMAC.

IN the meantime, great events had been taking place in the East. At the very beginning of the war, the Confederates seized the Nor'folk navy yard and the big ship *Mer'ri-mac*. For some time past there had been rumors afloat that they were changing this vessel into an ironclad, so strong that no cannon balls could harm it.

This was quite true, and the Confederates relied upon this ship to play havoc with the Union fleet in Hamp'ton Roads, at the mouth of the James River. When quite ready, therefore, the *Merrimac* steamed out, at noon, on March 8, 1862, while thousands of people stood on the shore, anxiously waiting to see what it would do.

The first vessel it encountered was the *Cumberland*. This ship defended itself heroically. The guns were fired until it sank, and the water ran into their mouths; but the Union sailors refused to surrender. It is said that when summoned to do so, the Union commander nobly answered: "Never! I'll sink alongside."

True to his word, he and his crew gallantly went down with their vessel, the Union flag still floating at the masthead. For months after it continued to wave there, because, the vessel having sunk in only fifty feet of water, the tops of the masts still rose above the waves.

The destruction of the *Cumberland* was quickly followed by that of the *Congress*, which ran aground, was set afire by red-hot cannon balls, and was forced to surrender. But when boats came from the *Merrimac* to take possession of it, the Union troops in a fort near by began to bombard

Burning of the Congress.

them. The Confederate officers loudly bade them stop, saying the vessel was theirs; but the commander of the fort defiantly answered: "I know the ship has surrendered; but we haven't;" and he went on firing in spite of all their objections.

Still, the *Merrimac* (which the Confederates had renamed the *Virginia*) was quite unharmed by all the shot poured upon her, and had lost only a very few men. She therefore went back to port that evening (March 8, 1862) with the firm intention of coming out again on the morrow, to destroy all the other vessels of the Union navy within reach.

The news of the sinking of the *Cumberland* and of the burning of the *Congress* filled Union hearts with dismay, for it now seemed as if nothing could resist the terrible Southern ironclad. But the President and Congress had been preparing for this danger. Several months before, they had given orders to John Er'ics-son, the inventor of the hot-air engine and of the screw propeller for steamships, to make a ship after a strange model which he had shown them.

The work was carried on in secret, and at the end of one hundred days the *Monitor* was all ready. When the huge *Merrimac* steamed out, on the next day, to attack the Union fleet, she met a small and strange-looking craft, which has been described as a "cheese box on a raft." But the "raft" was of iron, the "cheese box" was a revolving turret with two big guns inside it, and the little Union David, although manned by only a few very brave men, came boldly on to tackle the Confederate Goliath.

When the *Merrimac* tried to attack one of the Union

vessels, the little *Monitor* got between them, and now began the "most important single event of the war." The *Merrimac* vainly poured her fire upon the *Monitor*. The

Merrimac and Monitor.

heaviest cannon balls glanced off when they happened to strike its iron hull, which, being almost level with the water, could not easily be hit. Besides, the *Monitor* was so small that it circled round and round its huge foe, hurling heavy balls from its two big guns.

Still, after a while, a ball from the *Merrimac* struck the *Monitor's* pilot house and knocked a bit of lime into the principal officer's eyes. Blinded thereby, he was forced to give up the command; but his companions continued the battle with such spirit that, when evening came, the *Merrimac* went back to port, and never ventured out again.

At the news of this victory the Union people almost went mad with joy.

Thus, although the *Monitor* did not again take part in any great battle, it saved the Union at a moment of great danger. The inventor Ericsson won much praise for the good work his vessel had done, and since then many vessels have been built for our navy on about the same plan. In honor of the first ship, they are called monitors, too; but each of them also has a special name, like all other vessels in our navy.

XLI. THE PENINSULAR CAMPAIGN.

THE year 1862 brought many important events besides the duel between the *Monitor* and the *Merrimac*, as we have already seen. Still, there are several more of which it is well you should know, and which will surely interest you.

While the War of the Secession was raging on in the southern part of the country, the Sioux (soo) Indians in the West, who had always been troublesome, suddenly dug up the war hatchet, and invaded Min-ne-so'ta and I'o-wa. Here they attacked lonely farmhouses and small villages, killing and scalping nearly a thousand men, women, and children.

But the Indian revolt was soon ended by the arrival of Federal troops, and public attention was again all turned to the war in the South. Here, early in the spring of 1862, had begun the Peninsular Campaign. It is called so because both armies were on the peninsula between the James and York rivers; and while one was defending, the other was trying to seize the Confederate capital, Richmond.

The Union plan was that McClellan's army should march up from Yorktown, and McDowell's come down from Washington, while a small force guarded the Shenandoah valley to prevent the Confederates from attacking Washington. The Confederates, fearing for Richmond, gave up Norfolk to defend their capital. Besides, they burned all their naval stores, and even blew up the *Merrimac*, so it should never serve the Union again.

But, although clever, the Union plan was hard to carry out. McClellan had to take both Yorktown and Wil'liamsburg before he could proceed to the Chick-a-hom'i-ny, where he expected McDowell to

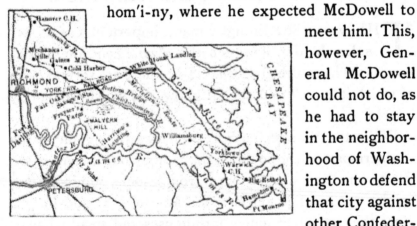

The Peninsular Campaign.

meet him. This, however, General McDowell could not do, as he had to stay in the neighborhood of Washington to defend that city against other Confederate forces.

These Confederate forces were under Stonewall Jackson, who, having heard that there was only a small force in the Shenandoah valley, marched up and down it, fought three battles there, and cleverly retreated after burning many bridges.

We are told that once, during this campaign, General

Jackson and his staff accidentally found themselves on the opposite side of the river from their troops. A few Union soldiers had already taken possession of the bridge between them, but Jackson rode boldly forward, and called out to the officer standing there: "Who ordered you to post that gun there, sir? Bring it over here!" The officer, at this tone of command, prepared to obey; and it was only when Jackson and his staff dashed safely past him to rejoin the Southern forces, that he saw he had made a mistake, and had obeyed the orders of the enemy.

Jackson's bold raid in the Shenandoah made the President fear for the safety of Washington; so instead of allowing McDowell to go on and join McClellan, as had been arranged, he bade him come back to defend the capital. Thus, you see, almost at the same moment both capitals were equally panic-stricken. In fact, when people at Richmond heard that McClellan was coming, they were so frightened that the Confederate Congress left the city, and Jefferson Davis's niece wrote to a friend: "Uncle Jeff thinks we had better go to a safer place than Richmond."

Heavy rains had made the roads rivers of mud, and McClellan, who had crossed the Chickahominy when it was only a small stream, now had a raging torrent behind him. The Confederates, seeing this, promptly attacked him at Fair Oaks or Seven Pines. Although their General Joseph E. Johnston was sorely wounded, and failed to win a signal victory, the Confederates killed so many Union men that they crippled McClellan's force.

Johnston being disabled, Robert E. Lee, son of " Light-Horse Harry " Lee of the Revolutionary War, now became the head of the Confederate army. General Lee had been

Robert E. Lee.

trained at West Point, had taken part in the Mexican War, and was a most able general. At the time of the secession he held a high command in the Union army, but he gave it up, thinking it his duty to serve his native state, Virginia.

Lee, whom the Southern soldiers affectionately called "Uncle Robert," now tried to check McClellan, and for seven days the two armies fought. They had encounters at Me-chan'ics-ville, Gaines Mill, Savage's Station, Frayser's Farm, Malvern Hill, and Harrison's Landing. Although the Union troops were never positively defeated in these battles, the Confederates generally had the best of it. Besides, they entirely prevented the proposed siege of Richmond, the object of the whole campaign.

XLII. BARBARA FRIETCHIE.

MCCLELLAN was ordered to take his army back to Washington by water; and Lee, advancing, fought another Union force, first at Cedar Mountain and then at Bull Run, where he won two brilliant victories, thus forcing the remainder of those troops to retreat and join McClellan. By this time the people in the North were so frightened that they felt the need of a larger army. Lincoln, therefore, called for more men, who eagerly volunteered, singing the new song: "We're coming, Father Abraham, three hundred thousand more!"

Encouraged by success, Lee now crossed the Potomac River and marched into Maryland, his army singing

"Maryland, my Maryland!" for the Confederates felt
very sure that people there would now desert the Union
to side with them. They were disappointed, however,
and McClellan, having found a copy of Lee's orders, set
off after him, and met him at An-tiĕ'tam, where a terrible
battle was fought. Here many men lost their lives, but
neither army won a real victory, though Lee soon after
returned to Virginia.

On his march with Lee toward Antietam, Stonewall
Jackson rode through Frederick, Maryland, where the

Barbara Frietchie.

Union flags had been
hauled down for fear
of the anger of the
Confederate army.
Still, there was one
old woman, Barbara
Frietchie, who wished
to show her love for
the Union, and a
famous story is told
of how she kept the
stars and stripes
proudly floating from
her attic window.

When the Confed-
erate soldiers came
marching through
the town they saw
the flag, we are told,
and, raising their guns and aiming carefully, broke the
flagstaff; but Barbara Frietchie quickly grasped the falling

pole and held it firmly upright, defiantly bidding the soldiers shoot her, if they must, but spare their country's flag. The story says that they could not resist this appeal, that Stonewall Jackson himself rode under the flag with bared head, and that his army followed silently, not a man venturing to insult the banner which the old woman so gallantly defended.

Barbara Frietchie's patriotism made every one feel proud of her, and our poet Whittier has told her story in a beautiful poem which you will like to read.

Although McClellan had received orders to follow Lee and meet him in another battle, there was considerable delay. The Northern people, who eagerly read the war news published in the newspapers, grew very impatient, and now asked that another, less cautious, general should be put in command of the Army of the Potomac. General Burn'side was therefore chosen, and he immediately attacked the Confederates who were intrenched at Fred'er-icks-burg. Here, in spite of the great courage they showed, the Union troops were beaten with great slaughter.

During this battle the Union army tried to storm the hill where a battery stood, and were mowed down like ripe grain by the deadly fire poured upon them by the Confederates intrenched behind a big stone wall. Six times the Union soldiers tried to dislodge their foes, but all in vain. The news of this awful battle, and of the loss of life it occasioned, caused great mourning throughout the country. When it reached Washington, Lincoln, who suffered keenly whenever he heard of loss of life and defeat, bitterly cried: "If there is any man out of perdition that suffers more than I do, I pity him!"

XLIII. LINCOLN'S VOW.

THE war which was to have been over in ninety days was still dragging on. When it began, Lincoln had no intention to interfere with slavery in the states where it already existed. Even later on, in writing to the great newspaper editor, Horace Gree'ley, he said: "My paramount object is to save the Union, and not either to save or destroy slavery. If I could save the Union without freeing any slave, I would do it; if I could save it by freeing all the slaves, I would do it; and if I could do it by freeing some and leaving others alone, I would also do that."

But, little by little, Lincoln saw that slavery was the real cause of the war, and that if it were not for the negroes, the Southerners who were on the battle field would soon be forced to surrender from lack of food. He also knew that most people in the North wished him to abolish slavery. They made this plain in countless ways, and hosts of Union soldiers tramped for miles to the tune of

"John Brown's body lies a-mold'ring in the grave;
His soul goes marching on!"

because they felt they were carrying out the good work Brown had so unwisely begun.

There was, besides, another question: France had promised to recognize the independence of the Confederates if Great Britain did; and just at this time it seemed as if the British, who needed cotton, might yet do so. The Southerners fully expected it, and openly boasted that "cotton is king." But, on the other hand, while Great Britain might side with the Confederates as long as the war was only against secession, she could not do so if the war was also against slavery, because her people were opposed to slavery, which was no longer allowed in any of her colonies.

In the very beginning of the war, Generals Frémont and Hal'leck both made proclamations freeing the slaves in the districts where they were stationed. But Lincoln knew that the right moment had not yet come, and therefore bade them free only the slaves they seized as contraband. As it now seemed to Lincoln that the right time had come, he made a vow that as soon as the Union won a victory he would make a proclamation emancipating, or setting free, all the slaves in the rebel states. Therefore, five days after the battle of Antietam, on September 22, 1862, President Lincoln announced that he would declare the slaves in the Confederate States free, if their owners did not lay down their arms and obey the Union by January 1, 1863. At that date, he issued another proclamation, setting those slaves free. This famous state paper was written entirely by Lincoln, who signed it on New Year's Day, after shaking hands with the many guests who came to wish him a happy New Year.

No slaves were freed, at that time, in the states or parts of states that were in the hands of the Union forces; but later on Congress proposed that a thirteenth Amendment be added to the Constitution, forbidding slavery in the United States forever. The necessary number of states finally accepted this amendment, which went into force in 1865.

The Confederate States paid no attention at all to the

Emancipation Proclamation, so the negroes dared claim their freedom only when the Union troops were near enough to protect them. Besides, the greater part of the colored people could not read, and did not even know they had been declared free until told the joyful news by Northern soldiers.

The first regiment of colored freemen had already been formed, however, and the proclamation was read aloud to them, too, very near the place where some of the South Carolinians had drawn up a law saying the negroes should be slaves forever. Although many people had predicted that negroes never could be trained to fight properly, they covered themselves with glory when the time came. Indeed, colored people bravely helped Union soldiers whenever they could, often risking their own lives to do so, and one of the most heroic deeds in all the war was done by a negro boy, at Fort Wagner, in 1863. This lad fell in a gallant attempt to climb the wall. Seeing one of the officers hesitate because he could not get up without hurting him, the poor boy bravely said: "I'm done gone, massa! Step on me and you can scale the wall!"

XLIV. THE BATTLE OF GETTYSBURG.

BURNSIDE, having failed to win a victory at Fredericksburg, was now removed in his turn, and the command of the Union army given to General Joseph Hooker, whom the soldiers called ".Fighting Joe." But at Chan'cellors-ville (1863) Hooker was stunned by a cannon ball, and as his army was thus left during several hours without a general, it was completely defeated. Owing in part, no doubt, to this accident, Lee won a brilliant victory over an army twice as large as his own; but he lost one of the bravest Southern officers, the gallant Stonewall Jackson. The latter was riding along with his staff, at nightfall, when his own men, mistaking him for the enemy, suddenly fired upon him, thus killing the man they loved so dearly.

Chancellorsville was the last great victory won by the Confederates in the Civil War, but their past successes had filled their hearts with hope. When Hooker retreated, therefore, Lee boldly crossed the Potomac and marched into Pennsylvania. His plan was to carry the war into the enemy's country and make the Northern people feel the hardships which the South had to suffer. Hooker, who had not expected this bold move, followed him in hot haste; but before he could overtake Lee, the command of the Union army was taken from him and given to General Meade.

It was the latter general, therefore, who overtook Lee at Get'tys-burg, on the 1st of July, 1863. Here was fought the greatest and most decisive battle of the whole war. It lasted three whole days, and about one third of the men engaged in it were killed or wounded. Both sides did wonders in the way of bravery on this occasion, and the Confederate General Pickett led a charge which will ever be famous in history. But in spite of their determined valor, the Confederates were finally beaten, and Lee was forced to retreat to Virginia, having failed in his second and last attempt to carry the war into the North.

So many Americans lost their lives at Gettysburg that

A Charge at Gettysburg.

part of the battle ground was changed into a national cemetery. The dead of both armies are buried there, and, besides many nameless graves, there are those of some of the principal men who fell during those three awful days (July 1–3, 1863). The regiments which took part in the battle have since erected beautiful monuments on the spots where they stood during that terrible but glorious struggle, when both sides proved their valor.

Every year, on the anniversary of the battle, speeches are made in Gettysburg Cemetery, but none of them have ever equaled the short address made by President

Lincoln, when he dedicated it the autumn of 1863. This speech, one of the simplest and most famous in our history, runs as follows:

"Fourscore and seven years ago our fathers brought forth on this continent a new nation, conceived in liberty, and dedicated to the proposition that all men are created equal.

"Now we are engaged in a great civil war, testing whether that nation, or any nation so conceived and so dedicated, can long endure. We are met on a great battle field of that war. We have come to dedicate a portion of that field as a final resting place for those who here gave their lives that that nation might live. It is altogether fitting and proper that we should do this.

"But, in a larger sense, we cannot dedicate, we cannot consecrate, we cannot hallow this ground. The brave men, living and dead, who struggled here, have consecrated it far above our poor power to add or detract. The world will little note, nor long remember, what we say here, but it can never forget what they did here. It is for us, the living, rather to be dedicated here to the unfinished work which they who fought here have thus far so nobly advanced. It is rather for us to be here dedicated to the great task remaining before us, that from these honored dead we take increased devotion to that cause for which they gave the last full measure of devotion; that we here highly resolve that these dead shall not have died in vain; that this nation, under God, shall have a new birth of freedom; and that government of the people, by the people, for the people, shall not perish from the earth."

XLV. THE TAKING OF VICKSBURG.

THE fact that the Union forces had won the victory at Gettysburg filled all Northern hearts with happiness, and they were soon to enjoy a new triumph. You remember that while the disastrous peninsular campaign was going on, Grant was on the Mississippi, where his object was to gain possession of Vicksburg. As already stated, this city stands on a steep bluff; it is more than two hundred feet above the river. It was, besides, well fortified on all sides, and very ably defended by the Confederate General Pem'ber-ton.

Grant soon saw that it would be best to attack Vicksburg from the land side; but to do that he had to convey his troops across the river at a point many miles below that city. The only fleet Grant had lay above Vicksburg, and as he did not like it to run the gantlet of the fire from the forts, he tried to find another way to get the gunboats down the river.

The west shore of the Mississippi River is very low, and there are so many bayous that Grant fancied they might perhaps afford a passage to his fleet. The gunboats, under his orders, therefore went in and out of every bayou, working their way over and under fallen trees, through mud and marshes, until the soldiers laughingly called them "Uncle Sam's webfeet." As no passage was found, an attempt was made to dig a canal. But to do this, trees had to be cut six feet under water, and the job was soon given up as hopeless.

Upon the failure of this plan, Grant saw that the fleet

must steam rapidly down the river past the forts. This was considered so dangerous an undertaking that the men were told that only such as wished need take part in the expedition. But the Union navy was so brave, and the volunteers so many, that all could not be accepted, and lots had to be drawn to select the number of men needed to man the boats. We are told that those thus chosen for dangerous duty were so proud of their luck that they would not give up their places to their comrades, some of whom vainly tried to bribe them to exchange places.

When all was ready, Porter's fleet rushed down the Mississippi, one dark night. But the Confederates had

Sailing past Vicksburg.

such bright fires kindled along the river bank, that the Union fleet was seen·as plainly as if it had been broad daylight, and a hail of cannon balls and shells was instantly poured down upon it.

Nevertheless, Porter safely ran the gantlet of the deadly Vicksburg batteries, and, having reached the spot where Grant's troops awaited him, carried them safely across the Mississippi. As soon as they had landed, Grant marched them to the northeast, so as to get between Vicksburg and the Confederate forces, under General Johnston, which were moving toward that city.

During the next seventeen days Grant defeated Confederate forces at Port Gibson, Jackson, Champion Hills, and Big Black River, and prevented Johnston from uniting with the army that was defending Vicksburg. Then he completely surrounded Vicksburg by means of his own army, a force under General Sherman, and the fleet commanded by Porter.

Thus hemmed in on all sides, Vicksburg suffered all the horrors of a frightful siege. Before it ended even "mule steaks" gave out, and people were reduced to such strange fare as mice, rats, and pieces of old leather. Meanwhile shells and cannon balls poured into the city from all sides, and as the inhabitants no longer dared stay in their houses, they dug caves in the soft, clayey soil, and went to live there.

The bombardment lasted forty-seven days, and we are told that little children grew so accustomed to flying bullets, and to the noise of exploding shells, that they ceased to mind them, and played out in the streets as merrily as if no siege were going on. But the grown people were very anxious, for the Union troops kept such a keen watch on every part of the fortifications, that when some one put a hat on the end of a stick, and held it for a moment above the ramparts, it was instantly riddled with bullets.

Besieging Vicksburg.

As he had no food left, was surrounded on all sides, and could not expect any relief, gallant General Pemberton was finally forced to surrender to Grant. So, at noon, on July 4, 1863, the Confederate flag was replaced by the stars and stripes in Vicksburg. The Union troops made the courthouse ring with the sounds of their new song, "We'll rally round the flag, boys," while "Old Abe," the pet eagle of one regiment, flapped his wings and screamed aloud, as in battle when the din grew greatest.

The news of the surrender of Vicksburg, with more than thirty thousand prisoners, reached Washington on the day after the battle of Gettysburg, and caused great rejoicing. Five days later Port Hudson surrendered also, and, as Lincoln gladly said, "the Father of Waters rolled unvexed to the sea." Besides, the Confederates west of

the Mississippi were entirely cut off from their companions on the east side, for Union men held the river.

Still, the war was far from over, and the hardships it forced
upon the people were daily growing harder to bear. When
it first broke out it cost the Union about one million
dollars a day, but by this time the expense was nearly three
times as much. To raise the necessary funds, Congress
little by little ordered internal taxes, and "revenue
stamps" were placed on photographs, pianos, and many
other objects which were not absolutely necessary. This
was a "stamp tax," like the one which helped to cause the
Revolution; but this time the representatives of the people
voted for it, and the people were willing to pay it.

Besides this, taxes were laid on other articles, large
sums of money were borrowed, and paper bills were issued,
which from their color came to be known as "greenbacks."
Every one knew that if the Union came out of the storm
safely, silver or gold would be given in exchange for these
bills. When the Union troops were successful, therefore,
no one objected to paper money; but whenever the Federals were beaten, the value of greenbacks fell, until at one
time a paper dollar was worth only thirty-five cents in coin.

XLVI. RIOTS, RAIDS, AND BATTLES.

UNTIL 1863 the President had been able to secure
enough soldiers by calling for volunteers; but the
time now came when Lincoln had to resort to drafts.
That is to say, all the able-bodied men in the country

between certain ages were forced to register their names, and from them a certain number in each state were selected by lot. These were obliged to join the army in person, or hire men to take their places.

The fact that the President issued such orders, although Congress had given him the right to do so, made some of the people so angry that there were draft riots in several cities. The worst of all, however, was in New York, where the rioters took possession of the city, attacked and brutally murdered some poor negroes, destroyed much property, and behaved so lawlessly that troops had to be called out to restore order. During those terrible days the excitement was intense; but the law-abiding citizens behaved so nobly that the mob was quelled after some bloodshed.

Drafts, which created such an uproar in the Union states, were also made in the South, where boys, and even old men, were made to serve, until it was said that "the Confederate army robbed both the cradle and the grave." There, too, paper money was used; but as the war dragged on, Confederate bills were worth less and less in coin. Owing to this, and also to the strict blockade, it took at one time about fifteen hundred dollars to buy a barrel of flour, and several thousand for a suit of common clothes. After the war was over, Confederate bills were worth nothing at all.

All through the war, Southern and Northern women proved equally ready to work night and day for the soldiers on their side. Some of them raised money by fairs; others made garments or delicacies for the sick; and many served as nurses in the hospitals or on the battle field. Even small children helped, and while the little girls knit stockings, the boys made lint, or picked berries which were made into jellies for the use of convalescent soldiers. The whole country suffered from the effects of the war, but while many families north and south were in deep mourning for their heroic dead, the worst suffering was borne by the Southern states, where most of the fighting took place.

The North knew very little of the actual hardships of warfare; for, with the exception of Antietam in Maryland and Gettysburg in Pennsylvania, there had been no great battles on its soil. It is true that General Bragg, the hero of Buena Vista, had made a raid in Kentucky, but he had been driven by General Bu'ell back into Tennessee. Besides, several other daring raids, mostly for plunder, had been made by John Morgan, a guerrilla chief. He had been with Bragg in Kentucky in 1862, and had even threatened the city of Cincinnati.

In 1863 this same Morgan raided Kentucky, and, crossing the Ohio, went into Indiana and Ohio, where he hoped that many men would join him. His quick movements and his fearlessness enabled him to do much damage and to get away again before any troops could be collected to crush him. During this expedition his men took horses, plundered mills and factories, and made the people pay large sums of money to save their buildings from being burned down.

The people were so exasperated by his invasion that they made a determined effort, and finally hemmed him in and made him a prisoner. He and six of his officers were locked up in the penitentiary at Columbus, Ohio, whence they managed to escape a few months later.

Morgan's Raiders.

Cleverly making their way through the enemy's country, these men contrived to get back to their own people, and joined the Confederate army in Georgia.

Some very funny stories are told about this Morgan and his men, who often indulged in harmless frolics. When the · people did not oppose them, they generally took only from the rich or well to do, leaving the poor alone, and sometimes even astonishing them by giving them some of the plunder.

While Grant was besieging Vicksburg, Bragg was in Tennessee, where General Ro′se-crans drove him from Chat-ta-noo′ga to Chick-a-mau′ga Creek. Here a desperate battle took place, and the Confederates were victorious; but General Thomas with his part of the Union army made such a firm and brave stand that he won the name of "Rock of Chickamauga." Some of his officers showed equal courage, for when one was asked how long he could hold a certain pass, he firmly answered: "Until the regiment is mustered out of service."

When the battle was all over, Thomas retreated to Chattanooga, where Bragg followed and besieged the Union army. Now began a hard time for the Union troops, for they had hardly enough food for the men. Besides, forage was so scarce that most of the mules died. Indeed, one soldier described a march near Chattanooga, saying: "The mud was so deep that we could not travel by the road, but we got along pretty well by stepping from mule to mule as they lay dead by the way."

There was so much danger that the army might retreat or surrender, that Thomas was put in command at Chattanooga, and Grant sent him orders to hold fast till he came. Thomas nobly answered: "We will hold the town till we starve." In a few days Grant reached Chattanooga, and soon after the army was reënforced by Sherman and Hooker.

Battles were now fought near Chattanooga, first at Orchard Knob and the day after on Lookout Mountain. As lowering clouds cut off all view of the summit during the greater part of this engagement, you will often hear it called the "Battle above the Clouds." The next day, the Union troops won a great victory on Missionary Ridge, so that at the end of three days' fighting the Confederates were driven away.

The next move made by Union forces was Sherman's raid across Mississippi, from Vicksburg, early in 1864. His aim was to destroy bridges and railroads over which

Lookout Mountain.

supplies could be sent to the Confederate army, and to burn mills and factories. He did this so thoroughly, and left so little standing at Me-rid'i-an, that one person remarked: "Sherman didn't simply smash things, but he just carried the town off with him."

XLVII. THE BURNING OF ATLANTA.

SHERMAN'S raid prevented the Confederates from again attacking Chattanooga, where the Union troops spent a quiet winter. When the spring of 1864 came on, Grant was made commander in chief of the whole army, with the rank of lieutenant general, a rank which had been given only to Washington and Scott before him. Grant had been so fortunate in all his efforts that every one felt great confidence in him, and while Lincoln said that at last he had a *man* at the head of the army, the rest of the people, referring to his initials, playfully spoke of him as "Uniformly Successful" Grant, "United States" Grant, "Unconditional Surrender" Grant, and "Uncle Sam's" Grant.

As soon as Grant received this appointment, he met Sherman, and they two together formed a clever plan to carry on the war. As there were now only two large Confederate armies, it was agreed that Grant should face Lee, near Richmond, while Sherman should beat Johnston, and then push on across Georgia to the sea, destroying all supplies on his way, so that the South should have to cease making war. It was further agreed that they should set out to do this on the same day.

Grant now went to join the forces in the East, and led them across the Rap-id-an' into the Wilderness, to begin his famous "hammering campaign." It was in May that his army started, and, sitting on a log by the roadside, Grant wrote the telegram which ordered Sherman to commence fighting.

As soon as Sherman received this dispatch, he set out, with about one hundred thousand men, to meet Johnston, with about one half that number, at Dalton. But Johnston placed his forces in the mountains and woods in good positions, and always retreated in time to avoid a disastrous defeat. Sherman, therefore, had to fight bloody battles at Dalton, Resaca, Dallas, Lost Mountain, and

Grant writes a Telegram to Sherman.

Ken-e-saw' Mountain, while driving Johnston back to At-lan'ta.

This sort of fighting—which was the wisest thing Johnston could do—made President Davis so angry that, hoping to settle matters by one big victory, he took the command away from Johnston and gave it to Hood. The latter was very energetic; but although three more battles were fought, and each army lost thousands of men in this campaign, Sherman went on, and soon entered Atlanta. Then he telegraphed to Washington the news: "Atlanta is ours, and fairly won."

Marching thus into the Confederate country, Sherman found the railroads destroyed by the Confederates, who

STO. OF GT. REP.—14

hoped thus to prevent his advance and to cut off his supplies. But he had a force of men who rapidly rebuilt the roads, and trains quickly followed his troops to bring them food and ammunition. The engineers who laid tracks and built bridges were so skilled, and their men worked so fast, that they really did wonders.

The Confederates were amazed to see how promptly the damage they had done was repaired. Once, when some one suggested blowing up a tunnel so as to check Sherman's trains, a man cried out: "No use, boys; Old Sherman carries duplicate tunnels with him, and will replace them as fast as you can blow them up; better save your powder!"

Hoping to prevent Sherman's doing any harm to Atlanta, or going farther south, Hood suddenly set out for Tennessee, thinking the Union army would follow to stop him. This, however, was just what Sherman wanted, and as soon as he was quite sure that Hood had gone, he sent word to Thomas at Nashville to look out for himself. Thomas, he knew, was calm and very deliberate. After keeping Hood waiting for about two weeks, General Thomas suddenly came out of the city, and in a hard two days' fight completely defeated him. In this battle the Confederates fought so bravely that when it was all over they had no army left wherewith to pursue Sherman.

Sherman, in the meantime, had gone steadily on, and had burned the rich stores and fine mills and factories of Atlanta. The churches and dwelling houses were not harmed, for Sherman's object was only to destroy the shops and factories which supplied the Southern army with arms, food, garments, or anything else.

XLVIII. THE MARCH TO THE SEA.

AFTER cutting all the telegraph wires, so no one could send news of his next movement, Sherman suddenly left Atlanta and set out for his famous " march to the sea." He had long been preparing for this. His plans were all made, and he sent on his sixty thousand men in four great columns. Their orders were to head for Savannah, three hundred miles away, to destroy all the railroads and supplies along a strip sixty miles wide, and to take nothing with them but the food they needed.

While the main army, therefore, marched steadily on, skirmishing parties overran the country, burning or breaking all they did not carry off. Last of all came the men whose duty it was to tear up railroads and burn bridges. They were adepts in this work, and finding that iron rails merely bent could be straightened out and used again, they adopted a new plan of destruction.

First, the railroad ties were torn up, piled together, and set afire. Then the rails were laid over the red-hot coals, so that the middle part of each one was heated red-hot. Two men next grasped a rail at either end, and, running to the nearest tree, twisted it around the trunk, thus making what the soldiers jokingly called " Jeff Davis neckties."

It was thus that the Union army left nothing but ruin and desolation behind it. This seems very wicked, but it is one way of making war, and Sherman thought it was wiser to stop the Confederates by depriving them of supplies than by killing so many men in pitched battle.

The roads were very bad during this five weeks' tramp, for the year (1864) was rapidly drawing to its close; but the men went merrily on, cheering their leader whenever

The March to the Sea.

he rode past them, and sturdily singing the familiar war songs.

The result of this move was just what Grant and Sherman had expected, and as soon as the army reached Savannah they stormed Fort McAl'lis-ter and thus forced the city to surrender. As telegraphs and railroads had all been destroyed, no news had been heard of Sherman and his sixty thousand men since they had left Atlanta. So

.there were many anxious hearts in the North besides the President's, and as week after week went by the suspense grew awful.

Knowing this, Sherman no sooner reached Savannah than he sent a dispatch by boat to Fortress Monroe, so it could be telegraphed from there to Washington. Some one standing near him cried that the message would probably reach the President on the 25th of December; so Sherman wrote to Lincoln: "I beg to present you as a Christmas gift the city of Savannah, with one hundred and fifty heavy guns and plenty of ammunition; also about twenty-five thousand bales of cotton." This message reached Lincoln on December 24, and the news, being flashed over telegraph wires, made many anxious Northern people spend a very thankful Christmas Day.

Sherman had first expected to take his army northward by sea; but after the capture of Savannah it was determined that he should march northward. Although he did not say a word of this plan, his men all suspected it. They were so impatient to go on that during their month's rest in the city they often called out when he rode past: "Uncle Billy, I guess Grant is waiting for us at Richmond."

Sherman was almost as impatient as his men; so as soon as he thought they were well rested, he led them up to Columbia, and then advanced, driving his old foe Johnston ahead of him, and beating him at A'ver-ys-bor-o and Ben'-ton-ville (1865). While he was doing this, other Union troops occupied Charleston, which, after a long resistance, had finally surrendered.

Sherman's aim was to join Grant and help him crush

Lee, who was still defending Richmond with the last large Confederate army. The roads were now worse than ever; but all were so eager to finish the war and go home, that the men cheerfully tramped on through mud and rain, waded through streams, and even fought one battle on ground covered with water.

Some of the swamps were so broad and treacherous that Sherman's army had to build corduroy roads through them. This was hard work, too; but the men all worked bravely, and cut down trees, whose trunks, laid side by side on top of larger timbers, formed a firm but very rough road. At Golds'bor-o, Sherman's army was joined by two other bodies of Union troops; and there, while the men were again resting after their hard labors, Sherman hurried off to meet Grant, at City Point, and plan the next moves with him.

———oo◦◦◦oo———

XLIX. SHERIDAN'S RIDE.

WHILE Sherman was going thus, first to Atlanta, then to Savannah, and finally north again, Grant had been very busy. No sooner had he got into the Wilderness—where woods and underbrush were so dense that one could not see far ahead—than he met the Confederate forces there; and he also met them at Spott-syl-va'ni-a Courthouse and Cold Harbor.

About fifty thousand Union soldiers were killed or wounded in these three battles. But Grant knew this was the quickest way to end the war, and wrote to Lincoln: "Our losses have been heavy as well as those of the enemy; but I propose to fight it out on this line if it takes all summer." The news of these losses was hard for the country to bear, and after one of these engagements Lincoln despairingly cried: "My God! My God! Twenty thousand poor souls sent to their account in one day. I cannot bear it! I cannot bear it!"

Next, Grant went southward to besiege Pe'ters-burg, hoping that Lee would come out of Richmond, which he intended to attack next. But Lee now sent General Jubal A. Early into the Shenandoah valley, to make a raid there. Early swept down the valley with a large force of cavalry, came within about five miles of Washington, then suddenly rushed up the valley again, carrying off large numbers of horses and supplies of all kinds.

This first raid was soon followed by a second, equally successful, the Confederates this time pushing on into Pennsylvania, where they set fire to Chăm'bers-burg. Knowing that these raids filled the hearts of Washington people with great terror, Grant now determined to stop them once for all. He therefore sent General Sheridan into the Shenandoah valley, with orders to burn and destroy everything, so that the enemy would find no food there for either man or beast.

General Sheridan set out in August, and after burning many barns and fields of grain, he found and defeated General Early at Win'ches-ter. The Confederate army retreated up the valley, while Sheridan followed, halting at Cedar Creek. On his way he destroyed everything, until he could say: "If a crow wants to fly down the Shenandoah, he must carry his provisions with him." As all seemed quiet, Sheridan went to Washington, where he had been summoned; but on coming back to Winchester, he fancied he heard distant sounds of firing.

Mounting his horse, Ri-en'zi, which had been his faithful companion for many months, Sheridan rode quickly out of Winchester in the direction of the noise. Before long he met the first fugitives, who told him that the army had been attacked and defeated by General Early, at break of day.

Sheridan now put spurs to his steed, and galloped along the road, swinging his cap to the soldiers, who watched him dashing past. He cheerily called out to them: "Face the other way, boys; we're going back!" The men, who had great confidence in him, now cheered him loudly, and, wheeling around, hurried after him to join in the coming fray.

Galloping thus for twenty miles, rallying the troops as he went, jumping fences and dashing through fields when the road was blocked by wagons or fugitives, Sheridan rode on, mile after mile. But all through that long gallop his noble steed never faltered, and the men, hearing his "Turn, boys, turn; we're going back!" followed him blindly.

When Sheridan finally came up to the troops, he encouraged them by crying: "Never mind, boys; we'll whip them yet. We shall sleep in our old quarters to-night." At these words the army quickly formed again, and when all was ready, Sheridan, at his officers' suggestion, rode down the line, to make sure that all the men would see him.

The sight of their familiar and trusted leader on his noble black steed roused the enthusiasm of the soldiers.

Gilbert Gaul, Artist.

Holding the Line.

(225)

When the signal came, they renewed the battle with such spirit that Early was defeated and sent flying out of the valley with a shattered army. This victory created a great sensation throughout the country. In speaking of it, Grant wrote: "Turning what bade fair to be a disaster into a glorious victory stamped Sheridan—what I have always thought him—one of the ablest of generals."

It may interest you to hear that the noble horse Rienzi, which so bravely galloped from Winchester to Cedar Creek, was treated with great kindness until his death in 1878. Then his skin was carefully stuffed and mounted, and placed in the Military Museum on Governors Island, New York, where it can still be seen.

Although Sheridan's campaign in the Shenandoah valley was the shortest, it was also the most brilliant in the whole war, for, while it lasted only one month, it put an end to all raids in the direction of Washington.

L. THE DOINGS OF THE FLEET.

THE Southern Confederacy was now in a bad plight; for, while it had won most of the triumphs in the beginning of the war, it had lately lost heavily, and its resources were exhausted.

Besides, its seaports had fallen, one by one, into the hands of the Union, and now it had hardly any left. In 1864, two years after taking New Orleans, Admiral Farragut went to attack Mobile (mo-beel'). He wrote home, saying: "I am going into Mobile Bay in the morning, if God is my leader, as I hope he is." True to his resolve, he ran into the bay, past the great guns of the Confederate forts, and in spite of the rams which tried to stop him.

To direct this battle, Farragut was tied fast to the rigging, and when one of his officers called out that they could not proceed on account of the torpedoes which had been sunk in the channel, he answered that this was not the time to think of torpedoes. Then, taking the lead, he bade his engineer run at full speed, and dashed safely ahead. Here, in Mobile Bay, took place a famous naval battle. The iron ram *Tennessee* was captured only after a hard struggle, and the port was blocked so securely that not a single vessel could pass in or out. But the city itself was not taken till the next year, at the end of the war, and with the help of Union land forces.

About two months after Farragut steamed into Mobile Bay and captured the iron ram *Tennessee*, another Confederate ram, called the *Al'be-marle*, played havoc among the Union vessels blockading the coast of North Carolina. It had already done a great deal of damage, and was getting ready to do more still, when Lieutenant W. B. Cushing proposed to destroy it while it was lying at anchor at Plymouth.

Stealing into the harbor one dark October night, Cushing and fourteen men drew close to the ram before they were seen. When only twenty yards away they were discovered and fired upon; but in spite of the bullets splashing into the water all around him, Cushing ran his small boat close up to the *Albemarle*, released his torpedo, and, bidding his men look out for themselves, set it off.

At that very moment a shot from the *Albemarle* struck

Cushing destroys the Albemarle.

his boat, which was dashed to pieces; but a second later a
frightful explosion was heard, and the ram was a wreck.
As for Cushing and his men, they were struggling in
the water in the darkness, surrounded by floating bits of
wreckage. Only two of them managed to escape, and
Cushing himself, although slightly wounded, swam bravely
ashore and hid in a swamp, where some kind-hearted colored people found him and brought him food.

After hiding there all day, Cushing got into a leaky little boat he found near the shore, and, in spite of weakness
and stiff muscles, paddled out to a Union ship, where the
sailors were anxiously watching for the return of his
launch. They saw him coming, but, failing to recognize
him in this sorry plight, sternly hailed him, crying:
" Who goes there? "

A weak voice answered: " A friend—Cushing; take me
up." The men, hanging almost breathless over the ship

railing, then cried: "Cushing! and the *Albemarle?*"
"Will never trouble the Union fleet again," answered the
same weak, hoarse voice. "She rests in her grave on the
muddy bottom of the Ro-a-noke'."

You can imagine with what joy this news was received,
and how eagerly hands were now stretched out to help
Cushing on deck. There, all crowded around him to hear
about it, and while the men mourned their lost companions, they heartily cheered Cushing, whose heroic deed will
never be forgotten.

In the meantime, Porter, after gallantly helping Grant
to secure the Mississippi, had taken part in an expedition
up the Red River (1863–1864). Here army and navy together tried to crush the Confederates. But the army
was beaten at the Sabine Crossroads, and the fleet became
helpless when the water in the river became low. Indeed,
before long the men perceived that there was not enough
water left to float their vessels down the stream.

Porter was about to blow up his gunboats, so they
should not fall into the Confederates' hands, when a Wisconsin lumberman suggested a plan by which they could
be saved. Under his directions, dams were built, and
the waters rose. Then the boats were sent downstream,
and, passing through the dams, which were broken one
after another, they safely reached navigable waters.

With another fleet, Porter then joined Butler's army in
besieging Fort Fisher, near Wil'ming-ton, North Carolina.
But the fort held out so bravely that Butler decided it could
not be taken, and returned with the army to Fortress Monroe. Porter, however, would not give up, and he was so
anxious to make a second attempt, that troops were sent

back under another general, and the fort taken, in spite of the heroic defense of its garrison (1865).

The war was rapidly reaching its close, for it was plain that the Confederates would not be able to hold out much longer. By this time they had little left in the East besides Virginia, North Carolina, and South Carolina. Feeling that they must soon stop fighting, the Southerners now made an attempt to end the war without shedding any more blood. At their request, an interview took place, on a war vessel at Hampton Roads, between Alexander H. Stephens, the Vice President of the Confederacy, and President Lincoln with Secretary Seward.

We are told that in the course of this interview Stephens, seeing Lincoln not willing to grant the terms he asked, urged that even Charles I. made certain concessions. To this, wishing to show that it was not wise to yield under certain circumstances, Lincoln quietly answered: " I am not strong on history; I depend mainly on Secretary Seward for that. All I remember of Charles is that he lost his head." Then, after a long talk, Lincoln said he could make peace only if the Confederates would lay down their arms, promise to obey Congress, and abolish slavery.

These terms the South would not accept, so the interview ended, and the war went on to the bitter end. About two months later, Lee, thinking the situation desperate, withdrew the Confederate troops from both Richmond and Petersburg, giving orders that all ships and ammunition be destroyed. When the Confederate army left Richmond, therefore, all the Southern rams on the James River were burned.

A colored man brought the news that the Confederate

army had left Richmond, and the Union troops immediately marched in. When they got into the town they found it was not so well defended as they had supposed, for many of the cannons were "Quaker guns,"—that is to say, logs of wood painted black so as to look like artillery at a distance. Still, as the colored man explained, they were "just as good to scare with as any others."

Lincoln, hearing that the Confederates had left Richmond, now went there on Admiral Porter's boat, and as no carriage was ready for him, he walked slowly up the street. When the negroes heard he was in town, they rushed to meet him, kissing his hands and fervently crying: "May de good Lord bless you, President Linkum!"

But when some of the Southerners, watching him, saw him return the col-

Lincoln at Richmond.

ored men's greetings by taking off his hat to them just as he did to the white people, they were offended, and said he lacked dignity. Those Southerners, however, had forgotten that Thomas Jefferson, a Virginia gentleman, used to do the same. When his grandson found fault with him for doing so, he quietly said: "You surely do not want me to be less polite than that poor man!"

Cavalry Charge at Five Forks.

LI. LEE'S SURRENDER.

LEE'S plan had been to force his way through the Union lines, and join Johnston farther south; but it was now too late. He was without food, and hemmed in on all sides by large armies. At the end of six days, therefore,—and after making as brave a stand as you can find in history,—he saw he must surrender. Sheridan had just won a last victory over his army at Five Forks, and Grant was rapidly moving toward Ap-po-mat'tox Courthouse. It was useless to fight any more, so, after exchanging a few letters, Grant and Lee met at a house which has since become historical.

There the two generals drew up the conditions of the surrender of Appomattox (April 9, 1865). Grant asked that Lee's army should lay down their arms and promise not to fight again until properly exchanged. But he allowed the Southern soldiers to take their private horses with them, saying he knew the men " would need them for the spring plowing."

When Grant noticed that General Lee wore a beautiful sword, which had been presented to him by his admirers, he also said that the officers might keep their side arms. This was both kind and thoughtful; and when Lee confessed that his men were starving,—having had little to eat but parched corn for several days,—Grant gave immediate orders to distribute rations among them.

The two greatest commanders of the Civil War then cordially shook hands; for, like all true-hearted men, they bore each other no grudge. They had been on opposite

House in which Lee and Grant met.

sides, it is true, but they thoroughly respected each other, for they knew they had done nothing but what they believed right.

The interview over, Lee went back to his army, and, with tears in his eyes, sadly said: " Men, we have fought through the war together. I have done the best I could for you. My heart is too full to say more." He then issued the necessary orders, and no sooner was it known in both armies that Lee had surrendered, than the men went to visit one another. Before many minutes, therefore, men in blue and in gray were sitting side by side, the Union soldiers sharing rations with their former foes in the friendliest way.

The very next day Lee made a farewell address to his men, who then went back to their homes, to work as hard as they had fought. Four years had now elapsed since the Civil War, or the " War for the Union," had begun. This war cost our country untold suffering, nearly a million lives, and about ten thousand million dollars. But it settled two important questions: that no state can leave the Union, and that slavery is forever at an end in our country.

On the fourth anniversary of the surrender of Fort Sumter, Anderson again hoisted the United States flag over its ruins. The war was so plainly over that joy all over the country was great, and even those who mourned were thankful that no more blood would be shed.

That evening, to please some friends who particularly wished it, President Lincoln went to a theater at Washington. While he was sitting there quietly in his box, John Wilkes Booth, an actor, stole in behind him. He noiselessly fastened the door, crept close to Lincoln, shot him through the head, and jumped on the stage, crying: " Sic semper tyrannis!" [So be it always to tyrants!] As he sprang, his foot caught in a United States flag draping the President's box, and he fell, spraining his ankle. Nevertheless, he sprang up again, crying: " The South is avenged! " and escaped by a side door, where, mounting his horse, he dashed away before any one thought of pursuing him.

Lincoln, in the meantime, had fallen forward unconscious. He was carried to a neighboring house, where every care was lavished on him; but he never recovered his senses, and quietly passed away the next morning. The people around him seemed stunned by this unexpected blow, and the whole nation, North and South, mourned for the murdered President.

When Lincoln's death became known, all rejoicing was at an end. Houses decked in bunting the day before were draped in deep mourning; for every one felt that he had lost a friend. At first people were terrified, too, because that same night Secretary Seward, although ill in bed, was attacked and stabbed several times. It was later discovered that a few wicked people had made a plan to murder the President, Vice President, Secretary of State, and General Grant, because they thought they would thus serve the Confederate cause.

But this wicked and foolish attempt failed, and those who had taken part in it were justly punished. Booth was pursued and overtaken in a barn in Virginia, and—as he defended himself and refused to surrender—was shot on the spot by one of his captors. The rest of the criminals were tried and either hanged or imprisoned for life.

———oo:o:oo———

LII. DECORATION DAY.

ALTHOUGH Lincoln was dead, and people were almost stiff with horror, there was no break in the government. Three hours later, Vice President Andrew Johnson took the presidential oath.

On the 26th of April, 1865, General Johnston surrendered the last large Confederate army to General Sherman, at Raleigh (raw'ly); and on the 10th of May, President Davis was caught in Georgia. Some say he tried to escape by donning a woman's waterproof, tying an old shawl over his head, and carrying a pail, as if on the way to draw water from a spring. But the United States soldiers seized him, and sent him to Fortress Monroe. There he was detained for two years, and then he was bailed out by the famous newspaper editor, Horace Greeley. But Davis was never tried before a jury, and when he died in 1889, in New Orleans, he was surrounded by his family and friends.

Those who had taken part in the Civil War were never called to account for their share in it, except that they were not allowed to vote or hold office for some time. The only person executed was the jailer of the An'der-son-ville prison in Georgia. He had treated the Union prisoners with fiendish cruelty ; and in punishment for this inhuman conduct he was sentenced to be hanged, because even a jailer should remember that prisoners are his fellow-

Libby Prison, Richmond.

creatures. So many prisoners were crowded into a small space in the Libby and Andersonville prisons, that the men suffered greatly, and many of them died there from hunger, filth, and disease.

The Confederacy being now a "lost cause," the United States army, numbering more than a million men, was disbanded. Grant's and Sherman's troops were reviewed at Washington by President and Congress. They formed a column thirty miles long, and as they marched up Pennsylvania Avenue, people from all parts of the country wildly cheered them. These soldiers deserved all the credit they received, for they had saved the Union. Now they were going home, to take up their daily work again, and handle the plow or pen with the same energy as they had handled picks and guns. The veteran officers of the Revolutionary War had formed the Society of the Cincinnati, and, following their example, the veterans of the Union army soon founded another society, which is known as the Grand Army of the Republic (G. A. R.).

The army was disbanded on the 24th of May, and soon afterwards some Southern ladies started a beautiful custom which has since become national. They visited the places where soldiers were buried, and, after decking with fragrant flowers the tombs of their own dead, spread blossoms also over those of the Union men.

There are now in our country over eighty national cemeteries, where nearly four hundred thousand dead soldiers have been buried. Every Decoration or Memorial Day these graves, as well as others, are visited and strewn with flowers, and little children eagerly listen to the speeches telling how bravely their grandfathers fought and died.

Before going on with the story of the great events which next happened in our country, you will enjoy hearing a few of the famous Lincoln stories, for you know he stands beside Washington on our book of fame. You have already heard, however, how poor he was, how hard he worked to get an education, and how he rose step by step until, from a rawboned rail splitter, he became the most famous President of the United States.

———oo⚬o oo———

LIII. LINCOLN STORIES.

LINCOLN was a true patriot in every sense of the word. In 1850, before any one suspected his name would be renowned, he once said,—speaking of some one who had passed away after spending a useless life,— "How hard, ah, how hard it is to die, and leave one's country no better than if one had never lived in it!"

When Lincoln first ran for office, and was defeated, some one asked him how he felt. Lincoln gazed at the speaker a moment in silence, and then said: "Like the boy who stubbed his toe: too bad to laugh, and too big to cry."

He was always gentle and tender-hearted toward every one, and very thoughtful about his wife and children, who simply adored him. The moment he heard he had been nominated for President, Lincoln caught up his hat, and started off, saying: "There is a little woman on Eighth Street who would like to hear about this."

In fact, he was not ashamed to own that a man's family is his dearest possession. Once, when asked just how much one of his acquaintances was worth, he answered that the man in question had a wife and baby which were

vice. Now, it happened that the President could not tell them his plans, as it was very important, just then, to keep them secret. Besides, it was quite impossible to take their advice. Still, he did not wish to offend them, so he resorted to what is probably the best known of all his stories, and, alluding to a famous tight-rope dancer, he said:

"Gentlemen, suppose all the property you were worth was in gold, and you had put it into the hands of Blondin to carry across the Niagara River on a tight rope. Would you shake the cable, and keep shouting to him: 'Blondin, stand up a little straighter! Blondin, stoop a little more! Blondin, go a little faster! Lean a little more to the north! Bend over a little more to the south!' No, gentlemen; you would hold your breath as well as your tongues, and keep your hands off until he was over. The government is carrying an immense weight. Untold treasure is in its hands. It is doing the very best it can. Do not badger us. Keep silence, and we will get you safe across."

The way in which he told this story made the gentlemen part with him in the most cordial way, whereas, had he stiffly told them that he could not impart state secrets, they would probably have left him in anger.

LIV. LINCOLN'S REBUKES.

LINCOLN could be firm and severe when there was occasion for him to be so, and he never allowed disrespect to God or disobedience to his generals. Two anecdotes will illustrate this. A man once came to him with a petition; before long this individual began to swear horribly. Lincoln gently, yet firmly, checked him. Still, in a few minutes the man swore harder than ever. Then Lincoln rose with great dignity, opened the door, and said: " I thought that Senator —— had sent me a gentleman. I find I am mistaken. There is the door, sir. Good evening."

Many of the Union soldiers had enlisted thinking the war would soon be over, and fancying they would surely be released at the end of three months at the latest. After the battle of Bull Run, an officer came to Sherman, and coolly announced that he was going home. Sherman reasoned with him a few moments; but perceiving that he

Sherman and the Soldier.

was defiant, and that several of his companions were inclined to follow his example, he said sharply: " Captain,
this question of your term of service has been submitted to
the rightful authority, and the decision has been published
in orders. You are a soldier, and must submit to orders
till you are properly discharged. If you attempt to leave
without orders, it will be mutiny, and I will shoot you
like a dog! Go back into the fort *now*, instantly, and
don't dare to leave without my consent."

There was such a firm look in Sherman's eye that the
officer went back to his post until he could find a chance
to make a complaint against his superior. Shortly after
this, President Lincoln visited the camp, and, meeting
Sherman on the way thither, invited him to take a seat in
his carriage. They now exchanged a few remarks, and
knowing the President would make a speech, Sherman
begged him to encourage the men to do less cheering and
boasting, and prepare to be " cool, thoughtful, hard-fighting
soldiers." When the carriage drew up before the ranks,
Lincoln made one of those simple, touching speeches
which, once heard, were never forgotten. But when the
men started to cheer him, he quickly checked them, saying: " Don't cheer, boys. I confess I rather like it myself;
but Colonel Sherman here says it is not military, and I
guess we had better defer to his opinion."

Then, as usual, he went on to explain that as President,
and therefore commander in chief of the United States army,
it was his duty to see that the soldiers were well and happy,
and that he was ready to listen to any just complaints. He
was scarcely through speaking, when the officer whom
Sherman had threatened stepped up to the carriage, say-

ing: " Mr. President, I have a cause of grievance. This morning I went to speak to Colonel Sherman, and he threatened to shoot me."

" Threatened to shoot you?" asked the President, looking at the man with his deep, keen eyes.

" Yes, sir; he threatened to shoot me."

Lincoln looked at the man again, then at Sherman, and, bending over, said to the officer in a loud whisper: " Well, if I were you, and he threatened to shoot, I would not trust him, for I believe he would do it."

This answer sent the man back to his post without another word; but later on Sherman explained the facts to Lincoln, who said: " Of course I didn't know anything about it, but I thought you knew your own business best." Sherman warmly thanked the President for the way in which he had settled the question, and added that it would have a good effect upon his men, some of whom could not realize that a soldier must obey his superior without asking why.

LV. A PRESIDENT'S SON.

LINCOLN was elected President twice. His first term ended in 1865, and in 1864, when the time came to elect his successor, many people were tired of the war, and doubtful whether all this bloodshed was not the effect of bad management. This was an anxious time for the country, and although Lincoln would have been only too glad to withdraw, and leave the awful responsibility to some one else, he knew it would be wrong not to stay at his post. When some one, therefore, asked his opinion, he said it hardly seemed possible that a stranger could steer the " ship of state " in such a tempest, and made even the most ignorant catch his meaning by saying : " I don't believe it is safe to swap mules while crossing a stream."

Lincoln was reëlected, as you have heard, and in his second inaugural speech he said these beautiful words : " With malice toward none, with charity for all, with firmness in the right,—as God gives us to see the right, —let us finish the work we are in : to bind up the nation's wounds, to care for him who shall have borne the battle,—and for his widow and his orphans,—to do all which may achieve and cherish a just and lasting peace among ourselves and with all nations."

Besides the nation's sorrows, which he took so sorely to heart that he spent many a night in agonized prayer or tramping up and down the White House, Lincoln had to bear a great private grief—the loss of his favorite child, Willie.

Fond of all children, Lincoln was devoted to his own boys. One of these, " Tad," as everybody called him, was still a little fellow. He was so devoted to his father that he followed him about like a faithful dog, climbing up into his arms to rest even when Lincoln was deep in business conversation.

This little lad always begged to go along when the President visited the army, so all the soldiers knew and loved him. He insisted upon wearing a sort of uniform, too, and when the news of a victory came to the White House, he was always beside himself with joy.

Once such welcome tidings came in the evening, and a

crowd assembled outside. It stood there, cheering loudly, and calling for the President to make a speech. One of the secretaries went to get Lincoln, and as the presidential party came into the room, they heard a scuffle, and saw Tad escape from the hands of a man who was trying to hold him. Rushing to the window, the child danced up and down before the people, waving his flag and cheering like mad.

The crowd shouted at the sight of the delighted boy, and, sharing his joy, cheered him again and again. Indeed, they were so amused that they could scarcely stop laughing long enough to listen to Lincoln's brief speech, which they had come there to hear.

Lincoln and his boy both delighted in the music of military bands; but while Tad preferred the Northern war songs of the day, "Dixie" was Lincoln's favorite tune. This was the most famous of the Southern songs; for, as the slave states lay south of the Mason and Dixon line, the South was known as "Dixie Land." Once, when Lincoln asked for this tune, some narrow-minded person remarked in a shocked tone that it was a Confederate air! Lincoln good-naturedly answered: "Well, General Grant has captured it now, I believe, so henceforth it is ours by the laws of war."

LVI. A NOBLE SOUTHERNER.

ROBERT E. LEE, the son of Light-Horse Harry Lee, of Revolutionary fame, was, as we have seen, the principal general and hero of the Southern Confederacy. He was one of the finest men in our country. Brave, good, handsome, and well-bred, he was educated at West Point, and distinguished himself in the Mexican War.

When the Civil War broke out, Lee sadly sent in his resignation from the United States army. He wrote to a

relative: "With all my devotion to the Union, and the feeling of loyalty and duty of an American citizen, I have not been able to make up my mind to raise my hand against my relatives, my children, my home."

Lee's Birthplace.

When war began, he was given a position of high trust in the Confederate army, and before long became its best general. Lee's influence over his men was so good that it has been said his army was as religious as Cromwell's famous Ironsides.

His family had lived so long in Virginia—where their beautiful home still stands—that he knew almost every foot of the ground. This knowledge proved very useful to him when the Confederacy bade him defend Virginia against the Army of the Potomac.

The Southerners of that region, who enjoyed fox hunting and hare coursing in times of peace, are said to have engaged in battle with the same zest. As they went into action they often gave vent to their long and loud hunting cry. The Northern soldiers called it the "rebel yell," but when old negroes heard it they shook their woolly heads, saying: "There goes Marse Robert, or an old hare."

Lee's Home in Virginia.

In spite of Lee's great ability as a general, and the successes which attended his army in the beginning of the war, things began to look very bad for the Confederates in 1864. By that time their supplies were so few that Lee and his staff lived on scant rations of corn bread, a few crackers, and bits of cabbage, with a little meat only twice a week. But, in spite of poor fare, none complained, and when Lee's servants tried to secure him better food, he quietly said: "I am content to share the rations of my men."

One day Lee had a dinner in his tent, and as he had several guests, his cook—who was ashamed to serve only a small dish of cabbage—borrowed a bit of pork to put in the center. This piece of meat was so very small that all the guests refused to touch it, hoping that Lee would

STO. OF GT. REP.—16

eat it himself. But he, too, ate nothing but cabbage, so the pork was safely returned to the person who had loaned it for the occasion.

The war was a very sad time for Lee; for not only was he forced to see all the suffering of his men, but he was anxious for many of his relatives, who were engaged in the war. Indeed, one of his sons was taken prisoner by the Union army, and when the Confederates threatened to execute some of the prisoners at Richmond, Lee was warned that his son should receive exactly the same treatment as was meted out to Union men.

While thus in captivity, this young Lee's wife and children were stricken with mortal illness. But although his brother offered to take his place, so he could hasten to their bedside, the exchange could not be allowed. You see by this fact not only how dearly the Lees loved each other, and what noble feelings were theirs, but also how cruel and sad a thing civil war necessarily is.

Lee's soldiers were all devoted to him. Every man in his army would gladly have laid down his life for him. When he started to lead a desperate charge at Spottsylvania, one and all shouted: "Lee to the rear!" vowing they could not fight if he were in danger. One of them even stepped out of the ranks, and, taking Lee's horse by the bridle, led him away. But as soon as the men felt sure their beloved general was safe, they showed him that, while afraid for him, they had no such dread for themselves, and made a most daring charge.

On another occasion, after many hours of hard work, Lee lay down by the roadside to rest until his army came up. But when the foremost men caught sight of him, they quickly passed the word down the long line, and the whole army filed past so noiselessly that the weary general's brief slumbers were undisturbed.

When the war was over, Lee—who had fought with all his might, but who was too high-minded to bear any malice—acknowledged that he was fairly beaten. He then set a good example for all his men by applying for pardon from the United States government. Besides, in his farewell address he said to his soldiers: " Remember that we are one country now. Do not bring up your children in hostility to the government of the United States. Bring them up to be Americans."

Lee also spoke and wrote on every occasion in the noblest and manliest way, saying: " I believe it to be the duty of every one to unite in the restoration of the country and the reëstablishment of peace and harmony."

When he became president of Washington College, at Lexington, Virginia, a Southern woman brought him her sons to educate. In the course of the conversation she made some bitter remark about the Union, for which he gently reproved her, telling her that there were none but Americans in the country.

Sad to relate, the women, on both sides, were far more unjust than the men, and, when the war was over, not nearly so ready to "shake hands and forget." Still, most men and women mean to do what is right, so we hope that before long the day will come when the past will be entirely forgiven, although not forgotten.

Probably the noblest words that Lee ever wrote were penned in 1868; they run as follows: " Whatever opinions have prevailed in the past with regard to African slavery, or the right of a state to secede from the Union, we believe we express the almost unanimous judgment of the Southern people when we declare that they consider these questions

Lee's Table as he left it.

were decided by the war, and that it is their intention, in good faith, to abide by that decision."

Lee was the president of the Washington College for several years. When he died, in 1870, the whole nation mourned for a truly noble man, and the university of which he had been president said that henceforth it would bear the honored names of two great Americans, and be called "Washington and Lee University." Lee was buried near the college chapel, where you can see a monument in his honor; and there is a fine one also at Richmond, the city he so gallantly defended.

LVII. HARD TIMES IN THE SOUTH.

YOU surely remember what a sad and trying time it was for the Americans right after the Revolutionary War. Well, after the Civil War it was even sadder and more trying. Every one felt this deeply, and while most people longed to do what was just right, they did not know where or how to begin. To remind every man, woman, and child in the country that one can always rely upon help from above, Congress decided that every American coin which was large enough should be stamped with the motto: "In God we trust" (1865).

Both armies had now been disbanded and had gone home. Northern men went back to comfortable homes, where the only drawback to their happiness was the thought of those who had died, and the pain they suffered from wounds received in battle. It was very different, however, with the Southern soldiers. Not only were they beaten,—a thing which only the noblest can bear well,— but they were ruined, had no government, and were forced to begin life all over again.

But the Southern men were made of such good stuff that in spite of countless hindrances,—more than you could understand,—they bravely went to work to make the South even better and greater than ever before. Men and women who had never done a stroke of work in all their lives now patiently learned to do everything for themselves, and earnestly tried to bring law and order out of chaos. Of course, this was not done in a day, a week, or a year; but in spite of a few mistakes, which could not be helped, since we are all human, the work was carried on day after day, and year after year, until a glorious "new South" arose.

Lincoln, as you know, claimed that the Southern states had never been really out of the Union. So he wanted each state to send members to Congress as soon as possible, and all to be as if the war had never taken place. Perhaps, if he had lived, things would have gone on far more smoothly; but he had been sorely tried during the war, and kindly death spared him some very hard work which remained to be done when it was ended.

Andrew Johnson, the seventeenth President of the United States, who took Lincoln's place, meant to do what was right; but he had never expected to be President, and was thrust into that position at a very uncomfortable time. He had been a poor boy, and was forced to work so hard at his trade as tailor that he had little time left to spend on books. Still, he did his very best, and was not ashamed to learn to write even after his marriage.

His efforts to improve were constant, and they met with such success that he was elected to share with Lincoln the highest place in the United States. Unfortunately, however, Johnson was not born with Lincoln's tact, and, while honest and good, was so outspoken and obstinate that he made many enemies.

No sooner had the Union army been reviewed and disbanded than President Johnson made a proclamation, offering full pardon to most of the people in the Southern states, if they would faithfully promise to "support, protect, and defend the Union."

He also put an end to the blockade, allowed trade to begin again, ordered the mails distributed all through the country once more, the laws obeyed, and the taxes collected. He also said that the Southern states could resume their places in the Union as soon as they elected men who would be true to the government.

But when Congress met, shortly after this, it did not approve of what Johnson had done. A quarrel began, therefore, between President and Congress, which grew worse and worse as time went on. The President wanted the Southern states readmitted right away; but Congress said they should not come back until the negroes were properly protected in their new rights.

The result of this quarrel was that Congress passed bills which Johnson vetoed. Still, they were passed again by a vote of two to one, and thus became laws without his consent. But Johnson vetoed so many bills, first and last, that his enemies called him " Sir Veto."

Congress also decreed that no Southern state should join the Union again unless it promised to give up all secession ideas, to protect the negroes and let them vote, and never to pay the Confederate war debt; or ask the nation to pay it. Besides, Congress insisted that no Southerner should be elected to office who could not make oath that he had taken no part in the Civil War against the United States.

This was very unwise, for most of the respectable Southern men had been in the army. When they heard what was required before they could again hold office, they naturally cried out against what they called the "ironclad" oath. Still, as they could not take it, they were shut out of office. Positions of great trust and importance were, therefore, filled by men from the North, who in most cases had no property in the South except what they brought in their traveling bags. Hence they are generally known as "carpetbaggers." These men were elected mostly by the colored people, who, as yet, had not received any education, and hence could not make a wise choice, and by a small class of Southern people, called "scalawags," because they were so dishonest that they would cast their votes for any one who paid them for it.

In spite of these unhappy conditions, eight out of the eleven seceded states soon managed to get back into the Union; but for years Southerners suffered more than words can tell from bad state government. Such was the disorder, that United States troops had to be stationed there to keep peace. But their presence, in many cases, only made matters worse. Besides, police work was just as distasteful to the soldiers as it was to the people, so both parties felt unhappy and sore.

By this time the quarrel between President and Congress had grown so bitter that the House of Representatives impeached him,—that is, accused him of acting against the law and making a bad use of his power. Johnson was therefore called before the Senate, where he was tried. But before he could be put out of office two thirds of the votes had to be against him. One vote proved lacking to make up this count, so he remained President to the end of his term, although he and Congress were now sworn foes.

On Christmas Day, 1868,—to the relief of the whole nation,—full and unconditional pardon was granted to all who had taken any part whatever in the war. This was a move in the right direction, and was followed, before long, by an act of Congress allowing most of the ex-Confederates to hold office again. The better class of the Southern people, now able to take part in public affairs, worked hard to redeem their states, and their noble efforts were soon rewarded. The years which followed the Civil War are generally known as the time of Reconstruction, or rebuilding the governments of the Southern states.

LVIII. THE ATLANTIC CABLE.

THE United States had been so busy, first with the Civil War, and then with the work of reconstruction, that many interesting events which had taken place passed by almost unnoticed. For instance, even while the war was raging, Napoleon III., emperor of the French, in spite of the "Monroe doctrine," sent an army into Mexico.

The United States then told him this was not right; but he paid no heed, and placed Max-i-mil'ian, an Austrian prince, on the Mexican throne. Later on, when the United States had a little more leisure, it sternly bade Napoleon withdraw his army, or it would show him that the Monroe doctrine must be respected.

At this warning Napoleon withdrew his troops, leaving Maximilian on the throne where he had placed him. But as the Mexicans did not want him to rule them, they rebelled, shot him to get rid of him, and again set up a republic (1867), which has gone on to this day.

After all the stories of wars and troubles which you have just heard, you will probably be glad to hear of the ocean telegraph, or the laying of the first Atlantic cable When Morse set up the first electric telegraph in 1844, he foretold that the time would come when dispatches would be sent across the ocean. This seemed great folly to every one then, but, as years went by, people began to see that wires could be laid in the water. Several short cables, or lines, were laid; but it was Cyrus W. Field, an American citizen, who determined to lay the first cable across the ocean.

He made careful plans, and in 1854 formed a company for that purpose. Several attempts were then made to lay a cable, but Field did not have the right machinery, and all his efforts failed. As the company's money was gone, Field now asked the governments of Great Britain and the United States to help him.

The day before President Pierce went out of office, a bill for the ocean telegraph was passed; but people were then so doubtful of its success, that had there been one vote less this help would have been denied to Field. This time, however, the work succeeded: a cable was stretched across the ocean, and the first official messages were exchanged between Queen Victoria and President Buchanan.

But after about four hundred messages had passed safely to and fro, and just as a grand celebration was held in honor of this event, the cable suddenly ceased to work. Still undismayed, Field began preparations for a new ocean telegraph; but, as the Civil War broke out, no one had any money to spare for such an undertaking, and it was not till 1865, when the struggle was ended, that the work could be resumed.

This last cable had been laid halfway across the ocean, when, owing to a flaw, it suddenly broke, and the end was lost in the bottom of the ocean! When an Englishman once asked Field what he would do in such a case, the latter said: "Charge it to profit and loss, and go to work and lay another." True to his word, Field now set to work again. This time a new plan was adopted: two vessels met in the middle of the ocean, and, after splicing the wires they carried, they set out in opposite directions to lay the Atlantic cable.

All went smoothly on this trip. The cable was laid, messages were sent to and fro, and events which happened on one side of the ocean could be made known a few minutes later on the other side. Not only had Mr. Field

Bringing the Cable Ashore.

succeeded in laying a cable, but he now also proved that a broken cable could be mended by sending a ship to the place where the broken cable lay. Its big grappling hooks sank several thousand feet below the surface of the ocean, were dragged about on the bottom, and finally caught the cable near the loose end. It was then carefully hauled up and joined to some cable on board, and the vessel then proceeded to lay the rest of that wire, too.

To accomplish his aim, Field had worked hard for more

than thirteen years, had spent all his own money, besides large sums supplied by his friends and the government, and had crossed the Atlantic thirty-one times. But his patience now reaped its reward. The cable proved so useful that fortune and honors were bestowed upon the man who alone had not lost courage, in spite of many failures.

Now there are more than a dozen cables across the Atlantic Ocean, and, before long, wires across the Pacific will complete the circuit of our globe. Cables also connect our country with many of the West Indies, and with South America.

In 1867, one year after the Atlantic cables were in perfect working order, and the same year that Mexico recovered her freedom, the United States bought Alaska from Russia for about seven million dollars. Secretary Seward urged this purchase, but Congress did not, at first, favor

Mining in Alaska.

it, saying that the United States did not need such an expensive " refrigerator."

Still, the furs, timber, and fishing were very valuable, and the seals alone brought in about two million dollars a year. Thus Alaska more than paid for its own purchase even before gold was discovered there. Since that discovery, the land, cold and uninviting as it may otherwise seem, attracts hosts of miners, who rush thither as they did to California in 1849, in hopes of making a fortune in a very short time. Many of them are now working hard along the Yu'kon River, where much gold has already been found.

When a new presidential election was held, in 1868, three of the Southern states were still unrepresented in Congress. The country this time elected Ulysses S. Grant, the hero of the Civil War, to be the eighteenth President of the United States. He was, as you know, a good, firm, and very silent man; but every one says he was a much better general than a politician.

Shortly after Grant's inauguration, a very important and interesting ceremony took place. Even before the war, a plan had been made to build a railroad all the way across our continent. This was absolutely necessary, because the " Pony Express " and stagecoaches were far too slow means of travel. Indeed, when California first asked to come into the Union, a member of Congress proved that a representative of California could spend only a fortnight each year in Washington, for he would have to be on the road all the rest of the time.

But the day of slow travel was nearly over. One railroad company began building westward from O'ma-ha, while another started from Sacramento to meet it. Although nine mountain chains had to be crossed, and trains had to go first up and then down seven thousand feet, the work was carried on with such energy that finally it was all done. On a certain day in 1869 the directors of the two roads set out, with their friends, and the two engines met at Og'den, in Utah. Here the last spike—it was made of gold—was driven in, amid great rejoicings.

People could now travel from the Atlantic to the Pacific in less time, and with far more comfort, than Washington had traveled from Boston to New York. Besides, the railroad was a great help to commerce, for goods from China and Japan could now be shipped direct to San Francisco or Sacramento, and thence be sent across the continent, reaching New York about a month after they had left the shore of Asia. Before long, too, this railroad, and others like it, were supplied with refrigerator cars, and now people on the Atlantic coast eat cherries, peaches, grapes, and many other fruits which have ripened on the other side of the Rocky Mountains.

LIX. THE BEST WAY TO SETTLE QUARRELS.

THE Union Pacific Railroad brought about many other improvements. Emigrants were no longer afraid to travel farther westward, where the government promised to give them farms, or "homesteads." They quickly settled all along the new railroad. Before long several prosperous towns arose in the far West, also, and train after train bore produce from Western farms to the Eastern market. Many of the broad prairies, where huge herds

Herd of Bison.

of bison once fed, are now plowed by steam, and immense fields of wheat can be seen stretching on every side as far as the eye can reach.

Thus, you see, our country was growing—growing fast. In spite of the war, where so many were killed, the census of 1870 showed that there were about thirty-nine million inhabitants in our country, and that wealth had increased as fast as the people. Railways and steamboats greatly helped commerce, and since the weather signal service was established, in the year 1870, fewer vessels have been lost at sea.

Still, while the East and West were prospering, the South had a very hard time to get on, for in some states the colored voters outnumbered the white. Schools had been started, but it would be some time before children attending them would be old enough to vote, and in the meantime ignorant negro voters and carpetbaggers were in control.

Bad and dishonest men so often got into office in this way that secret societies were formed in the South, to prevent the negroes from voting in regions where they outnumbered the whites. These societies formed what was called the " Ku-Klux Klan," and the members wore queer masks and frightful disguises.

Although at first intended merely to frighten and awe, but not to harm, the negroes, some members of the Ku-Klux Klan became very cruel before long. Negroes were whipped, maimed, and even murdered, carpetbaggers and scalawags were treated in the same way, and for a time there was a reign of terror in the South. But these methods were never approved of by the most sensible people. They knew that the only right way is to have good laws and an orderly government, and they worked very hard to secure both.

Two questions arose with Great Britain while Grant was President, which might have made trouble. But, instead of fighting, some of the best statesmen of both countries made a treaty at Washington (1871), saying that the difficulties should be decided by arbitration.

A board of distinguished men, therefore, met at Ge-ne'va, in Switzerland, to settle what are known as the "*Alabama* claims." You remember that during the Civil War a vessel of that name and other ships were built in England,—a neutral country,—and handed over to the Confederates, who used them to destroy many Union vessels.

After weighing both sides of the question, this board decided that a neutral country should not furnish vessels and arms to nations at war. As Great Britain had clearly been in the wrong in this case, she was condemned to pay the United States fifteen and a half million dollars as damages for property destroyed.

The second question—the water boundary between the United States and British Columbia in Pu'get Sound—was left entirely to the Emperor of Germany, who drew the line on the map where it now stands.

While Grant was President there was much talk about the Indians. The greater part of them had, little by little, been removed to the Indian Territory, where the Choc'taws, Creeks, Cher-o-kees', and Seminoles had houses and schools, and were fast learning to be very good farmers.

But, besides the orderly and industrious Indians, there were others who were as wild as their ancestors. The food furnished to these tribes by the government agents was not fit to eat, for most of the money devoted to this purpose was stolen by dishonest men. But the President had no idea of this until a Yale professor went to a Sioux Reservation to get specimens for the college museum. The Indians there called him "The-Man-who-came-to-pick-up-Bones," and their chief, Red Cloud, gave him samples of the food dealt out to the savages, making him promise to show them to the "Great Father" (the President).

The professor kept that promise; and when Grant saw the samples, and heard from some of the officers that the Indians had a right to complain in many cases, he decided that a change must be made. Since then matters have

STO. OF GT. REP.—17

(266)   The Custer Massacre.

gone on a little better. Various improvements have been made, and in the government schools you can now see many Indian boys and girls learning to be teachers, so they can help their people to become good American citizens.

Among the worst of the savage Indians, there were the wild A-pa'ches in Ar-i-zo'na, and the Mo'docs in Oregon, who, unable to agree with the settlers, and refusing to stay in their reservations, were finally forced to obey by the United States troops. This, however, was not accomplished until many Indians and a number of white men had been slain.

The worst Indian war at this time was with the Sioux in the Black Hills in Da-ko'ta. Gold having been found there, miners invaded the Indians' reservation. As the miners and Indians both drank, quarrels and fights soon arose, and, hoping to save bloodshed, the government tried to make a treaty with the Sioux to sell their land and go elsewhere.

The principal chiefs were Sitting Bull and Rain-in-the-Face, who refused to stir. They were then told that they must obey or the troops would force them to do so. But the Indians retreated into the Big Horn valley, where they got ready to fight. General George A. Custer, who had fought bravely all through the Civil War, set out in June, 1876, to attack them. But he divided his force, so as to strike them from two sides at once, and when he and his two hundred and sixty-two men came suddenly upon the Indians' camp he found that the Sioux. had been joined by many others of their tribe, and now, instead of a few hundred, were five thousand strong!

In a moment Custer's cavalrymen saw they could not

escape. Nevertheless, they dismounted calmly, resolved to die bravely at their post. The Indians came on, twenty to one, and stampeded the cavalry horses by fiendish yells and wildly waving blankets. Left thus, with nothing but the ammunition in their cartridge belts, Custer and his brave troopers fought until their last shots had been fired, and when the battle was over, every one of them lay there dead, but surrounded by many slain Indians.

Although badly wounded, Rain-in-the-Face boasted that he had kept a vow he had made, and had cut out and eaten Captain Tom Custer's heart! The heroes who died in the Custer massacre were buried on the spot where they fell around their gallant general, and a massive monument was erected in their honor. Besides, a statue of Custer is to be seen at West Point, where he learned to be such a good soldier.

———oo°o°oo———

LX. OUR NATION'S ONE HUNDREDTH BIRTHDAY.

GRANT served as President two terms, and it was while he was head of the nation, in 1870, that the last of the Southern states was again admitted to representation in Congress. The Union was complete once more, and all good Americans rejoiced.

His second election is interesting because it was the first time that all the electors were chosen directly by the people. Each state had always voted for electors in any way it pleased, but now all adopted the same way.

Several calamities took place in our country while

Ulysses S. Grant.

(269)

General Grant was President. For instance, one Sunday night in October, 1871, an upset lamp started a fatal fire in Chicago. This place had risen rapidly from a very small village and fort to a huge city. The blaze started near vast lumber yards, at a time when a strong breeze was blowing, and it soon developed into one of the worst fires the world has ever seen. In spite of heroic efforts, the flames spread and spread, until the city was a raging sea of fire.

Cinders fell in such showers that some of the terrified people had to take refuge in the lake. There they stood for hours, up to their necks in water, dashing it over their heads to prevent their hair from catching fire. For two days the fire raged, sweeping over about two thousand acres; and when it was over, Chicago was in ruins, and the people had lost about two hundred million dollars' worth of property. When it became known that the main part of Chicago had been destroyed, and that a hundred thousand people were homeless, help was quickly sent on to them. Every one contributed something, and the government forwarded tents and rations, so that the people should have food and shelter. Now, Chicago people have always been noted for their pluck. Without wasting time in useless laments, therefore, they went bravely to work to rebuild their homes and fortunes. Men who had been wealthy two days before, handled the pick and shovel to earn a living for themselves and families. Before long this energy bore good fruit, for Chicago is now the largest city in our country, except New York.

As if one fire had not been enough, unusually large forest fires next swept over Wisconsin, Minnesota, and

Michigan, in which many people lost their lives. The very next year, Boston was also visited in the same way, a large part of the city and about eighty millions' worth of property being burned.

Two of our principal towns thus suffered great losses by fire; but a third, New York, lost nearly as much by the "Tweed Ring." This was formed by a number of dishonest officers, who stole a great deal of the city's money. But they were finally arrested, tried, and punished, and their ringleader, or "boss," William Tweed, died shortly after in jail.

Awful fires, political troubles, and speculation did great harm to business, and brought about the panic of 1873, which was even worse than those of 1837 and 1857. But after a few years of "hard times," business again flourished, and the country became as prosperous as before.

The year 1873 is also noted for a change in our system of money. Before that time our money had consisted of both gold and silver—as much of each as the people would bring to the mint to be coined. But for several years very little silver had been brought in, and in 1873 Congress stopped the coinage of silver dollars.

Our nation was rapidly approaching its hundredth birthday, and centennial celebrations were talked of on all sides. First there were the centennials of the battles of Lexington and Bunker Hill, and then of the British leaving Boston. But it was rightly felt that the grandest of all celebrations should be held at Philadelphia, to celebrate the Declaration of Independence.

After some discussion, it was decided to have a World's Fair in Fairmount Park. Buildings of all kinds and sizes

Centennial Building.

were put up; exhibits were sent from all the countries of
the world; and many, many thousands of people went to
see all the beautiful and interesting things the Philadelphia
Exposition contained.

The most interesting of all these exhibits, however, was
the old "Liberty Bell," which had pealed forth joyfully

to proclaim the Declaration of Independence. Since that day it had rung
many times, but it was now quite
dumb. It had rung its last note on
Washington's hundred and thirteenth
birthday, and a huge crack showed
that it could never ring again. The
visitors were not only Americans from
all parts of our Union, but people
from foreign lands who came to see

Liberty Bell.

·what the Americans had done. They greatly admired the riches of our country in metals, produce, industry, and especially in useful inventions.

Since the *Monitor* fought the *Merrimac*, wooden ships had little by little been replaced by iron vessels, and railroads had greatly improved. Indeed, the Pullman cars were as unlike the first " coaches " as the modern steamships were unlike the Indian canoes. Bicycles and typewriters were then new and wonderful things; the telephone had just been invented by Bell, and electric lights by Ed'i-son.

This last-named inventor was once a poor newsboy on a train. As he was not afraid of work, he earned his own living, and being very quick to learn, never lost an opportunity to do so.

Once he saved the child of a telegraph operator from being run over, and when the grateful father offered to teach him telegraphy, he gladly set to work. This knowledge soon proved very useful. One day there was an ice jam between Port Huron and the town opposite. It was important to send a message, and Edison, who was always quick-witted, said he thought he could telegraph it by means of long and short whistles from a locomotive.

He therefore seized the throttle, and began to signal: " Hello, there, over the river!" But it was some time before the people on the opposite bank understood the meaning of these strange long and short whistles. When it finally dawned upon them, they were delighted, and gladly used this simple means of communication.

Little by little, Edison rose in his profession, and, studying scientific books, he decided that there must be some way

of using electricity to light cities and houses. As generally happens, he was first laughed at; but he persevered,
and hearing that one man was making great fun of him,
Edison good-naturedly threatened to avenge himself in
this way:

"I'll make a statue of that man, and I'll illuminate it
brilliantly with Edison lamps, and inscribe it: 'This is the
man who said the Edison lamp would not burn!'"

Although that statue does not exist, so far as I know,
you can see Edison lamps burning brightly on every side;
and since then the "Wizard of Menlo Park," as he is called,
has done countless wonderful things. Edison is still hard
at work in his great works at Menlo Park, in New Jersey;
for he is one of the men who cannot rest as long as they can
invent something which will benefit their fellow-creatures.

———oo;o;oo———

LXI. GOLD FOR GREENBACKS.

AFTER serving two terms as President, Grant started
for a long journey all around the world. He had long
wished to travel, and his fame, first as general and then as
President of the United States, won him a warm welcome
everywhere. He was received with all honor, was royally
entertained at many courts, and after visiting the principal
countries in Europe and Asia, he came back to San Francisco, where some of his former soldiers were the first to
greet him.

Grant was succeeded in the White House by Rutherford
B. Hayes, the nineteenth President of the United States

(1877). Hayes had taken a brave part in the Civil War, had been governor of Ohio, and was greatly respected for his many good qualities.

When called to be President, Hayes frankly said that in government positions there should be " no dismissal except for cause, and no promotion except for merit." Besides, he always thought and openly said that the South would get along much better if the United States troops were withdrawn. Still, owing to a dispute about the counting of votes, no one knew at first whether he or his rival Samuel J. Tilden had been elected. As the quarrel could not be decided otherwise, a commission of five congressmen, five senators, and five judges was chosen to settle the matter, and their decision was in favor of Hayes.

True to his principles, Hayes immediately called back the troops, an order which most people in the country considered very wise. Southerners were now left to settle their own affairs, and they have done it so wisely that no one has ever regretted Hayes's action, although some of his enemies had predicted that it would make trouble.

During Hayes's one term there were several great strikes among coal miners and railroad employees. These strikes spread all through New York and Pennsylvania, and even in the West. At one time there were more than one hundred and fifty thousand men out of work; and the strikers grew so unruly at Pittsburg that they destroyed much property, and ceased rioting only when the troops were called out to subdue them.

Already in 1868 our minister Bur'lin-game had made a trade treaty with China, but when Hayes became President, Congress passed a bill to prevent the Chinese from com-

ing over here.   Hayes vetoed this bill and in 1878 received
the first real Chinese embassy in the White House.   There,
their jewels, gorgeous costumes of finest silk, and gay peacock feathers caused a great sensation.

The most important event during Hayes's term was
that the government said it was ready to pay gold in exchange for every "greenback" issued during the war.
But now that the people knew they could get gold in exchange for the paper money whenever they wanted it,
they decided to keep on using bills, because they are so
much easier to carry than coin.   At the same time, Congress passed a Silver Bill, providing that the government
should buy and coin a certain amount of silver every month,
using sixteen times as much silver in a silver dollar as of
gold in a gold dollar.

Before Hayes's term ended, a dispute about fisheries
between Canada and the United States was settled in a
friendly way, by our paying Great Britain five and a half
millions for the right to fish along the Canadian coast.

Hayes and his wife helped the cause of temperance and
set a good example for the whole country, by refusing to
have any kind of wine or strong drink on their table in the
White House.

———oo°o°oo———

LXII. A CLEVER ENGINEER.

IF you glance at a map, you can easily see what a very
large stream the Missouri is, and what a vast extent
of land it drains.   In the northwest, where the land is
high and its banks steep and rocky, the current is very

swift. But as it travels onward it joins the Mississippi, which, when swollen by other streams, grows much wider, while, the land being lower, its current flows more slowly.

Near the mouth of the Mississippi, the country is often below the river level, and the waters are kept from overflowing these lowlands by means of walls or levees built

A Levee on the Mississippi.

along the river banks. These levees are built of piles, earth, and sand. They sometimes break, and then fields and houses are flooded.

After a hard rain, streams are swollen, and their waters are very muddy. But as they flow slowly along, the mud settles along the banks and in the river bed, leaving the water clearer. Being a very large stream, the Mississippi carries great quantities of mud and sand; and, while some settles along the way, a great deal is rolled down to the Gulf, where it drops near the mouth of the river, to form huge beds of mud. Such deposits prevent large ships from sailing in and out, and are therefore called bars.

Although the Mississippi has several mouths, they were all more or less blocked in this way, which proved very inconvenient, as only small ships could sail in and out of the stream on their way to and from New Orleans. The pioneer farmers along the Ohio and Mississippi built huge rafts of the timber they had cut on their farms, and, piling upon them the produce of their land, floated down the stream to New Orleans. There they sold raft and all, and slowly made their way home again on foot, carrying only the money they had earned, and their hunting knives and rifles. So much produce of all kinds came thus to New Orleans that it soon became a large and thriving city. It traded with various other ports in this country and in Europe, and before long many vessels laden with cotton, sugar, lumber, and rice sailed out of the Mississippi, and came back with goods from abroad.

The mud banks and sand bars proved a great hindrance even to these vessels, which often stuck fast there for hours or days. And although channels were cut, and the river bed dredged, the mud soon choked up the passages again, and all the money was spent in vain. People, therefore, began to wish that a way could be found to open a channel which would remain clear, and many clever engineers tried to think of a good plan.

At that time there was an American engineer named Captain James B. Eads. He, too, like many other great men, had once been a poor boy. When nine years of age he made his first trip in a steamboat on the Ohio River, and studied the engine so carefully that when he got home he made an exact model of it. This greatly amused his schoolmates, as did also a tiny locomotive engine which he had also made himself, and which was driven by a concealed rat.

At thirteen Eads was taken out of school, and he set out, with the rest of the family, for Wisconsin. But while on the Ohio their boat took fire, and when Eads reached the shore, he found that he had lost everything except the shirt, pantaloons, and cap he wore. Another boat soon picked up the forlorn family and carried them down to St. Louis, where the barefoot boy landed on the very spot on which he was later to build a wonderful bridge. As he had to earn his own living, Eads now found a place as errand boy in a dry-goods store; but, determined to learn, he spent all his evenings studying in the books he borrowed. Seeing how eager he was to learn, a kind old gentleman let him use his library, and there Eads found the first work on engineering which he had ever seen.

After spending five years in the dry-goods business, Eads got work on one of the Mississippi steamboats; and as it plied up and down the stream, he studied the river, and thus laid the corner stone of his fortunes. Before long he found a way to raise the cargoes of sunken ships, and, later, the vessels themselves.

By doing this he saved much property which would otherwise have been lost, and his ingenious contrivances won him fame as well as fortune. In 1861, when the Civil War began, the government gave him an order for some gunboats. He supplied seven within sixty-five days, and had them all ready when they were needed for the capture of Forts Henry and Donelson.

These gunboats also did good service at Vicksburg, and

it was partly owing to their help that Grant got control of the Father of Waters. In 1874, after seven years' hard work, Eads completed the huge steel bridge which spans the Mississippi at St. Louis. This is one of the most wonderful bridges in the world, and it was very hard to build.

The Eads Bridge at St. Louis.

To reach a rock foundation for the piers, Eads had to dig through one hundred and thirty-six feet of mud and sand,—a feat which many engineers said he could not accomplish!

The bridge was no sooner done, however, than Eads proposed to open one of the mouths of the Mississippi. During his journeys and studies of rivers in Europe, he had noticed that where a channel is narrow, the force of the current keeps it clear. He therefore laid his plan before Congress, which, after talking the matter over for about a year, gave him permission to try it. Eads spent the next four years in building two long piers, or jetties, from a natural mouth of the stream, far out into the Gulf. These jetties, which are more than two miles long and only four hundred yards apart, keep the waters from spreading as they used to do. The current is therefore much stronger and swifter, and as it sweeps along it carries the mud and sand far out into the Gulf of Mexico, where the water is so deep that they can settle without stopping any ships. Thus the river has deepened its channel through the bar so that the largest ships can always pass. This advantage is so great that it seems very little to have spent more than five million dollars to secure it.

After finishing this great piece of engineering, in 1879, Eads began to think of a ship railway across the narrow part of Mexico, but before he could carry out his plans, he died in 1887. He is known throughout the world for the Mississippi jetties, and every one greatly admires the patience of the man who educated himself while working hard to earn his own living.

LXIII. DEATH OF GARFIELD.

IN 1880 there was a new and very exciting election. The different parties were all eager, as usual, to have their candidates elected; but the Republicans had had much trouble in choosing theirs. While some wanted Grant for

a third time, others cried, "Anything to beat Grant,"
because they thought it wrong to let a man serve more
than eight years, Washington and Jefferson having both refused to do so.   Blaine, who had been Hayes's chief rival
in the Republican party four years before, and whom his
friends called the "Plumed Knight," was again suggested,
but his friend, James A. Garfield, was finally chosen, and
when the election was held he was successful.

The new President was a great favorite, and every one
respected him very much.   Although so poor that he was
once a "mule boy" on a canal towpath, Garfield nevertheless managed to educate himself.   By dint of great
efforts, he became the head of a college, and for this reason
he has sometimes been called the "Teacher President."
Later on he won great praise in the Civil War.   He took
part in the battles of Shiloh and Chickamauga, where he
shone by his bravery; and he was then elected a member
of Congress.

Garfield had barely been inaugurated (1881), when, as
usual, office seekers began to make his life a burden.
Still, sharing Hayes's feelings, he said he would not remove
men who were doing their work well; and he thus made
some people who wanted places very angry.

One morning in July, the President's son came boun-
cing into his room, and, taking a flying leap over the bed,
merrily cried, "There! you are President of the United
States, but you can't do that!"   The President laughed
at the boy's challenge, and a few seconds later proved he
could not be beaten, even in jumping.   That same day,
while in the best health and spirits, Garfield set out for
a train which was waiting to take him east.

Suddenly, an obscure man who had tried in vain to get a government position stepped up behind him in the depot and shot him twice in the back. Garfield fell to the floor. His friends rushed to help the wounded President, and carefully carried him home. But, in spite of the utmost skill, the doctors could not save the President, who daily grew worse.

He was such a strong man, however, that he lingered on until the middle of September. All through this long illness Garfield gave a most noble example to the whole country by his patience and courage in great suffering. Hoping that sea air would help him rally, his friends finally carried him to El'ber-on, New Jersey. Silent crowds collected at every station to see his car speed past, and the bulletin board was anxiously watched to find out how the President was standing the journey, for all hoped he would soon get better. But he was not to recover, and after a little more suffering passed quietly away.

After lying in state in the Capitol in Washington, the body of this " Martyr President "—for Garfield shares that name with Lincoln—was carried to Cleveland, Ohio, where an imposing funeral took place, and where his grave is often visited.

Garfield's murderer was caught very soon after he had fired those fatal shots; and while people were so angry that they wanted to lynch him, the police took charge of him and brought him before a jury. There were so many who had seen the crime that he could not have denied it, even if he had wished to do so.

At the trial, people found out that the murderer was such a wicked and stupid man that he fancied it would be a fine thing to commit a crime which would make his name known everywhere and prevent its being ever forgotten.

The Garfield Tomb, Cleveland.

His wicked wish has come true, but his name now stands in our history even lower than that of Arnold or Booth in the eyes of all good Americans.

It is true that Arnold was a base traitor, but for many years before that he had been a noble patriot, and he lived to repent of the wrong he had done. The murderer of Lincoln was the vile assassin of a good man, but he had thought so long over the sufferings of the Confederates that he was half insane when he killed the President.

When the murderer of Garfield was tried, his lawyer attempted to prove that this criminal did not deserve punishment because he was out of his right mind; but it was shown that he had been sane enough to plan the murder some time before. When the jury heard this, they decided that the law should take its usual course, and he was hanged.

All through Garfield's illness, Vice President Chester A. Arthur was in a very delicate position. By our Constitution he was to take the President's place only in case of the latter's death, resignation, or inability to discharge his duties. But it was at first impossible to decide whether the President would recover or not, and as no great event took place at that time to make it necessary, Arthur firmly refused to take Garfield's place.

But a few hours after Garfield had breathed his last, Arthur, who was known as " the first gentleman in the land," on account of his kind, true feelings and courteous manners, took the presidential oath.

While Garfield lay hovering between life and death, Arthur himself was also taken very ill. For a time it seemed as if the country would be left without any President at all. To prevent such a thing ever happening, Congress made a law (1885) saying that if President and Vice President both died, the President's place was to be taken by a certain member of the Cabinet. Therefore it is only in case the President, Vice President, and seven Cabinet members die, that our country can be without a head.

Congress also said it was high time to put an end to the " spoils system," by which each new President was annoyed by office seekers. So it was decided that a great many of the positions in the government offices were to be given only to such as proved themselves most capable, by passing civil-service examinations (1883).

LXIV. THE CELEBRATION AT YORKTOWN.

VERY soon after Garfield's funeral, and during Arthur's term, there was a grand procession at Yorktown, to celebrate " Surrender Day," or the centennial of Cornwallis's surrender, October 19, 1781, in the Revolutionary

War.　Visitors came thither from all parts of the country, and descendants of the three illustrious Frenchmen, De Grasse, De Ro-cham-beau', and De Lafayette, were invited to be present, as well as those of the German Von Steu'ben.

On that occasion, the corner stone of a beautiful monument was laid, and speeches were made in English, French, and German.　One of the guests present was the widow of President Tyler, who came forward to shake hands with President Arthur.　Many other noted people were there, and the crowd loudly applauded such heroes as Sherman, Hancock, and Fitzhugh Lee, who, having taken part in the Civil War, had many admiring friends among their former soldiers.

Besides illuminations, there was also a grand naval review, and when an English vessel came up, flying the Union Jack at its masthead, the whole American fleet fired a salute.　This showed very plainly that none but friendly and courteous feelings now existed between the two nations which had twice been face to face in war.

In 1883, after fourteen years of hard work and at the expense of nearly fifteen million dollars, the great Brooklyn Bridge was finished.　This bridge was planned by John A. Roe'bling, and constructed by his son.　It is one of the mechanical wonders of the world, and streams of people now constantly pass to and fro over it.　They can be seen on foot, in carriages, or in cars, for this structure has five separate avenues for those who go back and forth in New York between the boroughs of Manhattan and Brooklyn.

In 1884–85, New Orleans, the "Crescent City," the largest cotton market in the South, held an exhibition to celebrate the Cotton Centennial.　One hundred years be-

The Brooklyn Bridge.

fore, eight bags of cotton had been sent from Charleston to England. But now the South could well boast that "cotton is king," for more than two million bales were shipped in one year from the port of New Orleans alone.

The cotton crop is far greater, however, for, besides exporting cotton, the South supplies all the mills in this country. Most of the work in the cotton fields is still done by the colored people, who now get good wages. They are daily growing more self-reliant and thrifty, and whereas they did not even own themselves in 1860, they are now free and own several million dollars worth of property.

The New Orleans Exhibition was preceded and followed by smaller expositions of the same kind at Atlanta,

Louisville, and Nashville, all showing that the "New South" was growing fast. Not only were the cotton, sugar, rice, and tobacco crops far finer than ever before, but other things were now grown in great quantities in the South. Besides, many manufactories have been built, and shops of all kinds are seen in the South, where many of the towns are real "hives of industry."

Among the other grand changes which have taken place in the country, one of the most remarkable is that made in our mail service since the first postage stamps were used in 1847. It has grown better, quicker, and cheaper every year, the last great reduction being made in 1885, when Congress decided that all letters weighing one ounce or less should be carried from one end of our great country to the other for only two cents. Thus, a two-cent stamp will now carry a letter even from Florida to Alaska. The distance, as you can see in your geography, is very great, but Alaska is part of our country, and in 1884 it was provided with a government, and Sit'ka was chosen as its capital.

LXV. THE GREAT STATUE.

IN 1885, Grover Cleveland became the twenty-second President of the United States. He was the first Democratic President seen in the White House for twenty-four years. Even some Republicans voted for him in preference to Blaine, their own candidate, because they knew he would uphold the civil-service reform.

Cleveland, the son of a minister, was left alone at sixteen, without any money at all. But he was strong and very ambitious, and studied so hard in his leisure moments that he became a successful lawyer.

He practiced in Buffalo, took an interest in politics, and after being governor of New York, became President of the United States. Shortly after his inauguration, people were greatly interested to hear that he was engaged to a young lady noted for her charming manners and kind heart. Their marriage took place in the Blue Room, in the White House, and although there had been eight weddings there before, this one was considered the grandest of all, because the President himself was the bridegroom. When he and Mrs. Cleveland came home from their wedding trip, the bride was "the first lady of the land," and soon won the hearts of all who saw her.

The year after Cleveland's inauguration is known as "Strike Year," because many laboring men, who had joined a union called the "Knights of Labor," refused to work unless they received more pay and had shorter hours. Although the strike began in New York, it soon spread all over the country, north and south.

In some places, the men grew so excited that there were riots, and the troops had to be called out to suppress them. The worst disturbance of all, however, was at Chicago, where some anarchists—men who wanted to overthrow all the laws—not only excited the people, but threw a dynamite bomb when the police came to scatter them.

Several men were killed and wounded, and as pistol shots were heard in the mob, the police had to resort to force. Many of the strikers were killed, and others were seized, tried, and punished. But when the Chicago work-men found out later that their ringleaders were foreigners who wanted to upset all laws, they ceased to listen to them.

The strikes were hardly ended when a terrible earth-quake occurred, which extended from Florida to Cape Cod. At Charleston the earth heaved so violently that tall buildings were shaken down like toy houses. Many people were crushed in the ruins, while the rest fled for their lives to the open fields and squares, where they knelt in prayer while the earth shook beneath them.

There were several distinct shocks, and when all was over, many of the buildings in the city lay in ruins. All hearts were touched by the news of this calamity, and as soon as telegraph wires were up again, and trains could run into the city, help was sent from all parts of the country.

The Statue of Liberty.

While Cleveland was Presi-dent, our nation received, as a present from France, Bartholdi's (bar-tol-dee') statue of "Lib-erty Enlightening the World." It is one of the largest statues ever made, and represents a woman holding aloft a lighted torch. The torch is more than three hundred feet above the water. It is reached by a staircase built inside of the statue.

Sent over from France in sections, this statue was set up on Bedloes Island, in New York Bay, where a pedestal was prepared for it. Many people now go out to see this wonderful statue, and, after climbing up the stairs, stand near the windows set all around the statue's crown, and watch the ships pass to and fro in the harbor.

Among the laws passed during Cleveland's rule is one forbidding the Chinese emigrants to come into our country. Laws had already been made to stop their coming over in large numbers, but they were not well kept. The Americans did not want any Chinamen in the country, because those who came over here merely wanted to earn as much money as they could to carry back to China. They did not try to learn English, would not wear ordinary clothes, and had no wish ever to become American citizens. Besides, they worked for such small wages that they took work away from Americans. Most of them knew nothing of American laws or Christian religion, so they were greatly disliked, and one California politician hated them so that he began and ended every one of his speeches with the words: "The Chinese must go!"

It was while Cleveland was President that Congress began to carry out the plan made by Secretary Whitney of the navy. He said that our ships had long been out of date, and that we ought to have a better navy. Since then many fine war ships have been built, and we now have a fleet of some of the strongest war vessels in the world.

Another important engineering event took place while Cleveland was President. This was the blasting of a great rock which had caused many a shipwreck in the part of the East River, in New York city, called Hell Gate. Engineer Newton tunneled this rock, and arranged dynamite and electric wires in such a clever way that when his baby daughter touched an electric button, the whole rock was blown to pieces. This made the passage safe for ships of all kinds, and put an end to sad accidents on that spot.

After making his grand tour of the world, Grant, ex-President of the United States, invested his money in business. Unfortunately for him, business was something which he did not understand, and as his partner proved dishonest, Grant suddenly found himself almost penniless. To earn money for his family, he now accepted an offer for writing his " Memoirs," and worked hard to finish them, although he soon became very ill. Before long his sufferings grew intense, and the doctors found that he had a cancer in his throat, caused, we are told, by too much smoking.

Grant was then taken to Mount McGreg'or, near Sar-a-to'ga, N. Y., where the " Silent Man " wrote on and on, finishing his " Memoirs " only four days before his death. As he traced the last words, he sighed, " I am ready," for he felt that he had now finished life as well as his book. The last words he ever penned were for his wife, and that letter was found in his pocket when he had breathed his last.

After a private funeral at Mount McGregor, Grant's body was taken to New York, where it lay in state in the City Hall. Thence it was solemnly escorted by General Hancock and part of the Grand Army of the Republic to Riverside Drive, and laid in a plain brick tomb until a marble tomb could be built to receive it.

The funeral procession was eight miles long, and in it were seen the President, his Cabinet, and all the noted men who could be present. Veterans of the Civil and Mexican wars also took part in it, as well as other soldiers and sailors. That funeral showed that Grant's last and greatest wish, " Let us have peace," was granted, for among those present were many gallant Southerners, such as Johnston, Buckner, Hampton, and Fitzhugh Lee.

In 1897, twelve years after Grant's death, his tomb was

Grant's Tomb.

finished. At its dedication there was a procession even more imposing than the first; and many people daily visit the place where this great American rests in peace.

LXVI. A TERRIBLE FLOOD.

OUR twenty-third President (1889–93) was Benjamin Harrison, a grandson of "Old Tippecanoe," the ninth President. He, too, served in the Civil War, where his men loved him dearly. After the war, Harrison practiced law, served as a senator, and was chosen to fill the highest position in our country.

Six new states were admitted during his term: North and South Dakota, Mon-ta'na, Washington, I'da-ho, and Wy-o'ming. The United States then had forty-four stars in its "field of blue." In two of the new Western states, Wyoming and Idaho, and also in Colorado and Utah, women are allowed to vote as well as men, the people there having decided in favor of "woman suffrage."

New land was open to settlers under Harrison, for the territory of Ok-la-ho'ma, or the "Beautiful Land," had been bought from the Indians. As Oklahoma once formed part of the Indian Territory, the President had forbidden any white man to set foot in it until he gave permission to do so. But when it became known that the rich lands of Oklahoma would be open to settlers on April 22, 1889, hosts of people prepared to go there.

To make sure they would have a fair chance, they came on foot and in wagons, on horseback and muleback, and camped along the border. When the bugle gave the signal at twelve o'clock on the appointed day, they made a mad rush into the country. Before night more than fifty thousand persons had crossed the line, and by the next morning several "mushroom" towns had sprung up, newspapers had been printed and were ready for distribution, and all kinds of business had begun.

Of course, towns such as Oklahoma city and Guth'rie were at first only a collection of tents, clapboard shanties and huts, or prairie wagons, but before many months were over, banks, churches, and town buildings arose, and the people began to plan for street cars and electric lights.

Since then the growth of Oklahoma Territory has been so rapid that before long it will probably be ready to join the Union as a state.

The centennial celebration of Washington's inauguration was held in New York in 1889. There was another grand procession on this occasion, which passed under the Washington Memorial Arch, erected in honor of the centennial

The Washington Arch.

of the inauguration of America's greatest man as our first President. The places made famous by Washington's presence were all visited; and to commemorate his arrival, President Harrison, too, was rowed to New York in a barge manned by thirteen sailors. Not only did the army and navy figure in this procession, but all the trades and industries of our land were represented by picturesque floats, and there were large deputations of citizens and workmen.

This joyful celebration was soon forgotten, however, for, about one month later, a fearful calamity befell Johnstown in Pennsylvania. The dam of a reservoir burst after long rains, and a wall of water, forty feet high and about half a mile wide, rushed down the Con'e-maugh valley faster than any express train. A few moments before, seeing the dam was giving way, Engineer Parks rode madly down the valley, calling to all the people to flee. But, in spite of this warning, the waters followed him so closely that more than two thousand persons perished.

After the Johnstown Flood.

Houses were dashed to pieces, locomotives carried away like chips, and millstones weighing a ton apiece rolled along like pebbles. "Trees, brush, furniture, bowlders, pig and railway iron, corpses, machinery, miles and miles of barbed wire, and an indescribable mass" of wreckage rushed down the valley, formed a big whirlpool which crushed everything to pieces, and, sweeping on once more, made a jam at the railroad bridge.

Here, as the waters went down, the mass caught fire, and although there were still some living creatures caught in the ruins, they could not be saved. Money, food, clothing, physicians, and nurses were sent on as rapidly as possible, but the flood of Johnstown will never be forgotten by any who saw or heard it.

During that same month another misfortune visited the United States. This was a huge fire at Se-at'tle, which destroyed nearly all the business part of the town; but fortunately, in this case, very few lives were lost.

——— o○°○ o———

LXVII. LYNCH LAW.

IN 1889 was held the "Pan-American Congress," or assembly of delegates from the principal governments of North, South, and Central America. After meeting in Washington, where they settled a great deal of business concerning trade, the strangers visited about forty towns in our Union. They also examined many of the large mines and factories, and went home delighted with their journey and full of admiration for all they had seen.

STO. OF GT. REP. —19

While Harrison was President, Congress made laws granting more pensions to soldiers, and said that goods coming from abroad would have to pay duty as proposed in the McKin'ley tariff bill. A new copyright law was also made, whereby foreign artists and writers can be protected by American copyright, provided the conditions of the law are complied with and copies of their works are sent to the Congressional Library (1890).

In 1890 there were more Indian troubles among the Sioux in North Dakota. When told by their chiefs that the Messiah was coming to avenge their wrongs by killing all the white men, these red men grew so excited that an attempt was made to quiet or disarm them. They resisted fiercely, and were not subdued until a small battle had been fought, in which about two hundred Indians were killed.

That same year, a great change took place in Utah. When it belonged to Mexico, our government had gladly seen the Mormons go there, and did not care whether they had several wives or not. But when Utah was handed over to us it became a different matter. The laws of the United States allow a man to have only one wife, so the Mormons were told that they would never be allowed to join the Union until they made laws forbidding polygamy.

For a time they would not consent. But when they found they could not hold office, or sit on a jury, if they had more than one wife, they made up their minds to end polygamy. Some of the best men among them had never approved of it, and the Book of Mormon does not mention it. All Mormons still consider their book as sacred as the Bible, but they no longer follow the example given by ·igham Young, or allow any of their people to have more than one wife. Six years after the Mormons gave up polygamy, Utah was admitted· to the Union as the forty-fifth state (1896).

In 1890, the chief of police in New Orleans found that a few Italians in the city belonged to a secret society called Mafia (mah-fe'ah), whose object was to rob and murder. While he was trying to secure the wrongdoers they watched him closely, and, seeing that he suspected them, murdered him one night while he was walking home alone. Eleven Italians were therefore seized and nine of them brought to trial. But the jurymen were afraid or unwilling to condemn the criminals, though there was no doubt they were guilty. This so angered some of the citizens that they decided to take the law into their own hands.

Collecting at the foot of the Clay statue,—they evidently forgot he was the great peacemaker,—a few men began to make speeches which greatly excited the crowd. Before long, the mob marched off to the prison, seized a huge beam, and, rushing forward, battered in the door.

Warned of what was coming, and knowing they were not strong enough to protect the prisoners from the people's fury, the policemen set the Italians free, bidding them save themselves if they could. But it was too late; the mob came pouring in, and in a few minutes either shot or hung all the men. This was very wrong; for while the criminals deserved death, they never should have received it through lynch law. Every one who thus takes the punishment of a crime into his own hands shows that he does not respect our Constitution, which says that every man accused is to have the right to be tried by a jury.

Besides, this act of violence made trouble for the country. The king of Italy, hearing that several of his subjects had been murdered, suddenly asked for damages. Although our government explained just how the matter had happened, the Italian government insisted until the United States gave the men's families $25,000. But if people had quietly waited until the case was again tried, the criminals would have been punished by the law, no fault would have been found with us, and no money need ever have been paid. You see by that how much wiser it always is to respect the laws, and never to allow one's self to be carried away by speeches made by mob leaders.

In the year 1891, some of our sailors, walking through the streets of Val-pa-rai'so, were attacked by the people there, although they were doing nothing wrong. But there had been civil war in Chile (che'lä), and Chileans on both sides had asked for our help. They felt so angry because it had been refused that they attacked our sailors, killing two and wounding eighteen of them.

When our government heard of this it was justly angry. Chile was called upon to apologize and pay damages. At first, the South American republic refused to do so, but finally the affair was quietly settled to our satisfaction.

———oo꙳ꙫ꙳oo———

LXVIII. THE GREAT WHITE CITY.

CLEVELAND'S second election took place two years after the centennial census had been taken, showing that our nation had grown from about four million to about sixty-three million inhabitants. The voting process was carried on in a different way this time, because most of our states used the Australian system of balloting.

As you perhaps do not know what Australian balloting means, I must try to make it clear to you. Each voter receives a paper, called ballot, at the voting place, or polls. On this paper are printed the names of all the different candidates. The voter then goes into a little closet or booth, where no one can see him, marks and folds his ballot, and brings it out to be put into the ballot box. As no one knows how he has voted unless he chooses to tell, this system has served to check bribery, for politicians know that a man who is dishonorable enough to sell his vote is likely to lie, and they do not care to waste their money.

Cleveland is, so far, the only President whose two terms have not come together; he is the twenty-fourth, as well as the twenty-second, President of the United States.

You have probably heard so much about Columbus that you will not be surprised to learn that after celebrating all the centennials of the Revolutionary War, Americans began to think it would be right to do something grand to keep the fourth centennial of his discovery of America.

After much thought, they decided to have a monster World's Fair at Chicago; but as the plans were made too late to have it ready for 1892, the real celebration was put off till the next year. Still, in 1892, President Cleveland went to Chicago to dedicate the World's Fair, and in the spring of 1893 it was thrown open to the public. The newspapers had been telling so much about the coming fair, the vast preparations, and the beautiful buildings, that every one wanted to see them. But no one ever imagined anything half so beautiful as the Great White

World's Fair Buildings.

City really was. Several million people passed through its gates to view its wonders, and although many had seen fine sights before, all agreed that nothing could compare with the Chicago Exposition.

Not only were there exhibits of all kinds, from all parts of the world, but grounds and buildings were decorated with flowers and statues, and illuminated by electricity, until the place looked like fairyland.

Among the beautiful pictures and statues seen on all sides, were many showing some part of the life of Columbus. Besides, all the visitors were particularly interested by four queer-looking ships anchored in the lake. They had been sent from Norway and from Spain. One was an exact model of an old Vi'king boat, and the others of the *Pinta* (peen'tah), *Niña* (neen'yah), and *Santa Maria* (sahn'tah mah-re'ah), the vessels with which Columbus had first crossed the Atlantic.

Here, too, were exhibited many new inventions, and besides the wonderful things made by Edison, people admired the work of Tes'la, another genius in electricity. To show Americans how times had changed, the first and last locomotives stood side by side, Indian canoes, gondolas, and naphtha launches flitted about the lakes, and savages from some of the uncivilized parts of the world mixed in the crowd of loyal Americans and courtly foreigners.

In the year of the famous Chicago World's Fair, more strikes occurred, and in the course of the next year the workmen in some cities grew so unruly that the troops had to be called out. Many people thought that the business panic of 1893 was caused by the monthly coinage of silver; so Congress decided to stop coining that metal.

But this decision did not please everybody, and people took sides on the question. Some were in favor of the unlimited coinage of silver at the ratio of 16 to 1, although sixteen pounds of silver were now worth much less than one pound of gold. They were hence called "silver men," or "free-coinage" men. But those who did not believe in the unlimited coinage of silver, and insisted that gold was the best kind of money, were called " gold bugs," or " sound-money " men.

Meanwhile, as Cleveland and the Congress thought that the McKinley tariff was partly to blame for the trouble, it was changed in favor of another suggested by Wilson.

The Monroe Doctrine has been often mentioned in this book. It was again called into play in 1895. Ven-e-zuē'la and British Gui-a'na had quarreled over their boundaries. This was an old dispute, but it now seemed as if Great Britain would fight the Venezuelans. When the United States said this could not be allowed, the English were very angry, and there was some talk of war with us. But the statesmen luckily showed more sense than some of the newspapers, and the matter was wisely and quietly left to be arbitrated in 1897.

------oo;o;oo-

LXIX. THE EXPLOSION OF THE MAINE.

WHEN the time for a new election drew near, the silver men, including most of the Democratic party, proposed Bryan, while the Republicans, in favor of gold, nominated William McKinley. Both parties were greatly excited, there were huge processions everywhere, but

McKinley was finally elected by the citizens in favor of sound money.

Shortly after his inauguration, the Wilson tariff was set aside in favor of the Dingley Bill. The wheat crops having been unusually large in the West, the farmers earned much money, and newspapers showed that business was doing better day by day.

As you have read in this book, our country is made up of different pieces of land which came into our hands one after another. First, you know, we had only the thirteen colonies with the land to the Mississippi. Next, we bought Louisiana, or most of the land between the Mississippi and the Rocky Mountains. To this we added, little by little, Oregon, Florida, Texas, New Mexico and California, the Gadsden Purchase, and then Russian America, or Alaska. During McKinley's term we also added several distant islands to our possessions, as you shall soon hear.

It seems as if there must always be war somewhere. While all was going on smoothly with us, the newspapers told harrowing tales of the suffering in Cuba, where the people were fighting to win their independence from Spain.

Ever since the Spaniards set foot in the An-til'les, or West Indies, in the days of Columbus, they had tried to get all they could out of these islands, caring very little for the welfare of the people. Indeed, the natives were soon reduced to slavery; and when most of them had died under harsh treatment, negroes were brought to replace them.

Even the Spaniards born in those islands were forced to pay heavy taxes and to submit to the hard rule of Spanish governors, who would not listen to their complaints or let

them have a just share in the government. For four hundred years this state of affairs went on in Cuba, the largest
island in the West Indies, because although the people
there often rebelled, they were not strong enough to drive
the Spaniards out of their country.

Natives of Cuba.

Still, in spite of cruelty, oppression, and many raids from
pirates, Cuba, the " Pearl of the Antilles," proved so fertile that many of its inhabitants grew very rich. Before
the end of the eighteenth century, Havana, its capital,
was the largest and gayest city in the New World. It
was so important that when English and American troops
seized it during the last French and Indian war, the Spaniards gladly gave in exchange for it all the territory then
called Florida (1763).

The fact that Cuba is not one hundred miles away from us, and that many Americans own large estates there, has made us take a great interest in this island. Seeing that the Cubans would never be happy under Spanish rule, people from our country broke our laws to help them in their rebellions, and in 1848 President Polk offered to buy the island from Spain for one hundred million dollars.

Spain not only refused to part with this choice possession, but went on treating the Cubans so unjustly that in 1868 they again rebelled, and began a ten years' war. During this long struggle the Cubans did wonders; but they were so few, compared to the Spanish forces, that they could not win their freedom. In their despair they called upon the United States for aid, but Congress refused it.

Forced to lay down their arms once more, the Cubans now hoped Spain would prove less exacting. Still, cruel treatment drove many away, and more than forty thousand exiles sought refuge in the United States. Here Cuban refugees, merchants whose business suffered whenever there was war on the island, and a few humane Americans whose hearts were touched by the sufferings of the oppressed, kept planning how they could end Spain's rule.

When a new rebellion broke out in 1895, these people promptly sent help to their friends, hoping they would at last secure their independence. But although our government was again asked to help the Cubans, it declined to do so.

Still, when Spain heard that armed parties were carrying weapons and ammunition from our country to Cuba, she declared it was unfair, and threatened to make us pay damages. Spain was right: a country cannot allow its citizens to help wage war against a nation with which it is at peace. Our government therefore hired detectives, and kept revenue cutters sailing up and down our coast, to prevent the departure of any ships with war supplies for Cuba.

If you look at a map of the United States, you will see what a very long stretch of coast we have from Maine to Texas. It cost us much money to watch it, and as, in spite of all our care, the Cubans in our country managed to send out several secret, or filibustering expeditions, we soon saw we would not only have to pay the bill for guarding our coast, but would be asked to pay damages as well.

Besides, the fact that the Cubans received help from the United States made the Spanish feel very bitter toward us, and they would not believe we were trying to be fair. While they could not keep close enough watch over seven thousand miles of Cuban coast to prevent the landing of filibusters' cargoes, they nevertheless expected us to patrol our twenty-nine thousand miles of water front so carefully that no expedition could leave our country. In their anger, Spanish officials illtreated Americans in Cuba. Some were unjustly imprisoned, and others deprived of their property, and our consuls' complaints were unheeded.

Every country is bound to protect its citizens, wherever they may be. The United States, fearing the Americans in Cuba might be attacked in a sudden outburst of fury, now proposed to send a war ship to Havana, to protect our countrymen in case of need. Spain approved of this plan, promising that one of her war ships should visit New York, to show the people that the two nations were still on friendly terms.

The *Maine*, one of our finest cruisers, was therefore ordered to Havana, where it anchored over a spot pointed out by the Spanish authorities. It had been there only a very short time when a Cuban agent stole a private letter, written by the Spanish minister at Washington, and published it in all our newspapers. Of course this letter was never intended for the public, but when the insulting terms applied in it to our President became known, the minister resigned and left our country.

The night before he sailed, the *Maine*, while quietly anchored in Havana harbor, was suddenly blown up, and two hundred and sixty brave sailors lost their lives

After the Explosion of the Maine.

without a moment's warning. After two explosions close together, the ship sank, while boats pushed out hastily from shore, and from other vessels in the harbor, to rescue the survivors of this awful disaster.

Captain Sigsbee, commander of the *Maine*, telegraphed the news to Washington. He did not say anything about the cause of the explosion, but he begged the American people to suspend judgment until a further report should be made.

A few days later, several well-known Americans, accompanied by divers, were sent to Havana to examine the wreck. After six weeks' careful study, these men reported that the *Maine* had been destroyed by the explosion of a mine placed under it. They could not tell who did it, nor why it had been done; but as such mines are always in charge of trustworthy officers, many people thought that the accident was due either to criminal carelessness or to treachery on the part of the Spaniards.

In the meantime, the Spanish war ship *Viscaya* (veeth-cah'yah) had come into New York harbor for its promised friendly visit. On its arrival, the Spaniards heard with dismay of the stolen letter and the explosion of the *Maine*. Some of our newspapers were so bitter against the Spaniards, that our government, fearing lest friends of the dead sailors might try to injure the Spanish cruiser, had police boats watch it night and day; and most people breathed a sigh of relief when it sailed safely out of our port.

LXX. THE BATTLE OF MANILA.

MANY of the sensational newspapers, and a few thoughtless Americans, wanted our government to declare war just as soon as the news came that the *Maine* had been destroyed. But President McKinley had been in the Civil War, and, knowing how much suffering fighting brings on, he was determined to keep the peace if he could do so with honor.

Still, knowing war might come, and that we were not ready for it, he asked and received from Congress fifty million dollars to be used in preparations. Our long coast line was then ill-defended, our navy was smaller than Spain's, and we had but twenty-five thousand men in our army to meet the one hundred and fifty thousand soldiers in Cuba. Twenty days later, nearly all this money had been spent in getting ready for war, although the President still hoped to keep peace.

While he was secretly sending ammunition to the American fleet at Hong-kong' under Commodore George Dewey, and making many other necessary preparations, some of our fellow-citizens spent most of their time in talking against President McKinley. A few, forgetting the respect due to their chosen representative, not only abused him publicly, but actually burned him in effigy. The same foolish class of people showed their enmity to Spain by tearing down her flag and trampling it under foot. But by thus insulting even an enemy's flag,—when no one was there to defend it,—these people only showed how very ignorant and small-minded they were.

When all reasonable means had failed to settle our differences with Spain in a quiet way, and when the Americans in Cuba had been given time to leave the island, President McKinley sent a message to Congress. In it he related what he had done, gave all the information he had received about the state of affairs in Cuba, and said he would do whatever was decided best for the country.

Congress had been clamoring for war, and blaming the

President for not acting more promptly; but when called upon to take the responsibility of declaring war, and sending our army into Cuba, where it was certain many soldiers would die of fever during the unhealthful season, there was some hesitation. Still, eight days later, Congress decided that the Cubans ought to be free, and that a message should be sent to Spain, demanding that she recall her troops, and give up Cuba at once. The President was directed to use the army and navy, if necessary, to drive Spain away.

Notice of this action by Congress was given to the Spanish minister at Washington, who then left the country. But Spain would not let our minister at Ma-drid' deliver the message, which was sent as an open cablegram; knowing its contents, she sent him away, vowed she would never give up Cuba, and thus began war, April 21, 1898.

The President therefore ordered part of our navy to blockade the coast of the western part of Cuba. This was done to prevent any vessel from entering the enemy's ports with war materials or provisions. Our navy also had orders to seize every craft flying the Spanish flag, and our sailors kept such a sharp lookout night and day that in less than three weeks they captured thirty Spanish vessels.

The Spaniards having fired upon one of our ships from Ma-tan'zas, the forts there were shelled for fifteen minutes, and their guns were disabled. As the Spaniards had not done any damage to our ships, they were too proud to own their losses; instead, the Madrid newspapers made great fun of us, saying we had wasted our ammunition to kill one Spanish mule, which, they added, had been buried with military honors!

As soon as war was declared, President McKinley cabled to Commodore Dewey to destroy the Spanish fleet in the Phil'ip-pine Islands. This group of islands in the Pacific Ocean was discovered by Ma-gel'lan, in 1521, in the course of the first journey ever made around the world. Having taken part in a quarrel between two native princes, Magellan was killed and buried on one of the islands he had claimed for Spain. Several years later this group was visited by a Spaniard, who named it the Philippines, in honor of his master, King Philip II.

The Spaniards founded their first colonies in the Philippines and on the mainland of the United States during the selfsame year (1565), and soon after built Ma-nil'a, capital of the islands. With about the same area as Nevada, the Philippines have a greater population than any of our states, and are noted for their wonderfully fertile soil. The climate is so hot and moist all the year round, that crops ripen one after another, and fruits and flowers hang on the trees at the same time.

Under Spanish rule, most of the natives of the Philippines became Roman Catholics, but they were forced to work hard to send large cargoes of coffee, tobacco, rice, hemp, spices, and even silk and gold dust to Spain. They were treated so harshly that they too learned to dislike their Spanish rulers, and often rebelled. For that reason Spain kept a large fleet there, which it was important we should destroy or capture, as it might cross the Pacific Ocean to ravage our western coast.

Dewey set out, as soon as the orders reached him, to surprise and destroy the Spanish fleet near Manila. Although he knew the entrance to the harbor was mined, he

red boldly into it one night, and was already one mile
nd the first battery when discovered by the enemy.
es went off before and behind his five ships, which,
ever, passed on unharmed to attack the Spanish fleet.
hanks to the bravery of his men, and the poor condi-
of the Spanish fleet, Commodore Dewey in less than
hours' time wrecked eleven Spanish vessels, and killed
ounded nearly a thousand Spaniards. This victory,
May 1, 1898, in Manila Bay, is one of the most re-
cable in history, because, while such havoc was worked
he enemy's fleet, our own suffered very little, and only
t of our men were wounded.
ewey now sent a vessel to Hongkong, to cable the
s of his victory to Washington. He also sent word

that the city of Manila was at his mercy, but that he would need a force of soldiers to occupy it. Two weeks later, therefore, our first transports, or troopships, started for the Philippines, stopping at Ho-no-lu'lu, in the Ha-wai'ian Islands, where a feast was given to our soldiers.

———o○○○○○———

LXXI. HOBSON'S BRAVE DEED.

FROM the very first, it was plain to all that our eastern coast was in the most danger, for besides her fleet in the Philippines and gunboats along the Cuban and Puerto Rican (pwer'to re'can) coasts, Spain had many war ships near home. Fearing lest some of these vessels should attack our towns, and knowing we had not enough ships to defend them properly, the President ordered the *Oregon*, a Western battleship, to come to the east coast as fast as it could. This journey of fifteen thousand miles was accomplished without accident in seventy-one days. But every one feared the *Oregon* might be attacked by Spanish vessels in the South American waters, and there were great rejoicings when we heard it had reached Florida safely.

While the *Oregon* was rushing eastward, harbors were mined, forts garrisoned, guns mounted, vessels bought and armed, volunteers called and drilled, and funds raised. In a wonderfully short time our President had all the money he needed, and was at the head of a fine navy and an army of about two hundred and forty thousand men. While this army was getting ready, the navy was busy guarding our coast, watching the movements of the Spanish vessels, blockading the Cuban ports, cutting cables, capturing vessels, and from time to time shelling the shore batteries.

All at once, the news came that a Spanish fleet had started to cross the Atlantic, and until it finally ran into the harbor of Santiago (sahn-te-ah′go), on the southern coast of Cuba, great anxiety was felt lest it should attack some of our scouting ships or an ill-defended coast town. But as soon as we heard that the Spanish fleet under Admiral Cervera (ther-vā′rah) was in Santiago harbor, Commodore Schley's squadron went there to prevent its escape.

Meanwhile, three of our ships, cutting cables near Cardenas (car′dā-nahs), had been attacked; but although they soon silenced the Spanish batteries, it was with the loss of five of our brave men. Shortly after this engagement,— and before it was known where Admiral Cervera's fleet was,—Rear Admiral Sampson bombarded the forts of San Juan (sahn hoo-ahn′) in Puerto Rico, and did some damage to the enemy. The Spaniards bravely returned his fire, but their aim was so poor that most of their shots fell far from our ships. Soon after this, Sampson joined Schley near Santiago, and took command of the whole fleet.

The entrance to Santiago Bay is so long and narrow that, knowing it was mined, and protected by forts on either side, our government would not allow the American fleet to try to force an entrance. All our ships could do, therefore, was to shell the forts along the coast and keep watch day and night.

There was, however, great danger that if a hurricane arose, our ships would be obliged to run out to sea, or seek a safe port. The Americans knew Admiral Cervera would take advantage of such an event to run out of the harbor, and the navy was very anxious to find a way of blocking it so he could not get out.

Sampson therefore decided to run the *Merrimac*—a collier—into the channel at night, swing it directly across the narrowest part, and sink it there, thus making a barrier which could not easily be removed. The execution of this plan was entrusted to Naval Constructor Hobson, who, with seven brave volunteers, took the vessel into the channel one night.

Just as Hobson was about to swing the *Merrimac* around, he was seen by a Spanish patrol boat, and a shot disabled his rudder. It was followed by a deafening roar from the forts on shore; but although shells exploded all around him, and a mine went off under him, Hobson coolly gave his orders. The torpedoes were touched off, and as the *Merrimac* sank, he and his men were swept overboard into the seething waters. There, escaping death by miracle, they clung to the largest thing still afloat—an old raft or catamaran.

When the *Merrimac* went down, the Spaniards cheered wildly, thinking they had sunk an American war ship trying to steal into their harbor unseen. Many boats now put out from shore to examine the wreck, and Hobson, seeing no chance of escaping to the launch waiting for him at the mouth of the harbor, surrendered at dawn to the first officer he saw. This was Admiral Cervera, who, admiring his bold deed, sent word to our navy that the Americans were safe. But although our government took immediate steps to exchange prisoners, Hobson and his brave companions had to spend more than a month in Spanish prisons.

LXXII. SURRENDER OF SANTIAGO.

ABOUT a week after Hobson's heroic deed, a force of
American marines landed at Guan-ta-na′mo Bay in
Cuba, where they had to fight many hours to gain and
hold the position they wanted. They defended it bravely,
and the bay served as a harbor for the American ships.

General Shafter's army next landed a few miles from
Santiago, where he met General Garcia (gar-see′a), the
famous Cuban leader, who came to help him with a force
of determined Cubans.

A plan was then made for the attack on Santiago. It
was agreed that while the American and Cuban soldiers
closed around it on the land side, our navy should throw
shells over the hills and into the city. In carrying out this
plan, the Rough Riders—a troop composed of Western
cowboys and Eastern athletes—suddenly came upon a
strong Spanish force, and a few of them relieved their feelings by swearing. But when their leader shouted, "Don't
swear—shoot!" they ceased misusing their tongues, and
used their arms to such good purpose that they completely
routed the Spaniards. Advancing farther, our army fought
a brisk battle at El Ca-ney′, and made a memorable charge
up the hill of San Juan.

Having thus become masters of a position overlooking
the town, they planted their field cannon. But as they
knew their shells would do great damage, all the women,
children, and old men were allowed to leave the city and
seek a place of safety.

Just before the final shelling of Santiago was to begin, at

nine o'clock on Sunday morning, July 3, while our sailors were getting ready for divine service, the men on watch suddenly cried: "Cervera is trying to escape!" It was true; the Spanish fleet was coming out of the channel, which the *Merrimac* did not block securely, having swung only part way around owing to its disabled rudder.

As soon as the Spanish fleet was sighted, our ships prepared for action, and a few seconds later opened fire and closed in on the enemy. In spite of the running fire which the Spaniards bravely kept up to the very last, their vessels were soon riddled with shot, and, wreathed in flames, they sank or were run ashore to enable some of the men to escape. While one of the ships was sinking, our men started to cheer; but their captain quickly checked them, saying: "Don't cheer, boys; the poor fellows are dying!" Thus, at the moment of victory, he showed himself generous as well as brave by pitying the enemy.

The Oregon on July 3.

This second naval victory, which did very little damage to our men or ships, proved a crushing blow to Spain. Admiral Cervera, with all the Spanish sailors who had not been killed, fell into our hands, and his six fine war ships lay battered wrecks on the Cuban shore. Perceiving it would be useless to struggle any longer, Spain recalled her third and last fleet, which was on its way to the Philippines via the Su-ez' Canal, and gave General Toral (to-rahl') permission to save Santiago from destruction by immediate surrender.

On July 17, 1898, the American flag floated over Santiago; and seeing there was nothing more to be done there, General Miles set off with part of our army to conquer Puerto Rico. Almost four centuries before, this island had been conquered by Pŏnce de Leon, who sought there, as well as in Florida, the marvelous Fountain of Youth. He founded San Juan (1511), more than fifty years before the building of St. Au'gus-tine, the oldest city on our mainland.

San Juan was sacked near the end of the sixteenth century by the famous seaman Drake; pirates of various nations visited the island from time to time; and it was also attacked by British men-of-war. In spite of all this, however, the Spanish settlers prospered, and as they were better governed or more submissive than the Cubans, they suffered less from war. ·Their island is very fertile, and contains large coffee, sugar, and tobacco plantations; and their herds supply great quantities of hides and beef.

Landing on the southern shore of Puerto Rico, General Miles's troops met little or no resistance from the Spaniards, while the Puerto Ricans welcomed the Americans as friends. Our army now went by different roads to attack San Juan, on the opposite side of the island, where most of the Spanish forces had collected.

Meanwhile, Spain asked President McKinley, through the French ambassador at Washington, on what terms he would make peace. McKinley insisted that Spain should consent to withdraw from the West Indies forever, and to meet American commissioners in Paris, to discuss terms of peace. These men were to decide what should be done with the Philippine Islands.

After a little hesitation, Spain accepted these terms, and on August 12, 1898, a peace protocol was signed at Washington. This really ended the Spanish-American War, which had begun one hundred and fourteen days before. But before this news could reach Rear Admiral Dewey, our forces in the Philippines attacked and seized Manila, after a short battle, in which some of our men fell (August 13).

As soon as the protocol was signed, the Cuban blockade was raised and most of our ships were recalled to New York, where a great naval parade took place. But part of our army was kept in Cuba and Puerto Rico to maintain order and take possession of those islands when the Spaniards sailed home.

Although our navy won most of the glory in this brief war, it lost very few men; but our army, exposed to a climate which produces fevers, suffered far more from disease than in battle. This is, however, always the case in war; but while mourning for our dead, we must remember that it is just as heroic to die at one's post—wherever that may be—as to fall in battle.

Besides the heroic deeds already mentioned, and those

The Naval Parade at New York.

Copyright, 1888, by C. C. Langill.

(322)

every one talks about, there were countless brave actions done on land and sea. But while the heroes whose names we know are praised and rewarded, the others deserve no less credit. They too can enjoy the approval of their conscience, and feel with satisfaction that they have done the best they could for their beloved country.

As agreed in Washington, the Peace Commission met in Paris on October 1, 1898, and on December 10 signed a new Treaty of Paris. By this treaty, Spain gave up all her rights in Cuba, and ceded Puerto Rico and the Philippines to the United States, which in turn was to pay Spain $20,000,000.

It is said that the Spanish-American War cost us about two hundred million dollars and three thousand lives, while it cost Spain nearly five times as much. Besides adding to our territory, the war put an end to all jealousy between the North and the South, for old Union and Confederate soldiers, and their sons, now fought side by side under the same flag.

Many of the inhabitants of the islands won from Spain are supposed to be in favor of annexation to the United States. But whether they will adapt themselves to our rule, and become good American citizens, time alone can tell.

LXXIII. THE HAWAIIAN ISLANDS.

SINCE August 12, 1898, the Hawaiian Islands have belonged to the United States of America. They are a group of eight large and a few small islands in the Pacific Ocean, about two thousand miles from San Francisco.

We know very little about the early history of these islands, which were already inhabited by the gentle Ka-na'-kas when the Spaniards visited them in the sixteenth century. About two hundred years later, in 1778, Captain Cook, an English navigator, landed there, naming the whole group Sandwich Islands in honor of the Earl of Sandwich. The natives, however, went on calling them the Hawaiian Islands, after Hawaii, the largest of the group, and it is by this name that they are best known.

The natives worshiped Captain Cook as a god, and treated him so well that he went back there the following winter. But this time the Hawaiians were not so glad to see him, for his men had behaved very badly during their first sojourn. While repairing his ships, Captain Cook missed some tools, and knowing they had been stolen by the natives, he tried to seize one of their chiefs and hold him a prisoner until his property was returned. In the midst of the fight which this attempt stirred up, Captain Cook was separated from his men, who escaped when they saw he had been killed. He was buried on the island, where a monument has been erected over his remains.

During one of his sojourns he had received a visit from Ka-me-ha'me-ha, a young prince whose ambition was to conquer the other chiefs and rule over all the islands. He knew he could succeed if he had European vessels and arms, so he begged Van-cou'ver, who visited the islands for the third time in 1794, to show him how to build a ship. Vancouver greatly admired this young Hawaiian chief, who was so skilled a warrior that when six spears at once were cast at him, he " caught three, parried two, and avoided the sixth by a quick movement of the body."

The Hawaiians are so clever at imitating anything they see, that the young prince soon had a fleet of more than twenty ships. He bought arms from passing vessels, one of which he seized, killing all its crew except one man, whom he spared to show him how to use the guns. This man and another English-speaking castaway were so kindly treated by Kamehameha that they soon became his friends and principal advisers. Helped by these white men, Kamehameha became sole ruler of the islands, and, following their advice, he encouraged trade by treating all strangers as well as he could.

We are told that passing captains made the Hawaiian king presents of British and American flags, which floated in turn from his flagstaff. When the War of 1812 began, an American privateer ran into the port of Honolulu,— the capital of the Hawaiian Islands,—and the captain, seeing the British colors, indignantly asked what Kamehameha meant by flying the enemy's flag. To please these Americans the king immediately hoisted Old Glory; but a British man-of-war came along soon after, and Kamehameha promptly raised the British flag to suit the last arrivals. When his visitors had gone, however, he called his two advisers and asked them whether he could not fly both flags at once so as not to offend either nation.

They told him this would never do, but instead suggested a Hawaiian flag made up of the colors and emblems of both countries. So, while the field of the Hawaiian flag bore the British cross, the eight large islands were represented by eight red, white, and blue stripes.

In 1820, the first American missionaries came to settle in the island, where they were soon followed by many

Palace at Honolulu.

others. These men founded schools and churches for the Hawaiians, who had already given up many of their heathenish practices, such as throwing people into the burning crater of Mauna (mou'na) Lo'a to appease the anger of the awful goddess Pele (pā'lā).

During the reigns of five Kamehamehas, the missionaries converted most of the natives. Many foreigners came to settle on the islands, where they began planting sugar cane, rice, and coffee, built huge mills, and carried on a brisk trade. Many of these settlers were Americans, and the greater part of their trade was with the United States. As they and their children were the best educated people on the island, they soon won considerable influence, which they used to model the Hawaiian laws on those of the

United States, and to introduce American customs, methods, money, language, and schools.

After the British had made a vain effort to get the islands, the king offered them, in 1851, to the United States. But we had recently secured so much new territory that we refused them. Hawaiian kings therefore went on ruling as before, and when the fifth and last Kamehameha died, leaving no direct heir, the people elected Kalakaua (kahla-kou′a), a member of the royal family, who proved a very bad master.

Still, for a time, he respected the constitution made in 1864, which gave the Hawaiians the right to help govern themselves, and he made a trade treaty with the United States in 1875. But this king loved to spend, and could never get enough money. He took bribes from opium dealers, and when an agent from the Louisiana Lottery offered to pay him a large sum every year if he would only allow them to carry on there the business soon to be forbidden by law in the United States, he gladly consented.

But when Kalakaua tried to rule just as he pleased, thus depriving the people of the rights they had enjoyed, they became so angry that they rebelled and forced him to grant a new constitution and promise to govern by it. When he died, four years later, during a visit to San Francisco, his sister Liliuokalani (le-le-wo-kah-lah′ne) became Queen of the Hawaiian Islands (1891). The Americans were glad of this change, because she had been brought up by American missionaries, and had married an American named Dom′in-is. Being a Christian, they knew she would not encourage the people to become heathens again, as Kalakaua had done.

LXXIV. THE ANNEXATION OF HAWAII.

INSTEAD of favoring the Americans and missionaries, as every one expected, Liliuokalani soon showed that she too wanted to change the laws so as to rule just as she pleased. Like her brother, she spent much money, listened to the proposals of the Louisiana Lottery Company and of the opium dealers, and tried to change the laws so they could carry on their business in the Hawaiian Islands.

The better class of people on the islands knew that the lottery and opium eating would ruin the Hawaiians, and, led by Sanford B. Dole, an American born in the islands, they rebelled. The queen was made to sign a paper whereby she gave up her throne, but she added that the Americans had forced her to do so, and that the United States should judge whether they had a right to turn her out of her kingdom or not.

Dole and several other men on the island immediately set up a provisional government (1893), and sent men to Washington to offer the rich Hawaiian Islands as a free gift to our great republic. The Hawaiian question came up at Washington about a month before Harrison was to make room for Cleveland, and as everybody knew that the first of these gentlemen was for, and the latter against, the annexation of the islands, it became largely a question of time.

An attempt was made to rush a treaty through the Senate before the 4th of March. It failed, however, and Cleveland's first action was to withdraw the treaty and send a man to Hawaii to find out the wishes of the natives, be-

cause Liliuokalani insisted that they did not want to be
annexed, and that she would never have been deposed
had it not been for the American settlers and the United
States marines. The latter had been sent ashore to protect the lives and property of Americans during the revolution, but the queen declared they had helped the rebels
to dethrone her.

Now, it is very hard to find out the exact truth about
such things, and many people have stated that the man

Natives of Hawaii.

sent out to Hawaii by Cleveland heard only one side of
the story. However that may be, the President, upon receiving his report, felt sure that the Americans alone were
to blame for all the trouble which had occurred.

STO. OF GT. REP.—21

When a person or a nation has done anything wrong, the only honorable course is to apologize and try to undo the harm done. Cleveland therefore sent a man out there, with orders to help the queen recover her lost power. This American minister, however, found out that it could not be done without bloodshed, and that Liliuokalani meant to have some of the men who had taken part in the revolution put to death, and to take their property. He therefore wrote to Washington for further orders, and the President promptly answered that he would not compel the people to receive the queen if they did not want her, and that he would not uphold a woman who was not ready to show a generous and forgiving spirit. Liliuokalani thus lost his support, and, as the provisional government refused to yield to the queen, she had to withdraw to her private house, while the Hawaiians in power, seeing no chance of immediate annexation, set up a republic, with Dole as President.

Secretly helped by a few Englishmen, the Louisiana Lottery, and the opium sellers, Liliuokalani's friends now began to plot to overthrow the republic, and, it is said, they made arrangements to blow up the President and his Cabinet while they were at church.

We are told that this plot was discovered almost at the last minute by a man who stepped into the church and spoke a few words in President Dole's ear. The latter rose from his seat, after whispering in his turn to the men near him, who softly passed the message on. A few minutes later only the women and children were left in the building, but they too rushed out when they heard soldiers marching in the street.

Liliuokalani's friends and troops were promptly surrounded, and after a few men had been killed the rest surrendered. The queen was arrested, her stores of arms and
explosives seized, and the uprising of 1895 was at an end.
Fearing that the islands would not be able to resist an
attack from the British or the Japanese (who both seemed
inclined to pounce upon them), the Hawaiians again asked
to be annexed by the United States. They had proved
so quiet and orderly under a republican government that
the proposal was accepted, and the stars and stripes now
float over all the Hawaiian Islands, where until 1898 we
owned only the right to a coaling station.

PRESIDENTS OF THE UNITED STATES.

George Washington, that hero grand,
Was President of our dear land
Eight troubled years. Then Adams (John)
Preceded Thomas Jefferson.
He was elected twice, you know,
Like Madison and James Monroe.
John Quincy Adams, wise and firm,
Was next; then Jackson's double term.
Van Buren ruled when times were bad;
The death of Harrison was sad;
But Tyler came his years to close
Ere James K. Polk, in turn, arose.
Zach. Taylor of the Texan war
Soon left his place to good Fillmore.
Pierce and Buchanan both held sway
While slavery questions ruled the day.
That storm cloud burst while Lincoln steered
The "Ship of State," whose wreck he feared;
Scarce had he brought it safe to port
When crime his second term cut short.
Johnson was therefore forced, though loath,
To take the Presidential oath.
Grant of our nation twice was head,
Ere to the White House Hayes was led.
When Garfield's pain was o'er, at last,
His power to Chester Arthur passed.
Next Cleveland and Ben Harrison,
Whose place again firm Cleveland won
McKinley now rules land and main
And all the islands torn from Spain.

INDEX.

Key to pronunciation.—VOWELS: ā in lāte, ă in făt, â in câre, ä in fär, à in làst, ạ in fạll, ₉ in wạs, au in author ; ē in mē, ĕ in mĕt, ẹ in vẹil, ē in tērm ; ī in fīne, ĭ in tĭn, ï in polïce ; ō in nōte, ŏ in nŏt, ȯ in sȯn, ô in fôr, ọ in dọ ; ū in tūne, ŭ in nŭt, ᵮ in rᵮde, ᵮ in fᵮll ; ẏ in mẏ, y̆ in hўmn. CONSONANTS: ç in çent, e in ean ; ġ in ġem, g in get ; ñ=ny in barnyard, ꞟ = ng, N=ng, but is silent; qu = kw ; ꞩ = z. *Italic letters are silent.*

Eclectic School Readings

A carefully graded collection of fresh, interesting and instructive supplementary readings for young children. The books are well and copiously illustrated by the best artists, and are handsomely bound in cloth.

Folk-Story Series

Lane's Stories for Children.	$0.25
Baldwin's Fairy Stories and Fables	.35
Baldwin's Old Greek Stories	.45

Famous Story Series

Baldwin's Fifty Famous Stories Retold	.35
Baldwin's Old Stories of the East	.45
Defoe's Robinson Crusoe	.50
Clarke's Arabian Nights	.60

Historical Story Series

Eggleston's Stories of Great Americans	.40
Eggleston's Stories of American Life and Adventure . .	50
Guerber's Story of the Thirteen Colonies	.65
Guerber's Story of the English	.65
Guerber's Story of the Chosen People	.60
Guerber's Story of the Greeks	.60
Guerber's Story of the Romans	.60

Classical Story Series

Clarke's Story of Troy	.60
Clarke's Story of Aeneas	.45
Clarke's Story of Caesar	.45

Natural History Series

Needham's Outdoor Studies	.40
Kelly's Short Stories of Our Shy Neighbors	.50
Dana's Plants and Their Children	.65

Copies of any of these books will be sent prepaid to any address, on receipt of the price, by the Publishers :

American Book Company

New York   •   Cincinnati   •   Chicago

(15)

Carpenter's Geographical Readers

By Frank G. Carpenter

North America   Cloth, 12mo, 352 pages .   . 60 cents

Asia. Cloth, 12mo, 304 pages .   .   .   . 60 cents

This series of Geographical Readers is intended to describe the several continents, — their countries and peoples, from the standpoint of travel and personal observation.

They are not mere compilations from other books, or stories of imaginary travels, but are based on actual travel and personal observation. The author, who is an experienced traveler and writer, has given interesting and vivacious descriptions of his recent extended journeys through each of the countries described, together with graphic pictures of their native peoples, just as they are found to-day in their homes and at their work. This has been done in such simple language and charming manner as to make each chapter as entertaining as a story.

The books are well supplied with colored maps and illustrations, the latter mostly reproductions from original photographs taken by the author on the ground. They combine studies in geography with stories of travel and observation in a manner at once attractive and instructive. Their use in connection with the regular text-books on geography and history will impart a fresh and living interest to their lessons.

Copies of Carpenter's Geographical Reader will be sent prepaid to any address, on receipt of the price, by the Publishers :

American Book Company

New York   Cincinnati   ·   Chicago

(47)

A School History
of the United States

By John Bach McMaster

Professor of American History in the University of
Pennsylvania.

Linen, 12mo, 507 pages.   With maps and illustrations .   . **$1.00**

This new history of our country is marked by many
original and superior features which will commend it alike
to teachers, students, and general readers.   The narrative is a word-picture of the great events and scenes of
American history, told in such a way as to awaken enthusiasm in the study and make an indelible impression on
the mind.   From the beginning the attention of the
student is directed to causes and results, and he is thus
encouraged to follow the best methods of studying history
as a connected growth of ideas and institutions, and not a
bare compendium of facts and dates.   Special prominence
is given to the social, industrial, and economic development of the country, to the domestic life and institutions
of the people, and to such topics as the growth of inventions, the highways of travel and commerce, and the progress of the people in art, science, and literature.   The
numerous maps give vivid impressions of the early
voyages, explorations, and settlements, of the chief military campaigns, of the territorial growth of the country,
and of its population at different periods, while the
pictures on almost every page illustrate different phases in
the civil and domestic life of the people.

---

*Copies of McMaster's School History of the United States will
be sent, prepaid, to any address on receipt of
the price by the Publishers:*

American Book Company

NEW YORK   •   CINCINNATI   •   CHICAGO
(32)

To avoid fine, this book should be returned on
or before the date last stamped below

CPSIA information can be obtained
at www.ICGtesting.com
Printed in the USA
BVOW11s2342170817
492248BV00009B/265/P